The Infidelity Report

The INFIDELITY Report

AN INVESTIGATION OF EXTRAMARITAL AFFAIRS

Wendy Leigh

WILLIAM MORROW AND COMPANY, INC.
New York

Library of Congress Catalog Card Number: ~~84-60547~~ 84-61524

ISBN: 0-688-03930-8

Printed in the United States of America

First Edition

1 2 3 4 5 6 7 8 9 10

BOOK DESIGN BY ELLEN LO GIUGICE

To the only man in my life,
with love.

ACKNOWLEDGMENTS

I am very grateful for the professional advice and help of Dr. Ruth Neubauer of the American Association for Marriage and Family Therapy and to the following people for their informative interviews: Dr. Colin Beer, professor of psychology, Rutgers University, psychoanalyst Dr. Herbert Strean, psychotherapist Fredlee Kaplan, anthropologist Dr. Lionel Tiger, psychologist Dr. Robert Brannon of Brooklyn College, John Simon of *New York* magazine, Meredith Brown of *Soap Opera Digest,* television critic Jeffrey Greenfield, Detective John Johnston of Marital Investigation Service, Inc., Marvin Mitchelson, Aileen Mehlie, "Suzy," of the New York *Daily News,* Angie Bowie, and Prince Egon Von Furstenberg.

The book wouldn't have been possible without my advertisements in *The Village Voice, The New York Review of Books, Oui* magazine, *The London Sun, Soap Opera Digest,* and my lectures on infidelity at New York City's The Learning Annex. I also received invaluable input from countless radio and TV shows, including *PM Magazine, The Morning Show, Good Morning New York,* and from Bob Grant, Lenny Lopet, Steve King, Al Rentell, Michael Jackson, and many others.

With special thanks to my editor Pat Golbitz and her assistant, Jennifer Williams, to Robert Gottlieb of William Morris, to Joan Stewart, Michael Meller, Don Short of Solo, and especially to Sue Russell for her useful comments.

I'd also like to thank Via Nini designs and Joan Wieseneck at Saramique for allowing me to wear their clothes during TV appearances, and Rebecca Michael for her flawless secretarial and editorial assistance.

With many thanks to top makeup designer, Linda Mason for designing the makeup for the cover picture, to Angelina Capanna of Styles for doing my hair, and to London's ace photographer Peter Carrette for taking the photograph and teaching me Cockney rhyming slang along the way.

Contents

	Acknowledgments	7
	Introduction	13
One	*Attitudes Toward Infidelity*	23
Two	*Profile of the Cheater*	54
Three	*Profile of the Cheatee*	135
Four	*Profile of the Victim*	147
Five	*The Consequences of Infidelity*	189
Six	*Why Monogamy Is Better*	223
	Afterword	236
	Notes and Sources	251
	Bibliography	257

The Infidelity Report

Introduction

I am four years old and it is Christmas Eve. My father has been unfaithful to my mother and I am the first to know.

My mother is draping the tree with faded silver tinsel left over from last year. She is tall, slim, with hauntingly soft brown eyes, a beautiful version of Claire Bloom. My father sits on a couch, talking to his twenty-year-old secretary, June, who is spending Christmas with us because she is far from home. She is Irish, dumpy, pockmarked, and silent. Every now and again I look up from my doll's house and watch in fascination as my father's hand brushes June's. Then it's my bedtime and my mother takes me upstairs and reads me a fairy tale. I fall asleep as she says the familiar words, "And they lived happily ever after." In my dreams my father and June dance together under our Christmas tree.

I didn't see sparks fly, or hear lightning flash. I didn't even glimpse a hint of sadness in my mother's face. I just knew.

This book is about infidelity. Current statistics dramatically demonstrate that the face of marriage in America today is riddled with infidelity: 70 percent of married men cheat (*Playboy,* 1982)[1] and 50 percent of women (Atwater, 1982).[2] Infidelity has reached epidemic proportions, often leading to divorce, with thousands of children of divorced parents growing up without a role model for monogamy. Consequently, they find it virtually impossible to believe in the ideals of monogamy and "happily ever after." My own experiences of my father's infidelity made me acutely aware of the repercussions of infidelity and led me to investigate the topic on a universal level. I believe that by exploring the causes, methods, patterns, and consequences of infidelity we may perhaps be able to confront and vanquish the destroyer of any healthy relationship.

My childhood consciousness of my father's infidelity was precocious and acute and reverberated through the years into my adult relationships. By the time I was eight, I had already become a clear-eyed observer of my father's subterfuges and of my mother's reaction to them. I was still subjective though; I perceived my mother as perfect. She had lost her father at ten, was separated from her mother by war, and at sixteen had married my father. To me she was virtually a saint, I was passionately protective of her as I felt she had suffered so much. And I swore with childish ferocity that nothing would ever hurt her again. But eventually my father did.

First there was June, of the pockmarks, who didn't have two words to rub together; then there was Pam, who brought me cream buns and ate most of them herself. Then there was Margarate, then Judy, then Bridget, then separation, then divorce. I watched it all, infidelity after infidelity, as my parents' marriage crumbled and they became mortal. I watched and simultaneously gained my first credential for writing this book; I was living with a cheater and victim and was experiencing the dynamics of infidelity at an extremely close range.

Forsaking all others seemed like a fairy tale to me. A child of infidelity, I developed into an adult grappling with the image of my father's affairs. Consequently, I avoided marriage altogether. Determined not to fail, I was too scared even to try. On one hand, I expected perfection in marriage; on the other, I felt that I was doomed from the start. Having placed my mother on a pedestal, my reasoning went as follows: If my mother couldn't keep my father faithful, what chance have I got with any other man? Later, interviewing for this book, I found that many other children of infidelity felt the same way.

When I was in my early twenties, still afraid that someone I loved would be unfaithful to me, I tried to explain my father's straying by looking for failings in my mother which might have caused it. Unable to find any tangible ones, I picked the only unknown, sex, so that I eventually decided to attribute my father's persistent cheating to a lack of sexuality in my mother. By that time I was testing myself in relationships and having established in my mind the reason for my father's infidelity, I tried to combat possible infidelity in my relationships by cultivating wildness and super-sexuality. I vowed that no man would ever be unfaithful to *me* because I wasn't sexual enough. Consequently I spent my twenties being so hot that I nearly extinguished myself.

Still terrified that someone I loved would be unfaithful to me, I invented yet another strategy to avoid the possibility. I decided that if I were the one a man was being unfaithful *with,* I would be more exciting to him and he wouldn't be unfaithful to me. There was very little logic or conscious thought in my strategy, but I followed it faithfully, playing the part of the other woman with scarlet-lady perfection. I am not proud of my other woman role—and don't really want to dwell on it —but at the same time it does demonstrate some of the unhealthy drives that can be triggered off in the children of infidelity and also clarifies the process which led me to write this book.

First there was my long-term love, who finally drove me away by leaving his wife. Luckily he hadn't left specifically for me; I never wanted to marry him because then I knew I would run the risk of *becoming* my mother and having a husband who might be unfaithful to me. Next there was the "sexual addict" who used to phone his wife while he was with me and suggest her daily menu ("Darling, why don't you boil yourself an egg?"). I repressed my jealousy because, after all, at least *I* was aware of the situation. Far more preferable, I thought, than being unaware and floundering around in the victim's blindness to infidelity. At least I *knew* I was only getting half a man.

After the sexual addict came the millionaire. With high glamor, he whisked me from one European capital to another. In Switzerland he swore undying love, in Germany he declared that he would never leave his wife, and in London he begged ardently to be allowed to keep me. I was petrified. I didn't want him to leave his wife and I didn't want him to keep me. After all, if I were kept, perhaps I would be unable to keep.

I never wanted to marry my married men, and perhaps through them was, in a strange way, trying to conquer my cheating father. I also heeded the words of Cleopatra to Antony, who had been unfaithful to his wife Fulvia with Cleopatra:

> Why should I think you can be mine and true,
> Though you in swearing do shake the throned gods,
> Who have been false to Fulvia?[3]

If my married men cheated on their wives, why should their behavior alter radically just because they were now married to me?

Finally, I broke my illicit love affair pattern and started to concentrate on men who were genuinely available. Then I was unfaithful myself. I told myself, "Well, if my father cheated, why shouldn't I? If he didn't follow monogamy, why should I?" So I was unfaithful to a man to whom I had promised fidelity. My actions were partially triggered off by my overriding fear that he would be unfaithful to me. In the words of one of my interviewees for this book I wanted "to fire the first shot"—to be unfaithful to him before he was unfaithful to me. I was and I felt guilty and ashamed.

I don't know if I shall ever totally work through my fear of someone I love being unfaithful to me. I only know that even if I can't control my partner's behavior, I can control my own, and that I believe in monogamy for myself. After wildness and willfulness, sexual revolutions and love affairs, I finally believe that monogamy is better, and, at the time of writing, at least, am living up to my beliefs.

My own story served to illustrate some of the points that this book will make. Children of infidelity are acutely aware of its consequences, are often damaged and bruised by their parents' affairs, and repeat their mistakes in their own subsequent relationships. I found echoes of my own experiences and emotions as a child of infidelity when talking to men and women all over America. My findings were corroborated by Dr. Ruth Neubauer, marital therapist and President of the New York branch of the American Association for Marriage and Family Therapy (which has 10,000 members nationwide) who says, "You learn to expect in your own marriage what you have seen in your parents' marriage."

Thousands of men and women all over America have grown up, as I did, observing infidelity in our parents' marriages and consequently expecting it in our own. And most of us desperately wondered how to prevent that infidelity from occurring. This book was born because I wanted to investigate the phenomenon that had damaged me. To find out how and why people are unfaithful and how to prevent infidelity in my own relationships.

In my investigations, I found a world in which infidelity is viewed, reluctantly, as a part of life, a hazard from which few relationships are immune. I discovered, too, that there are no formulas to "keep" someone faithful, only ways of discovering the danger signs of infidelity. There are no magic spells which ensure fidelity, no model behavior patterns designed to guarantee living happily ever after in harmony.

The only clues I uncovered as a way of perhaps containing the infidelity epidemic lie within the realm of communication and confrontation. I found that although we all know that infidelity is lethal to relationships, men and women all over the country are unwilling to confront the possibility of infidelity occurring in their own personal relationships. They are aware of its prevalence in other people's relationships and accept that as almost a matter of course, yet act as if their own personal relationships are guaranteed to remain untouched by infidelity. Consequently, very few couples discuss the possibility of their own or their partner's infidelity. As psychotherapist Fredlee Kaplan (who is in private practice and is also clinical instructor and supervisor at the New Hope Guild Center in Brooklyn) points out, "Many people are unaware of how many problems or issues in their marriage they deny as important or they deny exist at all."

I found a climate in which men and women are afraid of infidelity but are nevertheless unwilling to deal with it in their private lives. On the whole, men who cheat are reluctant to confront the possibility that their infidelity could have consequences. Nor are they able to confront the possibility that their wives might be unfaithful to them. Women on the other hand, do confront the consequences of their own infidelity, but are afraid to confront the reality of their husband's infidelity.

Sexual revolutions may come and go, but human nature remains unchanged; everyone wants to be loved best and infidelity threatens that desire. I believe that as painful as infidelity may be, we should try and confront it. This book is an attempt to explore and reveal every aspect of infidelity in the hope of launching a debate that might lead to an honest confrontation of infidelity by men and women in their intimate relationships. By investigating and confronting infidelity, perhaps we may all begin to formulate ways in which we can be happier and more secure in our relationships.

Methods of Research

After exploring in depth my own conflicts regarding infidelity, I began researching the topic in general. I published a questionnaire in the June (1982) issue of *Oui* magazine aimed at the cheater, victim, and cheatee (third party). The questions were designed so as to elicit both general attitudes toward the subject as well as accounts of personal behavior. The questionnaire was also republished in "Oui Letters." The replies to the questionnaires produced some preliminary patterns which I then investigated further.

Oui sent me on a nationwide tour in connection with the questionnaire. I was interviewed on radio and TV shows in New York, New Jersey, Chicago, Dallas, Los Angeles, Boston, and Miami, and talked via phone-in programs to cheaters, victims, and cheatees, testing out some of my preliminary findings and gathering more material.

On the road, and throughout my research for the book, I was amazed at the willingness of people in all walks of life to talk to me about their private lives. In Los Angeles, I went out with the *PM Magazine* crew and filmed people on the streets discussing details of their own, or their partner's, infidelity. With media brazenness and self-confidence, we stopped passersby in downtown Los Angeles and asked them if they had ever been cheaters or victims. Most people talked to us, everyone was polite, and no one appeared to be shocked or surprised by the subject. In ten years as a journalist I've come to the conclusion that everyone wants to appear on TV or radio. This is probably partly due to vanity, and partly due to the media having become a familiar old friend to most viewers.

Like all journalists before me, I took advantage of the fact that the media seems to have become the church of our time in which everyone wants to worship. Just as people in the past paid homage to religion, men and women all over America seem desperate to expose themselves before the great god television—worshiping its power by confessing intimate details of their private lives.

People's willingness to confide details of infidelity to me over the airwaves also brought into sharp focus the contrast between people's eagerness to communicate with a stranger and their inability to discuss infidelity with their partner. Again and again, I was faced with statements like "I am terrified that my partner will be unfaithful to me." I always reacted by asking if they had discussed their fears with their partner. And the answer invariably would be no. Sadly, I was forced to conclude that many people are more prepared to be open with the media than with their own spouse. This inability to confront infidelity within a relationship seemed to be one of the major stumbling blocks to creating a monogamous relationship.

The tour convinced me that personal contact, even over the phone, was preferable to questionnaires. True, I had gotten responses from as far afield as Las Vegas, Arizona, from Alaska and from Arkansas, right through the alphabet to Z, but I was slightly skeptical about some of the responses and was careful to avoid crazies.

The questionnaires continued to arrive, as did feedback from the radio and TV shows. I taped every show I appeared on and used the resultant material as research for the book. The immediacy of the phone-in program continually reminded me of the rawness of the nerve I was striking. Many of the people I talked to were obviously suffering because of infidelity. One man even cried on air because of his wife's affair. Infidelity, and any discussion of it, obviously equaled insecurity and pain.

After the phone-ins, I believed more strongly than ever that we are, sadly perhaps, living in a world where people prefer talking to writing. This was evidenced by the fact that the talk shows yielded richer material than did the questionnaires. I decided that I would get the best, most vivid research if I followed through on my belief and interviewed cheaters, victims, and cheatees over the phone. Advertisements in *The Village Voice* and *The New York Review of Books* led to phone calls from men and women aged sixteen to seventy, from all over America.

I talked to each of my interviewees for up to an hour. If the caller's story seemed especially complex or representative, I arranged to meet them in person. In general, male callers were far less inhibited than female callers; a typical boastful cheater's introduction was very often "I'm calling from home because my wife is out right now." Women, however, were more cautious, but both men and women surprised me in many cases by giving me their home numbers in the eventuality that I might have further questions. A few of the interviewees said they were keen to take part in the project because they felt they were contributing to an important debate. Others wanted feedback from me regarding what I had found so far. One interviewee even offered to pay me if I would give her detailed advice because, she complained, therapists never talked back to her. Of course I refused, and in all my discussions on the subject made it clear to anyone I talked to that I was not a therapist and could merely discuss my findings with them.

The New York Review of Books and *The Village Voice* provided invaluable feedback and I repeated the advertisements regularly. I also advertised in *Soap Opera Digest* and lectured on infidelity at New York City's Learning Annex, gathering research material from students there. Once I had collected my own research material, I found that very clear patterns emerged. Certain themes and responses appeared repeatedly and make up most of the book.

My own research completed, I interviewed sociologists, anthropologists, and experts in the field of marital therapy. They and all the many people who have contributed to this book have enriched our knowledge of infidelity and relationships in our time.

ONE

Attitudes Toward Infidelity

Our grandparents' generation believed in monogamy; statistics compel the current generation to believe in the prevalence of infidelity. The figures indicate that infidelity is rampant in our culture. In 1948, Kinsey found that 50 percent of married men had extramarital sex.[1] That figure was substantiated again in 1979 when Yablonsky found that 50 percent of husbands are unfaithful.[2] These figures were topped in 1981 when Hite reported that out of 7,239 men, 3 out of 4 husbands had cheated during the first two years of their marriage and that 72 percent of married men were unfaithful.[3]

Female infidelity has been thoroughly documented as well. In 1953, Kinsey showed that 26 percent of wives had had one affair by the time they were forty.[4] In September 1975, *Redbook* demonstrated that this figure had dramatically increased; nearly one third of their married readers who had answered their questionnaire admitted to infidelity.[5] This was expanded on even more in 1981 when Linda Wolfe's *Cosmo Report,* which surveyed 106,000 women, found that 50 percent of married respondents had had extramarital relationships.[6] And in 1982, sociologist Lynne Atwater reported that 50 percent of women are unfaithful to their husbands.[7]

Why People Believe or Disbelieve in Monogamy

Perhaps men and women have always cheated. However, the prevalence of published statistics on infidelity in today's society makes it impossible for individuals to ignore the fact that their neighbor may not be monogamous. The majority of monogamous men and women I talked to observed that they were faithful simply because they had promised to be. Very few people (only 8 percent,) cited religion as the basis for their belief in monogamy, and the remainder explained that they were faithful because they wanted to honor the promise they had made when marrying.

A 1981 study by David Weiss and Michael Slosnerick found that the group of people *least* likely to believe in monogamy were men who disassociated sex from love and marriage and who also had permissive attitudes toward premarital sex. The researchers found that people who feel love is a necessary component of sex tend to believe in monogamy.[8] This finding was substantiated by sociologists Ira L. Reiss, Ronald E. Anderson, and G. C. Sponaugle who reported that people most prone to believing in extramarital affairs had a high incidence of premarital sex, but didn't have many religious beliefs.[9]

If the people who believe in monogamy do so because they wish to honor their marriage vows, are religious, and are unable to separate love from sex, then what about the 72 percent of men and 50 percent of women who make up the infidelity statistics? I wondered what prompted them to relinquish their belief in monogamy. I expected the answer to be simple and readily available. However, my expectations were startlingly confounded by every single one of my cheating interviewees. Each one professed, without a shred of irony, to believe in monogamy. Surprisingly, every cheater was unashamed to admit that he or she held one set of values (a belief in monogamy) but at the same time was prepared continually to undermine those values by their actions. As sociologist Minako K. Maykovich from California State University points out when writing about infidelity, "What people do is one thing; how they feel about it is quite another. The low correlation between attitudes and behaviour has been reported frequently in the literature, leading to a general conclusion that attitudes are not good predictors of behaviour."[10]

One wonders why cheaters feel compelled to pay lip service to monogamy, given the current awareness of cheating statistics. Perhaps part of the reason is that people are still unwilling to include themselves in the mass of statistics, in effect insisting, "I may be cheating, but as I believe in monogamy I am not part of the general cheating population." Perhaps, too, they are unprepared to give up the last vestige of respectability that a professed belief in monogamy upholds. Yet cheaters would almost be justified in pointing to America today and declaring that today's society is remarkably conducive to cheating.

One of the primary causes of today's cheating is *the relationship between fidelity and the state of someone's parents' marriage.* Twenty years ago, infidelity may have been hinted at, but because couples almost invariably stuck together and the mistress/lover was relegated to an illicit back-street role, children were less conscious of parental infidelity. In the past, extramarital affairs didn't inevitably lead to divorce, simply because divorce was less common. Today, however, divorce has become a fact of life (although it isn't always infidelity-based), and divorce and remarriage often confirm extramarital affairs that children may have suspected during their parents' marriage. When the cheatee becomes the second husband or wife, the fact that the infidelity occurred is confirmed.

As my own childhood experiences illustrate, growing up as the observer of one or both parents' infidelities can affect the child's approach to his own adult relationships. If the other man or woman becomes the child's stepparent, parental infidelity and divorce become inextricably intertwined in the child's mind. Although there are no statistics available on the relationship between infidelity and divorce (because of the new no fault laws), infidelity and divorce often appear synonymous to the child of a broken home. Anthropologist Lionel Tiger has coined the term *ominigamy* to describe the new kinship system which arises out of sometimes infidelity-related divorce and remarriage (often the result of infidelity). He writes in *Psychology Today,*

> In the old days people were titillated by the polygamous habits of Hollywood celebrities but few were tempted to emulate them. Parents, grandparents, aunts and uncles seem to be more important role models for children. When they keep changing partners, it will likely increase the child's sense of the tentativeness in all relations that the new system reflects.[11]

The way in which the parent conducts his relationships invariably influences the child, and if infidelity is part of a parent's marriage it can only serve to erode the child's own belief in monogamy and the promise of happily ever after.

It seems that many children of divorced parents tend to identify with either the cheater or the victim and then strive to emulate them in the way in which they run their own relationships. Sometimes the effect is positive, but often it is sadly negative. A twenty-three-year-old aerobics instructor from California managed to mingle the positive with the negative:

> Lots of people cheat. My own grandmother is having an affair with a married man and his wife doesn't know about it. My mother was unfaithful to my father and my parents got divorced. I felt my mother had deceived me and I hated her for cheating

> on my father. I respected him, you see. The whole situation made me want to be devoted to my husband when I finally got married and not see him get hurt like my dad was. I believe in monogamy —one man and one woman, together in love.

She so desperately wants to be different from her mother that the aerobics instructor wrote that she actually *allows* her husband to cheat on her "because I love him so much that I don't mind if he has lots of women, as long as he tells me about them." She has chosen to be hurt, rather than to hurt.

Tony, another interviewee, also reflects the effects of witnessing parental infidelity. He is married to a woman who doesn't satisfy him sexually. His mother was unfaithful to his father: "My mother always had uncles staying over, like 'Uncle Bill' or 'Uncle Joe.' I couldn't understand why this man who wasn't my father was sleeping with my mother." Tony, in a strange way, acted out his mother's past by repeatedly being unfaithful to his wife, but stayed married to her because she was sexually diametrically opposed to his mother. He says, "My wife is very religious and unsexual. In one way I don't like that, but perhaps I stay with her because she is so faithful and my own mother wasn't. Perhaps that is exactly what I want—a woman who will be faithful like my mother wasn't and who will cling to me."

Tony may be emulating his mother's cheating behavior; similarly, many men seem compelled to try and equal their father's sexual panache. Perhaps President Kennedy's notorious womanizing can be partly attributed to the model his father, Joe, set for him—flaunting his mistresses in front of his wife and even bringing them home for dinner. It is easy to conclude that Joe Kennedy's example didn't contribute to developing a belief in monogamy in his son.

Dick, a forty-year-old real-estate executive I interviewed, also admired and patterned himself after his cheating father. This is his story.

> My father was married three times. He was almost a professional cheater and I admired that. Even though he was married to my mother for twenty-five years, he was a real heavy-duty cheater. He was flashy, he would buy girls cars and would dress beautifully. My mother told me once that in a restaurant a waiter had said to her that she was pretty, but not as pretty as the other girl my father had brought in. I don't think it was right.

Dick may not have thought his father's cheating was right, but he certainly copied it. At twenty-one, he married, intending to be faithful. Within three months he had already gone to bed with his cousin. He divorced his first wife, married again, then discovered his new wife was cheating on him. He tried to win her back by using the methods with which he had seen his father manipulate other women—buying his wife a car and spending lots of money on her. None of that worked and Dick is now the epitome of the swinging bachelor; he is dating several girls at once without them knowing about each other—a nonmarital brand of infidelity. He says,

> I am really *up* when I am juggling five or six relationships at once. If one goes wrong then you always have the other one. I hate sitting down and talking to women—I prefer doing things. I'm big on clothes and hair in a woman. If she doesn't look like the girl in the *Land's End* catalogue, then forget it.

I asked Dick for his definition of love. "Love? Love is feeling sick. A lot of times I love women after they leave me."

Ellie, like Dick, had an unfaithful father. A thirty-two-year-old artist, she began to cheat on her husband when she was twenty-five. She says,

> My father was unfaithful and my mother turned the other cheek. But I knew all about my father's infidelity when I was young. My mother tortured us with it. My father owned a store and our

mother would take us there and we would watch him leave with his girlfriend. I don't know if my father being the way he was made me protect myself by cheating first. I would be devastated if my husband or my boyfriend cheated on me.

Valerie's parents divorced because of infidelity and she reacted very much in the way I did by becoming the eternal "other woman."

I grew up without the backdrop of a happy marriage. Years ago you stuck together no matter what, but my parents didn't. I've always had trouble with the idea of being a wife and I've always been the other woman. I am not sure what I am going to do about marriage. I want my marriage to be monogamous, but I don't know whether I shall be able to sustain that. I have a wandering eye. Hopefully I shall be enough of the kind of wife the man wants so he won't ever cheat on me. Or I'll choose a man who grew up thinking that you stay in a marriage no matter what.

Valerie seems to have unearthed the ideal formula for finding fidelity: Pick a man whose parents remained married despite everything, then the man will feel the same way. Or perhaps pick a man whose parents divorced but left him with the feeling that they should have stayed together. According to Valerie's reasoning those types of men will never stray. It seems a fool-proof recipe for guaranteeing a monogamous mate. Sadly, though, there aren't any formulas, just a few patterns which seem to form again and again.

Judging by the majority of my interviewees, it appears as if parental infidelity echoes through the years to children and determines how they handle their own relationships. Dr. Neubauer does say, "There is a healthy drive in human beings to observe their parents' infidelity, then say, 'I shall do the opposite.' " However, that same drive can also lead to unreal expectations in the children of infidelity who hope so much for perfection in their own relationships that they are often terrified of failing and consequently may never learn to relate at all.

There has been no research regarding the relationship between parental infidelity and attitudes toward monogamy. However, sociologists Richard A. Kulka and Helen Weingarten of the Survey Research Center at the University of Michigan published a landmark study in 1979 on the long-term effects of parental divorce in childhood on adult adjustment. They conducted two national cross-sectional surveys of children who had experienced parental divorce before the age of sixteen, and spaced the two surveys twenty years apart.

In both studies, Kulka and Weingarten found that people from backgrounds of parental divorce are significantly more likely to report having experienced problems in their own marriages than were subjects who came from intact backgrounds. They also found that children of divorce are more likely to admit feeling inadequate as spouses. Such children, report the researchers, admit to more problems in marriage, at the same time claim normal levels of marital happiness, and in general view the institution of marriage in a more complex light. Kulka and Weingarten conclude by saying that children from parental marriages which were dissolved by divorce or separation are more likely than children from intact parental homes to dissolve their own marriages voluntarily.[12]

Kulka and Weingarten's findings can also be applied to the children of divorce's reaction to infidelity. If they were aware of their parents' affairs, they are more likely to grow into adults conscious of the complexity and pitfalls of monogamous marriage. There are no data that prove children of unfaithful parents are prone to infidelity in their own relationships; however, my research strongly indicates that my generation's exposure to parental infidelity, coupled with parental frankness with children and parental infidelity-related divorces, contribute to this generation's departure from traditional monogamy. In very simplistic terms: Infidelity often leads to divorce, and divorce may lead to infidelity among the children of divorce. Children who experience their parents' infidelity may pattern their own behavior after their parents', causing the same process to begin again. And the infidelity/divorce/infidelity carousel whirls on more relentlessly than ever today, creating the ideal climate for cheating to take place.

Do People Believe Fidelity to Be a Realistic Expectation?

There is a split within people's expectations of fidelity. On a general level, a 1981 *Psychology Today* report on cheating asked the readers to estimate the percentage of married partners who have been sexually unfaithful. The overall guess was 52 percent. The report showed that 45 percent of married respondents admitted to affairs.[13] When I talked to interviewees about monogamy, 90 percent of them said they felt that monogamy was under seige and that fidelity was not a realistic expectation in today's world.

However, when it came to evaluating the realism of expecting fidelity in their own relationships most of the interviewees agreed that they expected their own relationships to be monogamous. In fact, in most cases, they had never even discussed fidelity with their mates. Every other issue was mulled over—attitudes toward children, family, vacations, work—but rarely did two people discuss their feelings about infidelity. Overall, I found that the majority of couples were playing ostrich politics, ignoring the rise in infidelity and preferring to take the stance that it would never occur in their own relationship. Fidelity was assumed but rarely discussed. Couples might "ooh" and "aah" over the current trend toward infidelity, but at the same time (even if one person is cheating) most people still maintained an attitude of "*They* may be doing it but *we* would *never* cheat." Individuals rarely countenanced the possibility of infidelity as a reality within their own relationships. In theory, the majority of people insisted that they believed in monogamy, yet when asked to evaluate the extent of infidelity in today's society most interviewees conceeded that cheating was all around them. While the majority of people surveyed initially committed to fidelity sincerely and didn't begin marriage planning to stray, present-day society is structured to make infidelity easier for them than it has ever been before. And so it seems vital to examine the reasons for today's infidelity-prone society.

The Decline in Religious Beliefs

One of the reasons for the increase in infidelity today is the decline in religious marriage services. The fact that two people promise before God to forsake all others doesn't, of course, automatically ensure fidelity, but the absence of a moral structure does tend to make infidelity easier. Researchers Reiss, Anderson, and Sponaugle reported that cheaters were mostly low on religious belief,[14] and the answers to my survey indicated that if cheaters felt guilty, their guilt was *not* motivated by religion. In the *Psychology Today* report, 85 percent of the self-confessed cheaters claimed to feel guilty about their affairs, and so did a high percentage of the cheaters I interviewed, yet when I asked them to explain *why* they felt guilty, the majority answered that they felt guilty because they had broken the promise of fidelity they had made to their partner. It seems that their guilt existed on a one-to-one level and not because they felt they had sinned against their religion. My interviewees were equally divided between Protestant, Catholic, and Jewish, yet none of them ever mentioned their religion when talking about infidelity. It is as if religion no longer has any influence whatsoever on the private behavior of individuals in their relationships.

The Rise in Hedonism

Life in the eighties is geared to instant gratification and naturally that quality spills over into the realm of relationships. Variety and the search for pleasure is one of the prime factors of life in today's America.

Take Janet and John, for example. They decide to spend an evening at home, watching TV. Thirty TV channels are available to them. But none of the programs tonight please them, so John leafs through his video-club catalogue and orders the latest movie to be delivered within the hour. In the meantime Janet has to decide about dinner; she doesn't feel like cooking, so she opts for having the food delivered from a local restaurant. Should Janet and John have steak, Japanese, Chinese, Italian, or Greek food, or just plain hamburger? The variety available is certain to please one or both of them. While they are waiting for the movie to arrive, John plays with his video game, while Janet tries on one of her ten gold necklaces. Finally the movie is delivered. After five minutes of watching it, Janet and John decide that they dislike it and snort some coke instead to increase their sexual pleasure. After sex, they both take a Quaālude to ensure that they will sleep soundly.

Much of our lives today are centered around pleasure and a hedonistic search for happiness. In the wake of the "me, me" era, many eighties' men and women still live by a desire to fulfill their individual needs rather than by the rules of religion or morality. It is true, however, that many people today are attempting to switch their focus from themselves to the couple unit as a means of attaining happiness. But the question often becomes, Which couple? The couple you are or the couple you *become* when you cheat? Often, if there is any flaw in the existing marriage or relationship, the individual's ever present tendency to search for pleasure can lead him or her to cheat.

It seems that everyone wants the best service, the maximum amount of pleasure. And if the partner they have fails to meet production standards and to continually deny pleasure, naturally the individual is motivated to sample another product instead. The hedonism of "self-satisfaction above all" seems to be essential to American life in our time. Again and again my interviewees mentioned the way in which the American dream and a hedonistic approach to life encourages infidelity.

A male cheater comments on cheating.

> I think cheating is very much a part of our culture, whether it is cheating on the speedometer or cheating on the taxes. Whatever you can get away with. Our expectations are so high in America today that we always feel we aren't getting enough. Cheating is an integral part of our culture and it inevitably leads to sex.

Another male cheater says, "Infidelity is really—'What I can get away with.' That's the covert American dream—to pull a fast one." And a female cheater agrees, "The American way of life is to get what you can out of life, and if it is to cheat, then you cheat."

Hedonism is riding high in America today and invariably leads to cheating. It is all related to the grass is greener syndrome. Why settle for the relationship you have when another one might make you happier? Why be faithful to one person when variety might be even more satisfying? All in all, why commit in the first place? In other words, why be faithful when infidelity might make you happier?

Many people, in fact, do believe that extramarital affairs lead to happiness. The sanctity of self-fulfillment seems to

49

override commitment in many cases. Psychologists Bukstel, Roeder, Killmann, Laughlin, and Sotile studied projected extramarital sexual involvement among a group of unmarried college students and found that individuals who planned to engage in extramarital sex, expected to find infidelity more emotionally and sexually satisfying than marriage. They assumed that extramarital sexual behavior would be more adventurous and would increase feelings of inner security. They also believed that their affairs would increase their social status and make them feel very independent. But, as the researchers point out, "this tendency to rationalize projected extramarital sexual behavior may be due largely to a lack of foresight about the possible negative outcomes."[15] It could be argued that instant gratification and hedonism don't mesh with foresight about the negative outcomes of our obsessive search for happiness.

The Sexual Revolution

The aftermath of the sexual revolution seems related to the increase in infidelity. Although sociologists Glenn and Weaver, in a survey of attitudes toward premarital, extramarital, and homosexual relations in the U.S. in the seventies say that "the so-called sexual revolution in the United States has been real, but that, at the level of espoused standards, it has been restricted to a decline in disapproval of premarital heterosexual relations. Attitudes towards extramarital and homosexual relations remain, in the aggregate, distinctly restrictive. Of course, there is not necessarily a close correspondence between behaviour and espoused standards."[16] Other researchers (Reiss, Anderson, Sponaugle) indicate that there is a relationship between the increase in premarital and extramarital sex and the fact that people who have a variety of sexual partners before marriage are more likely to cheat after marriage.[17]

I am a product of the sexual revolution and I wouldn't for the world have missed one second of wildness. I loved it all —the freedom and the self-indulgence—but in retrospect I am starting to realize that perhaps the sex code of the sixties and seventies might well extract a price in our relationships in the eighties.

The sexual revolution and the pill made sex guilt-free and fear-free for everyone. Sex became like a free-for-all in a candy store; suddenly everyone could gorge themselves, even if they ended up feeling sick. The pill made unplanned pregnancy almost obsolete and the modishness of unshockable sex made any excess almost elegant. Pornography was everywhere and taught us to fulfill our most lurid sex fantasies. Everything was fine as long as no one got hurt, and sometimes even if they did. Just as long as it felt good it was OK to do it or have it. Sex equaled elation and sophistication. Four letter words lost their shock value, and even their sexuality. Premarital sex became almost mandatory; after centuries of being forced to say *no* to sexual advances, it was suddenly overwhelmingly obligatory to say *yes*! A rainbow of sexual variety was celebrated in every conceivable shade imaginable.

And our experiments with premarital sex led almost inevitably to extramarital sex. Often, premarital sex bred standards of comparison, and these created higher standards of sexual perfection, so that if one's spouse failed to live up to perfection there were plenty of extramarital relationships available which would conform to one's high expectations. After all our premarital sexual adventuring, it became very difficult for some of us to settle for monogamy.

And even if we did momentarily commit to monogamy, why should the sexual carousel come to a halt? Why not, many of us reasoned, sample the lusciousness of infidelity? After the excitement and glamor of multiple partners why stagnate in the stability and sameness of monogamy? We had become so addicted to excitement and variety, why not "go with the flow," and sustain the pitch by biting into the forbidden fruit of infidelity?

So there it was. Premarital sex and an unlimited choice of partners who had taken us to dazzling heights of sexual ecstasy made it hard for us sexual revolutionaries to pick one partner and remain faithful to him. Our fevered pasts made it difficult for us to finally settle for monogamy. If our partner's sexual performance, over the long haul, failed to compete with past lovers, why not instead go out and sample more lovers? The sexual revolution bred standards of comparison, high expectations, a kaleidescope of changing partners, and halfhearted stabs at monogamy, followed by infidelity and chaos.

The sexual revolution has affected marriage negatively yet perhaps now that it has subsided, we may no longer be so frantic about premarital sex and in turn may find monogamy more satisfying.

The Women's Movement

In 1971, sociologist Robert N. Whitehurst in the *Journal of Marriage and Family,* put forward the following reasons for male infidelity:

> The separation of roles and functions, the disparate life cycle experiences, and the very different life-style of male-female involvements in the world outside tends to provide ranges of opportunities, new people and experiences that do not always make a marriage coalesce. The usual pattern of interaction in marriage promotes husband absence as an easy out—if and when things get difficult on the home front or when wives demand commitment and interpersonal response that husbands are not equipped to give. This often provides a rationale for wives to seek excitement,

romance, and thrills, but the position of husbands is already clear; if interested in extra-marital sex, his opportunities are already more than half made by his work setting or business or professional contacts.

The relative investment of male-female concerns has traditionally favoured women staying at home assigning priority to children, house then husband. This hierarchy does not preclude extra-marital sex searching, but in fact may at times encourage distance and the formation of new relationships. Different opportunity structures have always favoured the male, and they continue to do so, Numbers of hours freed from spouse, children and other kin has always limited wives, but new consciousness bred by women's liberation as a social movement may equalise this old trend.[18]

Eleven years after Whitehurst speculated on whether the women's movement might equalize the trend in infidelity, we are informed that the statistics for female infidelity almost parallel those of male infidelity. The working women of America are no longer—in theory at least—tied to unfaithful husbands, nor are they prevented by family responsibilities from straying themselves. Apart from the economic power that employment has given many women, the movement has, in effect, made female infidelity far easier.

On a very practical level: As the women's movement has opened up further fields of female employment in divergent areas, more women are working. This has created greater opportunities for women to cheat, given that we now all have access to the age-old male alibi, "Darling, I'm working late at the office." The high number of women in the work force also means that married men now come into contact with a greater number of women on a regular basis. Whereas in pre-women's movement days married men cheated mostly with women they met casually, in the eighties they are often likely to cheat with a female co-worker they meet on a daily basis. This obviously can lead to more profound, all-encompassing extramarital affairs.

The rise of female cheating, from Kinsey's 26 percent in 1948 to Linda Wolfe's 50 percent in 1981, seems to correspond with the evolvement of the woman's movement. Although one wouldn't want to equate liberation with infidelity, it is undeniable that female mobility and career success does create more opportunity for cheating.

The Media and Infidelity

Another possible cause for the increase in infidelity in our time may well be the media. In the 1971 survey conducted by Robert Whitehurst, "Violence Potential in Extra Marital Sexual Responses," 40 percent of the sample claimed that the mass media had an effect on them in a liberating direction in regard to sexual things, specifically to extramarital sex.[19]

Since Shakespeare created *Othello* and Tolstoi, *Anna Karenina,* infidelity has been a central theme of literature. However, in the seventies and the eighties, the debate has switched to television and media depiction of the extramarital affair has altered radically. Given that sociologists have proved that the media influences behavior and that it also mirrors trends, it is important to examine the changing reflections of infidelity projected by the media.

The Forties

The great romantic films of the forties clearly romanticized infidelity, but at the same time invariably preached that there was a price to be paid for adultery. Watching the forties filmed versions of the classics, audiences wept over the fate of the adultress who was inevitably punished by death (Anna Karenina and Madame Bovary). The other woman, too, was always punished for encouraging the married man to stray from the path of fidelity. In *Lady Hamilton* (Churchill's favorite film), Lady Hamilton, the scarlet lady, was portrayed as dying from starvation, suitably punished for her affair. In *Back Street,* too, a romantic tear-jerker, filmed in three different versions, the other woman suffered loneliness and the death of her married lover after a life-long affair with him.

Although the films of the forties may have romanticized the extramarital affair, the other woman was usually punished. So, often, was the straying husband. In *Intermezzo* Leslie Howard tries to recapture his youth in a mid-life affair with Ingrid Bergman. She suffers by eventually losing him and he suffers by watching helplessly as his daughter is struck down by a car.

Both cheating husband and cheating wife suffer in the great infidelity classic of all time, *Brief Encounter.* Neither is punished by death or illness, yet the Noël Coward script makes the point that their unconsummated contemplated adultery causes both the man and the woman a great deal of pain. As film critic John Simon observes, "In *Brief Encounter* and other films of the old days, adultery wasn't really mentioned. Infidelity was sacrificed for a greater good."

The Fifties

Infidelity in the movies was no longer depicted as a punishable offense, but was dealt with lightly and amusingly and never really focused on the subject. There were films like Alec Guinness' *The Captain's Paradise,* a comedy in which the captain takes infidelity to the limit by having two wives, and *The Seven*

Year Itch, another comedy in which infidelity is flirted with but never actually takes place.

Television, born in the fifties, also didn't tackle the infidelity theme. Jeffrey Greenfield, former TV critic for CBS *Sunday Morning,* remembers that the classic TV show of the fifties was based on the Hollywood production-code standards "which meant that there was no sex in the movies. Only twin beds and no suggestion of nudity. When Lucy had a baby in *I Love Lucy,* there was a big debate because the word 'pregnant' was not supposed to be used." TV was chaste, and the only reference made to infidelity occurred in situation comedies which never actually grappled with the issue.

The Sixties

TV still didn't deal with infidelity, but films like *Darling* (in which Julie Christie plays the amoral other woman who gets her man and survives, and Dirk Bogarde utters the memorable "swinging sixties" line, "Your idea of fidelity is not having more than one man in your bed at once," depicted infidelity as glamorous and not necessarily a sin that elicits the wrath of the gods. Mrs. Robinson in *The Graduate* cheats casually and doesn't suffer. Judy Geeson in *Three into Two Won't Go* plays the trendy other woman, awarding her married lovers sexual ratings along the way without encountering any retribution. The sixties marked the birth of the portrayal of adultery-without-suffering in the media.

The Seventies

By the seventies, infidelity was handled with sophistication. *Sunday, Bloody Sunday* was a cinematic breakthrough, with its portrayal of a bisexual man, juggling a male and a female lover. Infidelity was no longer solely the stuff that the classic romantic films were made of with the inevitable bitter sweetness of the husband or wife returning to their spouse. In *A Touch of Class* infidelity was treated as acceptable, sophisticated—if painful—fun. In *Shampoo* the cheating wife remained unpunished, although the "other man" was ultimately discarded. The films of the seventies no longer avoided the seriousness of the infidelity issue, but still didn't dwell on it in great detail.

Television in the seventies represented the biggest change in media treatment of infidelity and presumably had the heaviest impact. *Only with Married Men* was one of the first infidelity programs, which centered on a woman who only dated married men. *The Mary Tyler Moore Show, Mash,* and *All in the Family* dealt with extramarital sex at one time or another during the seventies. Jeffrey Greenfield remembers an episode of *Lou Grant* in the late seventies, which zeroed in on the media's burdgeoning obsession with infidelity when Lou Grant's son-in-law proclaimed that he planned to have an affair because "infidelity is all around us. You can't turn on the TV or pick up a book without reading about it."

The Eighties

Today infidelity is portrayed by the media as a fact of life, an element of relationships that isn't analyzed in detail. In the film *Shoot the Moon* infidelity is treated merely as the cause of divorce and is not explored any further. In the Anne Meara/Hal Linden, March 1983 drama *The Other Woman,* the program focuses on the age difference between Anne Meara and Hal Linden's young wife rather than on the infidelity itself. The way in which the plot is resolved (Linden confesses his affair, whereupon his wife owns up to hers) typifies the laissez-faire attitude toward infidelity projected by the media of the eighties.

The impact of the media on people's behavior was evident during my research. One female victim wrote to me saying, "My husband's affairs make *Dallas* and *Dynasty* look like Disneyland." She sounded almost triumphant; her life had overtaken art in terms of sensationalistic infidelity. Programs like *Dallas* and *Dynasty* certainly serve up graphic infidelity situations, and because of their opulent context, manage to glamorize infidelity. Daytime soaps, too, according to *Soap Opera Digest* editor Meredith Brown, also demonstrate a shift in attitude toward infidelity. Although they don't glorify extramarital affairs, soaps no longer portray adultery as an aberration that demands punishment.

As Jeffrey Greenfield remarks, there are very few shows on prime time TV today, that center on happily married people. The only couple which exudes marital fidelity and happiness are the Harts on *Hart to Hart,* but as Jeffrey wryly comments, "That seems to indicate that people can only be happily married if they have fifty million dollars."

The change in the media approach to infidelity from a melodramatic but moral standpoint, to virtually taking it for granted, inevitably reflects and influences the perspective from which the average person views infidelity. The media message is no longer, "Infidelity is bad and always causes suffering," but "Infidelity is inevitable." Infidelity is treated by the media as an everyday occurrence and this media trend contributes to the eighties' laissez-faire attitude toward infidelity.

Society's Attitude Toward Infidelity

Society's attitude toward infidelity has softened in the past ten years. One of the reasons for the current shift in attitudes may well be related to our contemporary belief that love excuses all. A 1977 study in person perception, "The Errant Spouse," by Hartnett, Mahoney, and Bernstein of the Virginia Commonwealth University, demonstrates that if a husband or a wife cheats as a result of love, their affair will be viewed more favorably. The married person was liked if he was in love but not if it was sex for sex's sake. If the cheating spouse was seen to be in love, the impression was favorable because they showed a capacity for involvement. The conclusions of the study were that a husband or a wife having an affair is perceived in a favorable light if they love the third party.[20]

Society may regard infidelity more leniently if love is involved, but other factors also contribute to our present-day permissive attitudes toward the extramarital affair. As stated before, the decline in religious belief encourages infidelity; so does the role model of parental infidelity, and our awareness, via statistics, of the prevalence of cheating. On a very primitive level, our awareness that infidelity is rampant makes it easy for the average person to rationalize their own infidelity (or any temptation to cheat) by saying, "Everyone else is cheating, so why shouldn't I?" Another factor in the rise in infidelity is our consciousness that infidelity is common among our most dazzling and respected public figures. Of course, infidelity has occurred in the realms of power since the days of Henry VIII and Anne Boleyn, who was executed for infidelity to a king. But it is only in the last ten years that the media has dared to chronicle the foibles of the famous. Up till now infidelity in high places was the subject of speculation but today the media is apt to openly confirm rumors. Public opinion has shifted radically in terms of infidelity-in-high-places since the sixties. And the way in which we react to adultery in public office naturally has some repercussions on the way in which we react to individual behavior in our private lives.

In the sixties even divorce was still frowned upon. I remember, in 1960, feeling there was a stigma attached to my parents' divorce and not wanting to tell my friends about it. Nelson Rockefeller, according to Jeffrey Greenfield (who was Robert Kennedy's speechwriter), probably lost the California Republican Primary in 1964 because his second wife, a younger woman for whom he had divorced his first wife, gave birth to their son two days before the primary.

If divorce was frowned upon in the sixties, infidelity in public life was anathema. Elizabeth Taylor was denounced in the House of Representatives by a congresswoman when she had her notorious affair with Richard Burton during the filming of *Cleopatra.* Both Burton and Taylor were married to other partners at the time and an enthralled public monitored their affair while the congresswoman announced that Elizabeth Taylor had "lowered the prestige of American women abroad and damaged good will in foreign countries."[21] Taylor's condemnation recalled public reaction to Ingrid Bergman's infidelity, when the Hon. Edwin C. John of Colorado called her "a powerful influence for evil." Joseph I. Breen, Vice-President of the Production Code Administration wrote to Ingrid saying that her actions "May well destroy your career as a motion-picture artist."[22] Infidelity in public life was tantamount to committing professional suicide.

Our current-day laissez-faire attitude toward infidelity among our public figures was perhaps partially formed by the startling revelations of President Kennedy's infidelities, first made public in the seventies. A stunned nation learned that Caesar definitely wasn't above reproach and that the late President had been, in the words of Jeffrey Greenfield, "a compulsive adulterer." Even at the time of his affairs, eye witnesses report, President Kennedy was blatant about his philandering. "One day I caught him messing around in the Cabinet Room in the White House," remembers presidential intimate George Smathers. "I asked him how the hell he thought he was going to get away with that kind of thing."[23] It seems that men in positions of great power, like President Kennedy, often have a compulsion to fly very close to the sun by flirting with the danger of discovery. The British press (who are quick to unmask the foibles and indiscretions of their public figures) printed a similar story of infidelity-in-high-office, when they revealed that the former leader of the Liberal Party, Jeremy Thorpe, was unfaithful to his wife with another man, in the shadows of the Houses of Parliament.

President Kennedy's infidelities were eclipsed and forgiven on the grounds that he died for his country. However, the tales of infidelity definitely paved the way for sagas of infidelity among the rich and the powerful. As Aileen Mehle, "Suzy," the society columnist, explained to me, when putting infidelity-in-high-places into perspective, "I don't think that because people live a higher life-style that they have a different kind of infidelity. Of course, an orgy or sexual kinkiness in a palace is more titillating than in a hovel. There has always been infidelity in all strata of society, the Peyton Place syndrome is found in every little town. It has always existed, it just seems more acceptable now."

Infidelity among our public figures certainly does seem more acceptable in the eighties. The Kennedy revelations were followed by the Wayne Hays and Wilbur Mills scandals, which did destroy both men's careers on the grounds of their infidelity, and once again focused the spotlight on infidelity among the powerful. Even President Carter contributed to the mass consciousness of infidelity by admitting in a *Playboy* interview to occasionally experiencing "lust of the heart."

Public opinion no longer condemns the infidelities of show-business stars. The reaction to Sylvester Stallone leaving his wife for Susan Anton (after having an extramarital affair with her) was decidedly mild and far removed from the pre-seventies public response to infidelity. Present-day celebrities may cheat on their spouses but the affair no longer damages their careers. As we watch our idols drift away from monogamy, the ripple effect may well be driving yet another nail into fidelity's coffin, conspiring to make infidelity in the eighties accepted as an inevitability.

Attitudes Toward Teaching Children About Monogamy

All my interviewees, even the most inveterate cheaters, claim that they will teach their children to be faithful in marriage. However, the parent's own behavior may transmit quite a different message which validates cheating as a way of life. If the parents are known to be cheating, their actions tend to make a mockery out of their teachings. However, if parental examples don't influence the child's attitudes toward monogamy, then pressure from peers certainly could.

The Relationship Between Peer Pressure and Monogamy

Peer pressure on men and on women in regard to fidelity is very different, leading to *different expectations relating to gender.* Little girls are brought up to implicitly believe in "happily ever after" and in Prince Charming, who will love them for life and be eternally true. During a girl's teens, there is no pressure on her to prove her sexuality or desirability by being promiscuous. Instead pressure is exerted through materialistic channels; a teenage girl's sexuality and attractiveness is probably more likely to be validated in the eyes of her peers by lavish gifts from her boyfriend than by having countless sexual flings. Even in post-liberated America, a diamond ring is still viewed as an affirmation of a woman's desirability to the opposite sex. Having multiple partners and being promiscuous before or after marriage still leads to accusations of sluttishness.

There is no peer pressure on women to cheat, but rather to find a prestigious husband. If anything, there is still a pressure on married women *not* to cheat, especially if they have children. If a married woman with children has an affair, one often hears the reaction, "How could she do that to the children?" Behind that lies the assumption that an unfaithful mother invariably neglects her children. Yet if a married father cheats, his affairs are viewed as having very little effect on the children and the concept of neglect as a result of infidelity isn't applied to him.

From childhood, many boys are educated to be womanizers, while their sisters are still educated to be wives. The message that infidelity is more acceptable for boys than girls is projected early in a boy's life. As he grows up, the adage "Boys will be boys" is said with a leer and a wink, but there is no female equivalent of the phrase. Children in the playground sing, "Georgie, Porgie, Pudding and Pie, kissed the *girls* and made *them* cry." Already the message is "Go for more than one girlfriend." Male promiscuity is virtually encouraged and laughed about.

As the boy begins to talk about sex with his peers, more seeds are sown for promiscuity that can later flourish into infidelity. Alan Gross of the University of Missouri investigated the male role and heterosexual behavior and says that

> early in adolescence, most boys recognize that sexual success is not "scoring" in the parked car, but describing real or imagined sexual exploits to a group of teenage cronies the next day at school or even the same night at the local drive-in. Thus, the sexual partner becomes a mere instrumentality used by boys to achieve status in the eyes of those who really count—the male peer group.[24]

Pressure from the male peer group to have sex with a variety of women persists as the boy grows older. If challenged to justify his polygamous attitude, many a man has pointed to animal biology as a means of proving that men are more sexual than women. This produces a great rationale for rampant male infidelity—"men are just made that way—they can't help it." However, the facts regarding the strength of male sexuality, as opposed to female sexuality, do *not* make an incontravertible case that men are biologically polygamous.

Dr. Colin Beer, professor of psychology of the department of Animal Behavior at Rutgers State University in Newark, makes the point that the animal kingdom isn't, perhaps, the best place in which to prove or disprove anything. "If you look at the animal kingdom," he says, "you can find evidence for any pattern you want to support; you find monogamy, you find promiscuity, you find the harem arrangement." Dr. Beer explains that monogamy in the animal world is related primarily to locale. That is, if the animals, for instance, eagles, are in an area where all other animals are excluded, they are more likely to mate for life.

Dr. Beer also found a relationship between fidelity and fecundity. "Coulson of Durham University has studied bond persistence and the relationship of it to breeding success and found that fidelity was related to fecundity and productivity. If the birds are productive they are more likely to stay together."

Two other studies on animals and fidelity demonstrate the lack of conclusive evidence for the case that infidelity is man's biological destiny. Dr. Beer says that there are examples of male harems, but that when the females come to heat, the younger male monkeys are turned on and sometimes the females will cheat. Female infidelity has also been observed in baboons. Hans Koummer's studies indicate that female infidelity is as frequent in the animal world as male infidelity. He has observed that very often a female baboon will become attached to a young male and will copulate with him behind a rock, so that the male she is supposed to be attached to won't see what is going on.

Anthropologist Lionel Tiger, on the other hand, puts forward an argument for males being biologically polygamous and says that man's sexual destiny evolves out of biology.

> Sexuality comes out of the reproductive system. It is embedded in the whole process. In order to reproduce often you expect the male to be more promiscuous. Before contraception the more times a male would copulate, the more chance he would have of producing an offspring. It is natural for the male to have as many sexual partners as possible, because that maximizes his chances of having offspring.

A desire to reproduce may present a valid rationale for male infidelity. On the other hand, the overall picture of male biology doesn't really provide a consistent reason for male infidelity. As D. Byrne asserts, in a paper, "Social Psychology and the Study of Sexual Behaviour," published in the *Personality and Social Psychology Bulletin,* "The belief that men have a stronger sex drive than women persists with no compelling evidence to support it."[25] Nevertheless, as Alan Gross observes, "Whether myth or biological fact, men and women generally believe and act as if sex is more central, enjoyable and necessary for males."[26] And as peers propogate that belief among each other, the resultant pressure provides part of the impetus which prompts many men to cheat.

Peer pressure is also apparent in the rash of sex magazines which appeared in the seventies and eighties, and which might be said to be partly responsible for the rise in infidelity among men. A combination of editorial propaganda and advertising in sex magazines project the ideal male as being a polygamous playboy. Frank, a married cheater of twenty-four I interviewed, told me,

> All one's life, men have the role of swinging n'er do well to live up to—the media image of playboy. Popular morality says boys will be boys, but once you hit a certain point in your life and

> marry you are supposed to cut out that image. Then there is the conflict between the settled individual and the playboy, both inhabiting the same body.

Other men, though, don't feel any conflict whatsoever between the married man and the playboy of popular pornography—this naturally can lead to infidelity. Keith, a thirty-one-year-old computer operator says,

> It is chic and hip and everyone can rationalize cheating. My goal is to satisfy as many women as I can. I've been with close to a hundred. I dislike the guilt and the fact that I lie to myself. Something inside of me says, "Hey, you've got it really good at home. Why go out and cheat?" Then the thrill-seeker side of me says, "Hey, you want to do it to feel satisfied and complete." Men find it more difficult to be faithful. My generation grew up believing that it was practically mandatory for our generation of man to cheat. What with the swinging sixties, sex was all out there, so why not go and get it?

Peer pressure to cheat via pornography, makes many of today's men believe that cheating is their destiny. Group sex and swinging, both extreme manifestations of promiscuity, have often been attributed to the fact that men succumb to pornographic projections of the ideal super-stud male. Anthropologist Gilbert D. Bartell investigated group sex among middle Americans and found evidence that many of the male swingers were propelled into swinging by the playboy image of the ideal male, popularized by the magazines of the seventies. He observes that by swinging, many men

> may now feel that they are doing what the "in" people are doing and living up to their playboy image. One of the most important negative aspects, as we see it, is the inability to live up to one's own psycho-sexual myth and self-illusions. This is particularly

> disadvantageous in the case of the male. They read about sexual behavior in the outer world, and they realize they are not participating in this elaborate sex life.

Bartell goes on to outline the fact that "in American society the male is expected to be a tremendous performer sexually and he must live up to his own publicity."[27] The attempt of many men to do so sometimes led them into group sex situations and often into extramarital affairs. Swinging may no longer be a strong element in the sex life of the eighties' male, however, extramarital affairs obviously are.

"The cultural underlay and the social setting increasingly allows if not openly encourages extra-marital sexual expressions," writes Robert N. Whitehurst in the *Journal of Marriage and Family.* He goes on to comment,

> It becomes evident that we find a vastly increased potential for extramarital contacts, open opportunities for sexual play, and vastly decreased internal and external restraints in the old sense of religious, community and familial controls over spousal acts. Social structures have become very much altered in terms of their ability to control, freeing people to act much more in alignment with their own desires. When we add the impact of mass media and the more positive orientation of self-fulfillment in a highly individualistic society, the peer support of certain extramarital sex activities and the tendency to seek a sense of community away from the established confines of social norms, we can anticipate a number of influences liberalizing and supporting a higher extramarital sex potential.[28]

On a subliminal level, society sends out the message that infidelity is permissable. We may all acknowledge the damaging consequences of cheating, allude to the negative repercussions of divorce, and deny that infidelity could ever infringe upon our own personal partnerships, but the fact remains that society's attitude toward infidelity, the sexual revolution, the decline in religious worship, peer pressure, and our reaction to parental infidelity, all combine to create today's liberal climate in which infidelity is accepted as a fact of life. Although society no longer hands out scarlet letters to cheaters it is important to be aware of the hidden pressures on individuals to reject monogamy.

The social stage is set to encourage infidelity. And if we want to understand the dynamics of cheating, it is vital to explore how and why the present-day cheater indulges in infidelity.

TWO

Profile of the Cheater

He is forty-two, married and imposing. She is twenty-three, single and experimenting with life. They meet by chance when he interviews her for a job as his secretary. Passion sparks over his repro-antique desk. He gazes at her with undisguised lust, while she trembles in innocent ecstasy, praying that the faint traces of sexual-arousal sweat won't stain her new Alexander's pantsuit. Urbanely he questions her about her ambitions, and coquettishly she avoids answering. Somehow he manages to convey his single state, mumbling that the children (whose photographs are so prominently displayed in the silver frames) are the offspring of his first marriage. Naturally, she never suspects that he is still currently married.

He, sensing her attraction to him, is tempted to seduce her. After nine minutes of serious soul-searching, he determines to follow the Pied Piper of temptation through to its logical conclusion. They lunch together the next day at Café des Artistes, sharing the desert platter which oozes fudge and chocolate charisma. He (Married Marvin, as we'll call him) charges lunch on his American Express card, and instructs his chauffeur to transport her (Swept-Away Cora) home to darkest Flatbush. When he arrives back at his office, Marvin commands his secretary to send Cora roses, thinks fondly of her for a few moments, then reminds himself not to sign the gift card.

That night, Marvin returns home to his wife (Petulant Patti) enshrined in their Scarsdale sanctuary. Toward midnight, he slips into his study and telephones Cora on the extension. While he is telling her that he feels it is more conducive to their fledgling passion if he hires another secretary, Patti picks up the living-room phone, whereupon Marvin hastily slams down the receiver.

Two days later, they lunch together again, Married Marvin and Swept-Away Cora, the unknowing other woman. When Cora archly asks Marvin for his home number, he mutters something about needing space, and she responds by nodding sympathetically. This time, they are lunching at Orsini's, Patti's favorite restaurant (although Marvin manages to expel that thought from his mind as the restaurant is only a block away from his office and oh so convenient). Flourishingly, Marvin presents Cora with a two-ounce bottle of Christian Dior's latest seductive scent, resisting his wish to shower her with Patti's pet perfume, Galanos. Over the fettucine, Marvin invites Cora for a weekend in the Bahamas. Blushing furiously, but mentally revamping her wardrobe for Paradise Island, Cora accepts.

Marvin and Cora meet at his office on Friday evening. The chauffeur drops them at JFK, where Marvin picks up the airline tickets at Pan Am, this time charging them to his MasterCard. On the plane, disaster nearly flattens him; Hysterical Herbert, Marvin's college partner in crime, is on the same flight. Marvin turns to his copy of *Time* and pretends not to have noticed Herbert. The plane lands in Nassau and from then on the weekend dissolves into pure enchantment.

Godiva chocolates and Dom Perignon champagne greet the couple in their suite. Johnny Mathis croons "Misty" through the hotel sound system. It's only a radio, but the effect is nevertheless evocative of perspiration-free passion. At dinner there is *langoustine* and *escaloppes de veau,* asparagus and *Omelette Norvégienne.* After coffee and amaretto, the couple retire to their suite. There, Cora languishes on silk sheets, draped in her duck-egg blue negligee, feeling like something straight out of one of Helen Gurley Brown's fantasies of the Cosmopolitan girl surrounded by romantic opulence.

True, there are a few false notes (as in the best *Cosmo* first-person romance in which the heroine ultimately discovers she is wed not to a Roman prince, but to a Sicilian smuggler of Oriental rugs). While Cora is in the shower she hears Marvin make a mysterious phone call. Patti, back in Scarsdale, also senses that the phone call is mysterious, Marvin having informed her only two days before that he was off for a few days in Flatbush with his dear friend from high school, Herbert. Half-heartedly, Patti had asked for Herbert's number, but pretended to be mollified when Marvin explained that Herbert had an antipathy toward telephones and therefore didn't have one. But then, Patti didn't care much. After all, she was fully aware of Marvin's extramarital excursions and was only waiting for his profit-sharing benefits for that year before filing for a quick divorce.

Meanwhile, Marvin has just finished making love to Cora and is lying on the slightly rumpled sheets next to her, plotting his next move. How will he tell Cora that he is married given that he plans to continue the affair on a monthly basis? Marvin actually isn't too worried, fully primed as he invariably is with lines like "My wife doesn't understand me" and "Of course, I never touch her sexually—we gave that up twelve and a half years ago." The next few months unfold euphorically in Marvin's jaded mind. Lunches and weekends with Cora, the odd present designed to ease her single state, accompanied by an always unsigned gift card. Perhaps some lace underwear, and definitely gallons of French perfume. And Cora, in return, will be honor bound to love Marvin and be forever available to him. Maybe Marvin will even set her up in her own apartment. The silk sheets rustle as Marvin drapes his arm around Cora and drifts off into a self-satisfied sleep totally befitting his dream extramarital affair.

Dream extramarital affairs. They don't ever happen. Although I don't want to suggest that every single infidelity is bathed in excruciating squalor, according to my research, silk sheets and champagne are very far removed from the average extramarital affair. And so are most of the other elements of the Marvin/Cora affair. The reality is, for the majority of cheaters, very different. So let's look at the norm by replaying the Cora/Marvin scenario.

Marvin is forty-two; Cora is thirty-five. He is a shoe salesman, and she works at one of his accounts. They have known each other for five years but Marvin never managed to summon up the courage to ask her out. When he finally does, he makes it abundantly clear to Cora that he is married and has no intention of leaving his wife.

Cora is willing to go along with the situation. She is divorced, doesn't want to get remarried and is quite prepared for a fling with Married Marvin. Cora gives Marvin her home number, fully understanding that he can't reciprocate by giving her his. A week later they lunch at a diner in another part of Manhattan, holding hands under the Formica table.

Two days later it is Cora's birthday and Marvin mails her a Hallmark card, signing his name in bold letters at the bottom. He brings Cora a pair of red patent-leather, high-heeled shoes crafted in his company's latest best-selling style. He also presents her with a bottle of Galanos, his wife's favorite perfume.

When Marvin gets home to Patti, his wife of fifteen years, she senses that her Marvin is acting friskier than usual, but is unprepared to draw conclusions from his behavior, simply ignores it, and instead worries about the baby's croup. She doesn't even register his tardiness or question him at all.

So the affair continues as it began—a typical, modern extramarital affair.

Marvin, of course, is home late because he and Cora have finally consummated their affair. The event was destined to happen the day before, but just as Cora and Marvin were leaving Beefsteak Charlie's after work (where they had popped in for a brief preconsummation hamburger), they had bumped into Herbert, Marvin's old college mate. Marvin had risen to the occasion and introduced Cora as a business colleague, propelling her straight into the nearest cab, and then waving good-bye. But finally tonight is the night.

It is six o'clock. Marvin and Cora, following a prearranged plan, take separate cabs and meet at a motel, just outside the Lincoln Tunnel. Marvin pays eighteen dollars for the room, giving the cashier the money in notes. Cora hovers in the shadows, careful to note the key number. Five minutes later, she knocks on the door of Marvin's room. Inside, she finds him sitting on the red bedspread, staring nervously at the Utrillo print of the Arc de Triomphe which hangs beside the cracked mirror. Cora undresses in the bathroom, remembering to rinse out her mouth with water sipped from the plastic cup provided by the motel. Marvin, meanwhile, has undressed in the bedroom. Cora walks toward him, and in a few minutes they make ardent love on the slightly graying creased polyester sheets.

After an hour, Marvin and Cora leave, finishing their cigarettes, Marvin arranging to meet Cora at the same motel in a week's time. Never, at any point during the rendezvous does Cora question Marvin on his sex life with his wife. However, if she had, he would have told Cora the truth: They sleep together and usually have sex once every two days.

Of course some extramarital affairs are flamboyantly glamorous and filled with exotic details, but the second Marvin/Cora scenario is typical of the extramarital-affair settings that I encountered in my interviews.

Why waste time with Marvin and Cora at all? Why bother examining the methods and context of the average extramarital affair? Because, I believe by looking at the components of today's affair, we may learn how to spot the danger signs when they appear in our own relationships.

First, though, there are some general signs which may indicate infidelity. John Johnston, a detective who works on marital cases for one of Manhattan's biggest investigation agencies, Marital Investigation Service Inc. (which has nine East-Coast offices), summarizes the warning signs to look for that may point to a cheating partner:

> One sign is if you have been married to someone for a long time and all of a sudden, the patterns are broken. A husband might always come home at eight, then suddenly it is nine. All of a sudden she has new friends, a loss of weight, new clothes, a different hairstyle. There is a sudden mystery and excuses like "I will be out at a card game, but there is no place where you can reach me."

Other interviewees repeatedly cite general clues of infidelity; unexplained phone calls and letters, talking about a member of the opposite sex obsessively, friends and neighbors who drop cryptic hints. Those may be the general signs, but it is by examining the specific tactics of cheaters that we can gain insight into the ways and means of infidelity. Luckily, for the purposes of this book, cheaters are extremely boastful about the cunning they employ to cheat and get away with it, providing extensive clues to the modus operandi of the seasoned cheater.

I have divided extramarital affairs into three basic categories:

a. Hit-and-run cheating—The one-night stand
b. Commercial-sex cheating—Sex with a prostitute
c. Secondary-relationship cheating—A long-term extramarital relationship with one person.

How and Where the Cheater Met the Cheatee

Detective Johnston, who has dealt with over one thousand cases of marital infidelity, reports that roughly 50 percent of cheaters are involved with co-workers. Given the time spent at work, the opportunities to establish relationships with co-workers are manifold. Any profession which includes contact with the opposite sex can be a prime breeding ground for extramarital affairs.

Obviously the more mobile a person's profession, the more opportunity he has to meet people with whom to be unfaithful and also to arrange alibis. Cheating is far more difficult to schedule for anyone in a strict nine-to-five job. Not only do they have very few chances to sneak away for assignations, but their spouses expect them to return home at the same time each day.

On the other hand, I found that a great number of cheaters work in free-lance professions, or jobs with flexible hours (the police force or the transportation business). I also discovered that there is a relationship between someone's professional skills and his propensity for cheating. According to my research, salesmen and attorneys prove to be the most prevalent cheaters. There are possible explanations as to why both professions are conducive to cheating. A salesman boasted to me that he could sell anyone anything, which included selling his wife the idea that he was faithful to her. Salesmen may be ace cheaters because they are in a more goal-oriented profession and are accustomed to instant gratification in their careers, which could contribute to their dedication to winning what a salesman described to me as "the cheating game." Attorneys too (members of a profession in which verbal skills are of paramount importance) are polished at exercizing their verbal talents by wooing cheatees as well as convincing victims of their own fidelity.

Other "unfaithful" professions include show business, journalism, teaching, and other professions which necessitate verbal ability. And naturally professions which include periods of travel away from home. Many of these professions (like selling) provide expense accounts which help male and female cheaters to lure cheatees by entertaining them lavishly on the company which employs them. And for both male and female cheaters, traveling for career purposes provides the ideal opportunity to cheat far from home, without the danger of complications or being seen by friends or acquaintances.

Apart from the obvious reason of proximity and daily personal contact, the office affair may begin for other, more complex reasons. Perhaps the husband or wife is in a profession far removed from the spouse's sphere, an area in which the spouse has no interest. Enter the co-worker, who not only is excited by the profession, but also may have some expertise or knowledge which he can pass on to the cheater. Not only does the cheater have opportunity to cheat, his participation in the same profession as the cheatee gives the couple parity of interest, and makes an affair all the more likely.

The common cliché (pre-liberation era) was that the boss might cheat on his wife with his young (usually blonde) secretary. The wife, therefore, was always wary of her husband's underpaid right hand. How much more threatening then, is the female executive, a potential *other woman,* who is the husband's professional equal? The same applies to cheating wives who work. Before the advent of the working woman, the cheating wife might be suspected of infidelity with an inferior, someone who called at her home on an errand, but rarely with an equal. Now, work has become the best way in which a woman as a potential cheater can meet a cheatee who is *her* professional equal.

Cheaters also meet their cheatees at singles bars, a phenomenon of the seventies. Discoteques have declined in popularity, but previously were also a prime meeting place for cheaters and cheatees.

Apart from work, the chance encounter is the most common way in which the married cheater meets the other man or woman. However, a new, more calculating trend has evolved in the permissive eighties, a surprising channel whereby married people can attract lovers.

The New York Review of Books, The Village Voice, and *New York* magazine, all carry advertisements placed by both men and women who solicit partners, blatantly stating that they are married. Many of the ads lead with "Married Man" or "Married Woman." *The Village Voice* prints at least five advertisements from married people each week and the fact that advertisements such as these produce replies from both the single and the married is very indicative of the climate of the cheating eighties.

A married woman, Barbara, contacted me in response to one of my advertisements for cheaters. She herself, she told me, had advertised for a lover in a previous issue of *The Village Voice.* She specified in the advertisement that she was looking for a married boyfriend. Barbara was hesitant and nervous when she talked to me, but confessed that she felt unhappy.

> I feel sad that my marriage has brought me to this, but I feel I have to look outside of my marriage for my own sanity. I feel I need someone else to bring out the best in me. My husband is a workaholic and very self-centered. I love him and I think that he has some positive qualities, so I don't want to break up the marriage. I advertised in the paper because I don't have the time to go out and look for someone. I definitely want a married man because I am not ready to leave my marriage. I am looking for someone who is supportive to my ideas, who is sensitive and attractive. I am not cheating for sex, sex will just be a by-product.

I think advertising for someone in the paper is ideal; that way I can get right to the point of what I want.

Barbara told me that she had 150 replies to her advertisement, but was cagey about revealing details concerning the respondents.

In contrast, Cliff, another married advertiser, was far more forthcoming and shed some light on the kind of replies a married cheater gets when he pleads in print for a partner. Cliff is in his fifties, has been married for twenty-eight years and is a businessman.

I started advertising in *The Village Voice* because I once fell in love with a woman and it was a very, very painful experience. I've had the ad in *The Voice* for three years and have put it in six times during that period. I've got replies from all over the country. I call the women and make appointments to meet them. There is no mystery when someone answers my ad. I try and meet women from all walks of life.

I heard from a woman whose husband was a public figure. She was scared to death, but she just had to answer my ad. I hit her solar plexus. She couldn't help herself and as afraid as she was, she still answered. I got one woman who answered who is married, works three days a week, and got hold of her closest friend to have me write to her address with my phone number. She told me how sexual and warm she was and how she thought I was the kind of man she wanted to meet. How she misses intimacy. A lot of the women who reply are divorced but don't want to get married again. They feel that if they find the right kind of married man, they won't be smothered or hassled and will still have their freedom.

Many of the single women who answer the ads are turn-offs. Some of them are looking for a sugar daddy. One woman answered who is divorced with kids, and wanted me to pay her. Another said she was twenty-five, beautiful, and a college student and wanted to meet someone generous. Not for me.

Personal advertisements are the newest way in which the cheaters of the eighties meet their cheatees. However, one of the most startling discoveries I made is that approximately 20 percent of men and 30 percent of women cheat with family friends or relatives. The reason why women cheat with friends or relatives may be the fact that there is still a certain amount of danger inherent in picking up a stranger. Women (with a few exceptions) prefer the safety of the familiar. A female cheater I talked to, for example, was unfaithful to her husband with the best man at their wedding. Another woman cheated with her brother-in-law. Dave, thirty-one, found his twenty-seven-year-old wife was having an affair with his best friend. "I called him up and told him it was a rotten thing to do," remembers Dave. "He said she was coming on to him for a long time. I believe him because she is very sexual."

Betty, a female cheater, talks about infidelity with a family friend and makes it sound almost cozy.

> I am friends with his wife and they are both friends of my husband. We all go out at night to meetings and club activities, then it is easy for my boyfriend and I to disappear and go off to a hotel. I don't think there is anything wrong with it. We are just friends and sex is part of the friendship that developed.

A male cheater, from Arizona, felt the same way: "The cheatees were all friends of my wife and I knew most of their husbands socially. We met during the day and other times when I didn't have to defend my whereabouts."

Cheating with an in-law is surprisingly prevalent. Mike, thirty-five, cheated with his sister-in-law a year after he and his wife got married. "The affair went on for four years. She came on to me. Maybe it was a psychological thrill for her," ponders Mike. "Having sex with me must have been exciting for her. I was working nights and my wife was working days so her sister and I would go to each other's houses."

Mike doesn't seem to feel guilty about his affair and said,

"I don't think my wife knows; I think she would leave me if she found out about her sister."

Peter, a construction worker was unfaithful with his sister-in-law four months after marriage.

> The affair started when my wife was out of work and went on for a year. Her sister was very dominant and when I was with her I dressed up in women's clothing. The most exciting thing, though, was that she was my *wife's* sister. Eventually, though, my wife found out and we got divorced. I didn't marry the sister.

In-law infidelity is taking sibling rivalry to its farthest possible conclusion. And one wonders about the nature of "the psychological thrill" that brothers or sisters feel when they cheat with their sibling's spouse.

In theory, most cheaters say that they prefer to cheat with other married people. As one cheater puts it, "That way they have as much to lose as I do, if we get found out." But in practice, cheatees are divided fairly equally between the married and the single.

The Way in Which the Cheater Explained His or Her Primary Relationship to the Cheatee

We have seen that some cheaters of the eighties far from disguising their marital status, literally advertise it. In today's world very few married men or women start an affair by hiding the fact that they are married from their cheatee. I remember in my "swinging sixties" teens still hearing horror stories from older, saddened, sophisticated girls, which climaxed in the punchline, "And after all that, I discovered he was married." Yet, only about five people I surveyed admitted that they lied to their cheatee about being married.

A few interviewees told me that they even tried to turn their marital status (which used to be a negative) into a plus. One experienced male cheater proudly announced to me that his favorite come-on line to a woman usually was "Would you like to have dinner with a married man?" and that he rarely met with any rebuffs. The fact that married men are no longer compelled to lie about their marital status is a reflection on the current state of the mating game.

Where Cheaters Cheat

Very rarely on a tropical island or in a luxury suite according to my research. The majority of cheaters in America today, unlike Marvin and Cora, can't manage the extramarital vacation, but instead slip away for one hour trysts at a local motel. Only 20 percent of the cheaters I surveyed slip away on illicit weekends. And if they do, most cheating couples register under their own names. The pseudonyms, Mr. and Mrs. Smith, seem to be dead in the eighties. Today's cheater brazenly registers in motels or hotels under his or her real name, although I did encounter the unusual case of the real-estate magnate who proudly informed me that when *he* cheats, he registers in motels under the names of his business competitors.

The second Marvin and Cora scenario highlights one of the cheater's number one rules. If he does cheat in a motel/hotel room—or even if he takes his cheatee out to lunch—he always pays cash, with the aim of preventing telltale credit card slips appearing on the breakfast table at home along with the morning mail. The practiced cheater always carries plenty of cash.

Cheating, and where the cheater and cheatee consummate their relationship, is often related to income. The *Playboy* (January 1983) survey reported that 70 percent of unfaithful men and 41 percent of unfaithful women earn more than

$60,000 a year. Although their high income may also be coupled with a mobile job (and also more opportunity to cheat), the *Playboy* finding underscores the fact that cheating can be expensive.[1] While you don't have to be rich to cheat, money certainly helps.

When it comes to the one-night or one-hour stand, money can obviously make the difference between tussling in the back seat of the car (a happening reported by many cheaters) or relaxing in the local motel. The days are over in which the guilt-ridden married man feels compelled to shower his mistress with gifts to "soften her single state" and even to set her up in an apartment so that she can be permanently available to him. Today's other woman no longer demands payment for having an extramarital affair. However, any man who conducts an extramarital affair on a long-term basis finds that he has to be able to afford two Christmas presents (for wife and girlfriend), two birthday presents, two Valentine's Day presents, and so on. (And if the gift, as in Marvin's case, turns out to be perfume, experienced cheaters recommend that the cheatee be presented with the identical scent as the victim so that when the cheater arrives home from his cheatee, he won't smell of any strange perfume.)

Women, too, need money for extramarital affairs. If the woman has children, she often has to afford home help, which will free her to meet her lover. If she is working, she may also need cash to pay for cabs to that midtown rendezvous and perhaps new clothes with which to titillate the secret man in her life.

Cheating definitely is expensive not just in emotional terms but in pure dollars and cents. The economic recession may prove to be monogamy's number one ally, making it too expensive for many a potential cheater to stray. Indeed the current economic crisis may force many people to spend longer hours on work, leaving little time to juggle with the intricacies of the extramarital affair.

Alibis for Cheating

Without a doubt, even the most casual affair requires that the cheater weave an extremely tangled web. It is surprising how much brainpower is channeled into cheating and getting away with it. In a few cases, it almost seems as if cheaters are more excited by the thrill of cheating and not getting caught than by the actual affair itself. Some cheaters I talked to took great delight in fabricating complicated alibis to cover their cheating.

The classic cheating alibi, used now by both men and women is "Darling, I'm working late at the office." I found in my research that 48 percent of women and 42 percent of men use going out with a same-sex friend as a cover for time spent cheating. Detective Johnston says that the most prevalent excuse he hears from cheaters (after working late and going out with friends) is the "I need some time to think" excuse.

> Clients always call me up with that one. The husband, for example, calls up and says, "I don't know what is happening to my wife. We have been married for twenty years and now she is suddenly telling me that she needs time to think. She says she wants to go down to the Jersey Shore by herself. She doesn't want to tell me where she is—she just wants to go for the weekend." But of course, she is not by herself but with another man.

Johnston's data, and my own interviews, completely negate the idea that cheaters use friends as alibis without telling them about it. An experienced cheater never uses a Herbert for cover, as Marvin did, without informing him beforehand. And if cheater and cheatee accidentally did meet a family friend, the cheater would respond by switching to a prearranged plan and introduce the cheatee as, for example, "My cousin's best friend, Bill, from out of town."

Cheaters tend to use alibis that can't be verified. They might tell the victim that they are going to a particular bar for a drink with the boys, but after the event tell the victim that "the boys" didn't like the bar so they went to another one on the spur of the moment. That way, if the victim happens to check with the bar, the cheater is covered and can say the venue was changed at the last minute. Another uncheckable alibi, which Detective Johnston says is mainly used by men, is that they fell asleep in the car by the roadside and so arrived home three hours late. As Johnston observes, with a cynicism born out of dealing with the identical alibi in countless cases, "I drive constantly, and the only people I ever see sleeping by the road are truck drivers. I never see any husbands."

Another classic cheater's alibi is the hobby. About 20 percent of cheaters use hobbies or sports as an excuse for time spent cheating. However, the majority of cheaters exhibit great deviousness in picking the particular hobby which will provide their alibi. Some of the cheater's well-chosen alibis include working out at a health club, where naturally there is no telephone on which members can take calls. Another bonus from the health club alibi is that the cheater can explain his lack of desire for sex with the victim by saying that he or she is exhausted from a stiff workout that evening at the club. The outdoors is also a favored cheater's ploy; birdwatching or sailing are popular examples, both sports where the cheater cannot be contacted (and checked up on) by telephone.

Once the cheater has established his alibi for the evening, he still has to tackle the possibility of detection when he arrives home. Many cheaters don't drink, to avoid "spilling all" when they arrive home after a romantic cheat. Others cautiously run Scotch tape over their clothes before they go home, in an attempt to remove any hairs from the cheatee that might be sticking to the fabric. Then there is also the major

—if clichéd—male cheater's problem of lipstick stains in the wrong places. A cheating expert I interviewed tells me that he circumvents that one by tactfully informing all his girlfriends that he detests lipstick. Consequently none of them wear it, and so the danger of lipstick stains is averted.

The majority of cheaters are remarkably cautious (although Marvin in the first story made a point of not putting his passion on paper), but an incredible 50 percent of my sample actually send their illicit lovers postcards, birthday cards, letters, and even poems. Fifty percent of today's cheaters ignore the maxim: Never put anything in writing. We may not be too far from the day when Hallmark starts to manufacture greeting cards which read "From your married lover." Cheaters, apparently, are just as sentimental as anyone else in the throes of a passionate affair. A more cynical slant, however, is that some cheatees report that they *demand* that the cheater commit his or her love to writing, as a way of proving trust.

Communications in general can often be used to the cheater's advantage. Current awareness of cheating is running so high that one Dallas man, Mason Zelazny, has even invented an alibi for veteran cheaters to use. So far, six American restaurants have purchased his $2,000, "What's your excuse?" telephone booth. Clients pay one dollar for two minutes of convincing background noise to be played into the telephone, while they talk to their spouses and proffer suitable excuses for not being at home on time. Cheaters can pick either the noise of a traffic jam, a thunder storm, a beauty parlor, or an airport lounge to substantiate their alibis.

Marvin may have used his home-phone extension to call Cora, but the majority of cheaters rarely telephone their cheating partners from home. If, however, this does become inevitable, the cheater of today is helped by call-waiting, a modern innovation. One interviewee told me that he was talking to his cheatee when his victim came into the room. Instead of slamming the phone down in guilt, he was able to click it and say, "I was talking to my mother but lost her on call waiting."

That way he appeared less suspicious. The film, *Sunday, Bloody Sunday* illustrated the importance of not being too friendly with the answering service; the service accidentally informed the victim of the cheater's whereabouts.

Some cheaters go so far as to leave a trail of false clues for their victim to find. A female cheater I interviewed told me that each day she laboriously scribbles into a fake engagement diary, then leaves the diary around for her victim to discover. The engagements cover the time when she is cheating, and add a touch of authenticity, she feels, to her alibi.

Another jaded male cheater keeps a secret notebook, in code, listing his victim and cheatee's likes and dislikes so he doesn't mix them up. He revealed his tactics to me with evident relish. Many cheaters approach cheating as a kind of challenge to their ingenuity. To them, success at remaining undetected is a tribute to their intelligence.

Unless an extramarital relationship is long-standing and based on mutual trust, very few cheaters allow themselves to be photographed with their cheatees. But in our video age, a new area of danger has emerged. The chances of being unknowingly video-taped or filmed as part of a crowd scene, are increasing, as one cheater learned to his cost. While walking in the streets of New York with his girlfriend, a married man was totally unaware that he had stumbled into the filming of a crowd scene. A year later, he and his wife were at the movies, watching the film, when he and his girlfriend appeared on screen, strolling hand-in-hand. The film was used as part of the divorce evidence.

Whether or Not the Cheater Was Open with the Victim About His or Her Cheating

Do men and women enter marriage making it clear that they plan to cheat? My research suggests that while some marriages evolve into open relationships, very few start out that way. Of course there are one or two exceptions like the case of Simon, a fifty-year-old attorney.

> I've been married for twenty-seven years, but I was unfaithful to my wife the day after we got married—with a girl I met in law school. I thought I should get married to have children, but I was honest with my wife from the start. I told my wife that I planned to cheat on her. I wouldn't have married her if she had said that she wouldn't put up with it. I'm not dishonest.

Simon and his wife didn't embark on an open marriage in the classic sense, because his wife never really believed that he would cheat.

> My mother told my wife that I would never change, that I had been having sex since I was twelve, but my wife didn't listen. She insisted that she would change me. She didn't. She knew what she was getting into. I view our marriage as a contract; if I lease an apartment from you and openly tell you that I am going to light a bonfire in your apartment, you still lease it to me and I then really do light a bonfire in the apartment, there is literally nothing you can do about it. You can't sue me because I made my intentions clear from the start.
>
> Polygamy was the thing in the Bible, almost everyone—right from Abraham had multiple wives. I support my wife well. I don't hit her. When I go out and she asks me where I am going I just tell her "Out." And she puts up with it. I don't know if she cheats, but if she does—fine—I'm not jealous.

Simon's story is unique. Unless a couple has ventured into the realms of swinging or open marriage (which will both be discussed later) the subject of fidelity is rarely broached. The victim's reaction to an extramarital affair will be explored in the next chapter. However, the overall finding regarding whether or not the cheater is open with his victim about his cheating, is a resounding no, hardly any cheaters are.

In many ways, the reasons are obvious; if a spouse declared his desire to cheat when committing to marriage his or her partner would naturally question the sincerity of the commitment to marry in the first place. A question I heard again and again when exploring the topic was "Why get married if you start out planning to be unfaithful?" Unfortunately, the majority of people don't seem to plan at all, but merely drift into infidelity, as we shall see in case histories of the cheater.

The Relationship Between Cheatee and Victim

If, as in the majority of situations, the victim is not aware that the spouse is cheating, their relationship with the cheatee will be one of complete innocence. The cheatee may, of course, hate the victim (because he or she wants to replace them), but the way in which the cheatee relates to the victim is largely determined by the cheater. Most cheaters make it clear to the cheatee that any threats or revelations to the victim will only result in anger on the cheater's part and won't lead to a dissolution of the marriage. This usually prevents the cheatee from disclosing the affair to the victim.

If the cheatee isn't a relative or friend (which as we've seen, many cheatees are) the majority of cheaters try to ensure that the victim and cheatee never meet. However, a few male cheaters appear to be titillated by their two loves meeting—without the victim being aware of the truth. A male cheater explains,

> I feel great when I am in public with both of them. I suppose it makes it hard for my girlfriend, being with my wife, but the fact that my wife does like her, makes it easier for me to cheat and not feel guilty. I suppose I have the feeling, somewhere inside, that

> if my wife discovered our affair, she would almost approve, because she knows and likes my girlfriend. But apart from that—when I am with both of them I feel doubly loved.

Some cheaters deliberately manipulate the relationship between victim and cheatee and enjoy the results. Shana Alexander's book *Very Much a Lady: The Untold Story of Jean Harris and Dr. Tarnower* describes the motivations and actions of a man involved in a triangle situation who contrived to create jealousy between the wife figure in his life, Jean Harris, and his younger mistress, Lynne Tryforos. "Many observers surmised that Tarnower deliberately encouraged each woman to be jealous of the next, in order to feed his own ego." writes Shana Alexander.[2]

Diana Trilling's book *Mrs. Harris: The Death of the Scarsdale Diet Doctor* comments further on Dr. Tarnower's manipulation of the relationship between "wife" and mistress.

> Whatever his seriousness as a physician, in his private life he was in the business of indulging some profoundly unserious notion of what constitutes manhood. There is something disturbed and disturbing in the sexuality of someone who plays women off against each other as he played these women of his.[3]

Shana Alexander's analysis of Dr. Tarnower's motivations adds to our understanding of the cheater's attempt to incite rivalry between wife and mistress. She tells us that a Moroccan driver once mentioned to Tarnower that he had two wives. Tarnower asked him why. The driver replied, "Because I can't afford four. But even two is much better than one. With two, both try a little harder." Apparently, Dr. Tarnower repeated that same story on many occasions, and Shana Alexander, commenting on the rivalry Tarnower engineered between girlfriend and wife figure, observes, "And some, worldly as the Moroccan limousine driver, understood the enjoyment it can afford a vain and ageing man to watch two attractive desirable women fight over him tooth and claw. They thought it simply turned him on."[4]

According to Dr. Neubauer, certain men (and there seems to be no parallel syndrome among cheating wives) deliberately encourage a conflict between wife and mistress because "the fact that two women fight over the guy makes him feel great. He wants both of them to fight over him because he is quite a guy." The male fantasy of having two women compete for his favors is reflected in the underground sex world of New York where men pay nude women to wrestle with each other in brothels, or watch nude women fight one another in places like Plato's Retreat.

The cheater who makes sure that wife and girlfriend are aware of each other's existence knows that both women will be on their mettle, constantly trying to please him. The rewards of such tactics are tangible and obvious. However, there can also be another unconscious payoff for him. Men who indulge in pitting wife against girlfriend may themselves have been victims of sibling rivalry. Their mothers may have forced them to compete against a brother or a sister for her love. As a result they tend to construct their adult relationships so that the women in their lives compete for their love—just as they did for their mother's.

At the other end of the spectrum, a few men confess to harboring the fantasy of going to bed with wife and mistress at the same time. Some cheaters, usually the ones involved in long-term secondary relationships with women who are practically second wives, admit they would "love to go to bed with my wife and my girlfriend at once. I often fantasize about it." Another cheater wistfully says, "I wish my wife would be more open-minded. If only she would have my girlfriend come and live with us. To have sex with her and with me." One wife and girlfriend actually fulfilled that genre of fantasy by presenting their mutual lover with a ménage à trois—a birthday present from both of them. The girlfriend enjoyed the experience most because she was bisexual. Eventually, both the wife and girlfriend split up with the husband, and he is now monogamously involved with a third woman.

Although the occasional married man exists who fantasizes sleeping with victim and cheatee at once, I never encountered a parallel syndrome among female cheaters. Not one of them say that they want a ménage à trois with husband and boyfriend, although a few women say that they fantasize about their lover when having sex with their husband.

The Effect of Cheating on the Cheater's Sex Life with the Victim

Cheating effects the cheater's sex life with the victim on many different levels. First there is the purely physical fact of making love to more than one partner in a day. However, most cheaters seem to be managing quite well; the *Playboy* (January 1983) survey found that half of the married men and women who answered the questionnaire admit to having had sex with two different people in a twenty-four hour period.[5] In my sample, I found that generally men have less of a problem having sex with their wives after being with their mistresses than married women do after being with their lovers. Men cite not wanting to arouse suspicion as one of the main reasons for rushing home and having sex with their wives. Women, on the other hand, seem to have more psychological problems. Sally, a forty-year-old cheater says,

> I always avoid having sex with my husband after I have been with my boyfriend. A bit of that may be because of guilt, but the main reason really is that I don't want my husband coming inside of

me straight after my boyfriend has. I know it sounds strange, but it just doesn't seem right.

The cheater who fulfills unusual sex fantasies with his cheatee, also has sexual problems when returning to his spouse. If the same fantasies have never been lived out in the marriage, very few cheaters repeat their extramarital sex practices (if they are unusual) within their marriages. Some cheaters want to but can't because they feel that their spouses would be suspicious if they suddenly initiated a new type of sex. Jackie, a female cheater, circumvented the problem in the following way: Her lover had taught her that she enjoyed giving oral sex, something she had always hated. After a year, her extramarital relationship broke up, but Jackie found that she enjoyed oral sex so much she wanted to continue it with her husband. Knowing that he would be shocked and perhaps suspicious, Jackie announced that she wanted to try and conquer her dislike of oral sex "because I read an article the other day in some magazine on how to enjoy giving oral sex and so I figured I might as well try again." Jackie's husband was overjoyed, yet remains unaware of his wife's affair.

Some sexual practices, however, don't transfer so well from cheatee to victim. Bill, a married cheater, had during the twenty years of his marriage, rigorously suppressed his sadistic impulses. Then he began an extramarital affair with a woman who had masochistic tendencies.

I used to have sex with her in the rear-entry position, and while I penetrated Julia, I'd spank her. Nothing heavy, just light slaps. But then, when I made love to my wife after that, I constantly had to fight back the desire to spank her. I'd get all tense and the whole thing ruined our sex life, which up till then hadn't been too bad.

Many cheaters, in contrast to Bill, don't *want* to enact the same sexual practices with cheater and cheatee. They deliberately pick partners who are very different sexually from their spouses and in their minds rigidly separate them. The motivation of these cheaters who suffer from the madonna/whore syndrome will be explored more fully later in this chapter.

Dr. Herbert Strean, psychoanalyst and author of *The Extramarital Affair* talked to me about the effect cheating has on the cheater's sex life with his victim. Generally he has encountered one major trend: "If the cheater has a long-term extramarital affair, they often move further and further away from the wife/husband—partly because there were probably sexual conflicts in the marriage in the first place. It is very frequent that an extramarital affair leads to the cheater having less sexual interest in the husband/wife."[6]

Why People Cheat

If we attempt to examine and confront the multitude of motivations for infidelity we perhaps may begin to understand and deal with our own or our partner's temptations to stray.

The question why people cheat will be answered in a variety of ways throughout the book, most particularly by the profiles of cheaters in this chapter. I have dealt in the preceding chapter with the reasons why I believe cheating is so prevalent in today's society but for a general overview of the age-old reasons for infidelity, I asked experts in the field of marital therapy for their opinions of why people cheat.

Dr. Neubauer cautions that before examining why a person cheats it is imperative to look at the relationship. "Every relationship problem is not just one person. You can't say 'she cheated.' You have to say, 'What did she not get in our relationship that she is looking for.' "

I asked Dr. Neubauer to evaluate why some cheaters race from one-night stand to one-night stand.

Someone like that has not matured enough to know that real love is not only being loved but feeling lovable and good enough about himself, to be able to extend himself and love and care for the other. People who run from one relationship to another may fear intimacy and closeness because they are not sure that they really deserve it. This often goes back to early childhood experiences. Love and attention was either not given adequately, or it was given at times—then seemingly arbitrarily withdrawn.

A typical experience is what happens to the firstborn child. He was king of the roost. Then his sibling arrived and suddenly mother gave more attention to the new child. As a result, he gets jealous, misbehaves, the parents get angry—then more love is withdrawn. This can be a traumatic experience which makes the child learn early not to trust or expect love.

Many people cheat because they never got what they wanted from mother or father and don't trust that they will ever be able to get it out of any one relationship. He has never learned that he is an important enough person to demand undivided love and attention and to be comfortable with it. He doesn't think he can make it with one person.

Sometimes cheating can happen because the person is still in a symbiotic relationship with the parent and it seems impossible to replace them. Or, on the other hand, the parent can be too self-involved and doesn't give enough love to the child. Then in adult life the person won't know how much to expect in a relationship. Then they learn to run before a relationship becomes really intimate as a way of forestalling disappointment and hurt.

Dr. Neubauer says that if someone cheats throughout a marriage she would ask him what he is getting out of the marriage. "You can't get deep fulfilling satisfaction in one relationship if you keep spreading your attention around. So, if a person keeps cheating I would question what the marriage is to begin with. And the person may be afraid of intimacy and closeness and has never learned that mature love depends as much on giving as getting."

A common reason for cheating, according to Dr. Neubauer, is marrying too young. High-school sweethearts who marry and have never had an experience with other people sometimes feel they are missing something. So they go out and have an extramarital affair. My research bears this out; many cheaters I talked to had, indeed, married in their teens and cheat out of curiosity or a need to rebel against the marriage they have known for most of their lives.

Dr. Neubauer also suggests that people often cheat as a way of increasing self-esteem; a new lover may obviously flatter the cheater's ego and a new romance may regenerate the cheater. This relates directly to sociologist Robert N. Whitehurst's remarks on infidelity in the *Journal of Marriage and Family.* He writes, "An increasing body of research shows that often there is a decrease in marital communications with length of marriage, a tendency for spouses to see fewer likeable traits and more negative ones, and for an increase in complaints due to the natural processes of male-female involvements that tend to make us appear different as spouses from the romantic people we supposed we married."

In other words, extramarital affairs may rekindle romance lacking in a long-term marriage. Whitehurst also cites other reasons for infidelity. "The interhabituation pattern of long association with one person naturally leads to some extinguishing of the intensity of sexual response. Although we receive much security in the predictability, recognition and response with the spouse, our needs for new experience is complex in this sphere of sexuality."[7] As the profiles of the commercial sex cheaters will show, familiarity often destroys sexual fantasy and excitement, and if they are unwilling to relinquish these elements of their sex life, they may well be tempted to cheat. Infidelity can often be activated by a desire for sexual adventures and more variety.

However, it would be a mistake to assume that infidelity is primarily sexually motivated. It may start out that way, but many long-term extramarital relationships are maintained because of intellectual, social, and emotional reasons. As Richard, a male cheater in his fifties explains, "I cheat because my wife doesn't have enough interests. If she were interested in some of the things I am, then I wouldn't cheat. I enjoy relationships with women who are intellectual, who are interested in travel, law, the stock market. If I were married to a woman like that, I would be faithful."

Richard may think he would be faithful, but Dr. Strean doesn't agree. The principle behind his Freudian-based theories of why people cheat is that infidelity isn't motivated by external factors, but that the cheater himself is a conflicted individual who would carry his internal conflicts with him into any marital relationship.

> Why people stray is usually unconscious and is born out of needs that are totally unconscious. I look at cheating as a symptom of marital stress and internal conflict. I look at infidelity as I would any neurotic symptom; an addiction, a phobia. The reasons why people cheat are so complex that most people aren't really aware why they are having an affair.

Dr. Strean outlines some of those reasons.

> A lot of people have residues of conflict from the first years of life. They can't really allow themselves to trust, to depend, to be depended on. This enters into their marriage. Also some people turn the spouse into a powerful figure. This results in them wanting "more space." They have formed a symbiotic relationship with the spouse that they have to run away from.

The powerful-spouse theme is related to another reason Dr. Strean gives for infidelity.

> Many children have been taught their do's and don't's very harshly. There is a tendency to view the spouse as a parent who is always controlling them. And to fight their feelings of being controlled, many people rebel and cheat.
>
> In some cases, if the spouse is made into a powerful parental figure, the person can't allow themselves to be turned-on sexually, but can only be sexually excited outside of marriage. The spouse is totally associated with mother or father, and is seen as virtually putting a noose around the person's neck—while the boyfriend or girlfriend is viewed as exciting.

Throughout my research I have continually encountered men and women whose behavior validates Dr. Strean's remarks. They have transformed their husbands or wives into parental figures, then many of them proceed to rebel and cheat, yet always feel secure in the belief that their spouse will never leave them. After all, a parent never deserts a child, no matter how naughty the child is. The cheater who views the victim as a parent figure also often expects unconditional love, saying to himself, "No matter how much I cheat, I will always be loved." The cheater's profiles will illustrate this statement in detail.

Another, more complex reason that Dr. Strean gives for infidelity is latent homosexuality.

> In the process of growing up, every boy or girl always wonders what it is like to be a member of the opposite sex. If someone wants to be a member of the opposite sex, then they may reverse roles unconsciously with the spouse. For example, if a man who wants to be a woman unconsciously turns his wife into a man—he may feel very uncomfortable. This often prompts the person to cheat—as a way of affirming their sexuality.[8]

Fredlee Kaplan, marital therapist, describes another motivation for infidelity, for embarking upon what I have termed the secondary relationship, a long-running extramarital liaison with one person.

> The triangling in of a third person in the marriage is an indication that there is either a problem between the couple that has been long standing, or a problem that has emerged from something new. The person who has the affair either doesn't perceive the problem and denies it, or if they perceive the problem—are denying it by turning to a third person. The affair becomes another mask over the marital problem and is a way of coping with the pain in those problems.

The majority of my interviews with secondary-relationship cheaters show that secondary relationships are indeed maintained as a way of avoiding confrontation with marital problems. Although many secondary relationships start as sexual flings, if they develop into sustained long-term relationships they function as safety valves within the marriage. A cheater may realize on a deep level that there is something radically wrong with the marriage, but instead of dealing with the problems (and risk, perhaps, breaking up the marriage itself) he goes out and tries to compensate for the qualities that he hasn't got within the marriage, by cheating with a third party. The secondary relationship, as we shall see in the interviews with secondary-relationship cheaters, is truly the triumph of love over sex. The long-term secondary relationship may fulfill intellectual, emotional, and friendship needs in the cheater that his legal marriage is completely unable to supply.

Infidelity and Gender

I started my research believing that given women's liberation, male and female methods and motives for committing infidelity would be identical. Past research in the field, however, told quite a different story. In 1969, sociologists D. W. Gurgul and F. Furstenberg reported that men and women experience affairs differently, that women have described their affairs as more emotional, and men have described their affairs as more sexual. They also reported that female affairs last longer and are more frequently associated with a decrease in marital satisfaction.[9] The research may date back to 1969, but in 1984 my findings are identical. The men I interviewed are prone to extramarital affairs of the one-night stand variety, and the women are more likely to get emotionally involved.

My research also validates Dr. Robert Athanasiou's 1970 findings that men begin their extramarital affairs earlier than women, have more sexual partners than women, and are more interested in mate swapping and group sex than women are.[10] I firmly believe, as sociologists Shirley Glass and Thomas Wright observed in the *Journal of Marriage and Family,* that "since men and women experience love, marriage and affairs so differently, it is important that data in the area be analysed for the effects of sex difference."[11]

What are the major differences between male and female cheaters? The most dramatic difference I found is that many men are unfaithful just for the sake of it, whereas most women cheat reactively. The profiles will illustrate this, and they will also attest to the fact that male and female cheaters have radically different capacities for analyzing and confronting their own infidelity. Women, I have found, tend to speculate endlessly on their partner's reaction to the affair and on the possible consequences of their extramarital relationship. Men, in contrast, don't seem to give much thought to the possible repercussions of their infidelity, usually telling themselves that there won't be any. The male cheater rarely speculates on whether or not his wife knows about his infidelity, or what she would do if she discovered the truth. Talking to the majority of male cheaters, I got the impression that they were all married to deaf-mutes, and that very few cheaters have any curiosity whatsoever regarding the workings of their wives' minds and emotions, or their own motives for infidelity.

Psychologist Robert Brannon of Brooklyn College (who specializes in the study of male sex roles) says that he could have predicted my findings on male/female introspection with regard to infidelity.

> A variety of studies have shown that women are more introspective about relationship issues. Women are better able than men to predict how a partner sees them. They are better at empathy and they are socialized to care more about relationships. In the thirties Helene Deutsch pointed out that the lives of men and women are very different in the sense of what matters to them. A man knows that to him, power and work are going to matter. But a woman knows that a big part of her life is going to be love and relationships, so naturally she will be introspective about those things.

Dr. Brannon's remarks bring to mind Lord Byron's lines from the poem *Don Juan.*

> *Man's love is of man's life a thing apart*
> *Tis woman's whole existence.*

Those words may no longer be valid for a great number of women in post-liberated America, but in some cases old emotional patterns die hard. Therefore, women who center their lives around their relationships and marriages will naturally be more introspective and thoughtful about anything affecting those relationships—including their own infidelity.

There is also the question of economics as a cause for female introspection. If a woman is supported financially by her husband, she may be more wary about his reactions to her infidelity. That statement appears to be anti-feminist, but it may well be that when a woman's economic survival depends on her husband's goodwill, she is less likely to cheat casually and is more liable to ponder over her motivation for having the affair and to try and predict its consequences.

Part of the low level of male introspection about affairs may also be because men don't feel obliged to justify their infidelity, either to themselves or to their partners. As we have seen, male infidelity is almost expected, even in today's world.

Many male cheaters are unafraid of the consequences of their affairs because their experience has taught them that infidelity need have no consequences. These are often the men who have witnessed their father cheating on their mother, who has then uncomplainingly endured the infidelity. Such an experience is common. Although women also come from backgrounds with cheating *mothers* (as the victim chapter will demonstrate), male victims usually don't put up with their wives' affairs knowingly. Therefore, most women will have seen that their mothers' infidelity had a destructive result—teaching them that infidelity does have negative consequences. However, sons of cheating fathers usually don't learn that lesson.

If a man has grown up observing the machinations of a cheating father and a compliant mother, he may tend to believe that he too will be able to cheat and get away with it. His reasoning may run as follows: "My father cheated on my mother and *she* didn't leave him. Given that my mother never left my father because of his infidelity, my wife will never leave me because of mine." The prevalent pattern of a cheating father and a compliant mother can lead many men to cheat without fear of consequences. My own family history mirrors this common pattern.

My grandfather was a larger than life, florid Viennese charmer who habitually wore a red carnation in his lapel and lavishly handed out large bottles of Chanel No. 5 to every pretty girl he met. My grandmother, small, dark, and intense, spent forty or fifty years passively and resignedly waiting in the wings while my grandfather cheated outrageously with musical-comedy actresses and nightclub singers. My father consequently grew up aware of my grandfather's debonair cheating. So naturally, when he married my mother, my father did the same and cheated his way through the marriage, assuming that his wife would put up with his infidelity. My father was convinced that he could follow his father's example and be unfaithful and always get away with it.

As it turned out, he couldn't, and my mother divorced him, much to the concern of my paternal grandmother who begged her not to, insisting "All men cheat." My mother did leave my father, and for many months he was stunned, refusing to confront the consequences of his own infidelity. Even when the divorce papers were issued, he tore them up, declaring, "She will always be my wife, no matter what."

That statement of my father's (something I had heard as a teenager) echoed through the years, carrying with it a message which my interviewees relayed again and again; many male cheaters view their wives in the role of mother. While they cheat they seem to regard their infidelities as escapades which will never seriously infringe on their marriages and which will never deprive them of their wife's love. "She will always be my wife" is extremely close to "She will always be my mother," which translates to "My wife is like my mother. She will always be my wife just as my mother is always my mother. And like my mother, my wife will love me unconditionally and will never desert me." This seems to explain many male cheaters' beliefs that their wives will never leave them.

For the most part though, the male cheater is usually so caught up in his cheating game that he doesn't reflect on what his wife would do if she found out about his affairs. However, there is still an element of wife-into-mother present in the way in which some cheaters handle their wives. Almost like children they test how far they can go. In some cases they almost seem elated that they are able to "put one over on her." Julia, a female victim, points to the sly-child syndrome in many male cheaters: "I asked him why he had been unfaithful. He said he just was and had no excuse. I said, 'If you had no intention of being faithful, why did you need to create the impression that you would be, and then do it behind my back like a bad boy?' "

The Commercial Cheater

Commercial infidelity is predominantly a male phenomenon. As Glass and Wright suggest in the *Journal of Marriage and Family* (all evidence I have gathered points to the same conclusion), "Female affairs are mainly emotional, and male affairs are mainly sexual."[12] Other findings related to their statement are those of sociologist Maykovich, who writes, "They (American women) do not approve of extramarital sex, but once exposed to an opportunity they are inclined to be emotionally involved,"[13] and of Bell, Turner, and Rosen, sociologists who surveyed 2,262 women who report,

> It undoubtedly continues to be true that the personal and social taboos against extramarital sexual involvement are stronger for women than for men. It is also true that extramarital sexual events don't occur just among married women in a random way. The sexual involvement is not simply a random event, but is a result of personal feelings, attitudes toward one's marriage, sexual feelings and general values toward life.
>
> In fact extramarital sex as a single event is not the common pattern. The [average] number of times a woman had sexual relations with each extramarital partner was almost six times. Only 16 per cent of the women had limited themselves to one sexual experience. By contrast, one third had extramarital coitus

> more than ten times with each partner. The evidence clearly implies a willingness to maintain a series of experiences with the sexual partner.[14]

My research shows that a small proportion of married women are breaking the traditional patterns and are having one-night-stand sex (the next section will discuss those women), but it is patently true that any woman who is prone to the casual sexual encounter will find it very difficult to satisfy her needs via commercial sex.

It is undeniable that female prostitution makes it easy for men to cheat. If a man wants to be unfaithful for "just sex" the world is his erotic oyster loaded with goodies designed to satisfy his every sexual whim. Everything available is conspiring to tempt him to stray. Streetwalkers are everywhere, so are brothels, which today are openly advertised in underground newspapers.

If a man wants to cheat without involvement, society is organized to fulfill that desire in the form of female or male prostitutes (for homosexuals). Commercial sex makes cheating eminently easy and tempting for men, and to many males, the hooker is a classic fantasy that they feel compelled to act out at least once in their married lives. George, a male cheater, explains,

> For some reason I had never gone to a hooker in my life. It struck me as very exciting. I saw an ad in *Screw* for a place on the Upper East Side. The first two times I paid sixty dollars, the third time, one hundred. I was worried about picking up an illness, but found that hookers are cleaner than most. The first place was a nicely furnished apartment. You walk into a room and there was just a mattress, a little table and a chair. The first girl was fattish, with a nice face and figure. She gave me a lot of oral sex to the point of orgasm.
>
> Something made me go to hookers. I cheated for sexual rea-

sons. That's really why I went to hookers. I really didn't feel I wanted any emotional involvement with the woman I cheated with. I love my wife and I don't want her to find out about my cheating because it would hurt her.

George's story illustrates both the lure of the hooker and what has come to be known as the safety-valve model of deviance, a theory first developed by social scientist Kingsley Davis who comments, "The attempt of society to control sexual expression, to tie it to social requirements, especially the attempt to tie it to the durable relation of marriage and the rearing of children, or to attach men to a celibate order, or to the sexual expression on love, creates the opportunity for prostitution."

Davis, as we have seen, blames society for prostitution, but then goes on to state that, in effect, prostitution provides men with a safety valve from the so-called tensions of monogamous marriage: "The craving for sexual variety, for perfect satisfaction, for novel and provocative surroundings, for ready and cheap release, for intercourse free from entangling cases and civilized pretense—all can be demanded from women whose interest lies solely in price."[15] In other words, commercial sex provides men with the opportunity for infidelity without entanglement, for sexual variety without consequence. Before we examine exactly what that means to male cheaters, it is important to look at the married women of the world who don't have the safety valve of commercial sex available to them.

Basically, if a woman wants to cheat, she either has to run the risk of the one-night stand with a stranger, or she becomes involved in a longer-term relationship. As we have seen, researchers (and my findings) indicate that most women want sex with emotional involvement. However, this might well be due to a chicken and egg effect. Do men indulge in quick commercial sex merely because it is available, or is it available in such profusion because men crave commercial sex so deeply?

In other words, if society didn't provide commercial sex for men, would they need it? If there were no prostitutes available as safety valves for married men would they sublimate their desires to cheat without involvement and maintain monogamous marriages, or would they then become emotionally involved with their extramarital partners as women do? There is no way of answering these questions conclusively except to look at the parallel position of married women who may want to stray. Commercial sex is only available to women in a limited way; consequently, the only way they *can* be unfaithful is to risk a hit-and-run encounter with a stranger, or in classic female manner—get involved. One could argue that the availability of commercial sex for men encourages them to cheat without involvement, and that the absence of commercial sex for women encourages them to cheat only *with* involvement.

It is true, however, that in post-liberated America, some male prostitutes for women do exist in urban cities like Los Angeles, New York, Miami, and Las Vegas. The fact that there are only a few male prostitutes may not be because there is no demand for them but because, according to sociologists Duane Denfield and Michael Gordon, "Males prostituting themselves for females has never been common, perhaps merely because apart from their economic positions, males are constitutionally less suited for frequent and prolonged intercourse."[16] Physically, a male prostitute is unequipped to take on many clients per day and in pure economic terms won't make much money by renting himself out on an hourly basis in the same way that female hookers can. It is easier for a male to patronize a female prostitute; it is also easier for a woman to *be* one.

If a female cheater does find a prostitute and plucks up the courage to patronize one, he will be expensive. A man can buy oral sex for about twenty-five dollars in any major U.S. city, but a woman will have to search, suffer embarrassment, then pay up to one hundred dollars for the same act. In other words, even if women do seek commercial sex as a safety valve from their marriages, it is expensive, difficult to find, and embarrassing to arrange.

However, I did talk to Suzie, a married cheater in her late twenties, who had an encounter with a male prostitute in Las Vegas.

I had always fantasized about paying a man to have sex but I never quite knew how to arrange it. Then a female friend from work and I went to Vegas and we saw ads for male escorts in one of the papers. I wanted to try it because my husband never gives me much oral sex. I never got used to having it and it took me ages to orgasm through getting oral sex. I always knew that I'd like it, but I never wanted to ask my husband to go on for as long as I needed. But I thought a male hooker would be a great way to try—to see how I'd like having it for a long time.

My girlfriend chickened out at the last minute, but she stayed with me in the hotel room while the man from the escort agency came over. It was very embarrassing really. He was a little bald man who got there and asked me what I wanted. I told him I wanted to "spend the evening with a man." He asked if I wanted to go out or stay in and I said "stay in." Then he asked me if I wanted him to be with me. It was awful, but I managed to say no and told him that what I really wanted was a dark man, very big and hairy.

The man arrived about an hour later. I was already undressed because I knew that I only had an hour and I didn't want to waste any time. I was shaking from head to foot when he knocked on the door, but when I saw him I couldn't believe how gorgeous he was. Sort of like Englebert Humperdinck. The agency had told me it was seventy-five dollars just to see him, plus a tip for sex. I tried not to think of any of that. I told him I wanted oral sex and he got undressed and kissed me. We had oral sex till I came—then we had proper sex.

I felt uncomfortable really. He kept telling me I was pretty, but I knew he was lying and that made me feel bad. I also could tell that he was trying to kill time by talking a lot. I've heard that female prostitutes do that to men, so I avoided that. But I did ask him why he was a hooker and he spun me some long story that sounded phony. He also told me that most of his clients were married. I gave him a twenty-dollar tip and he seemed quite pleased. I hated doing that, paying for it. But the worst bit really was when we had sex. I know he didn't really come. That he faked. And I felt terrible. I know female hookers do that all the time to men, but perhaps men don't mind.

I've talked to sophisticated women in New York, Los Angeles, and London, who say they have fantasized about paying for sex—having an extramarital fling without involvement—but I believe that many of them would react like Suzie. Apart from asking a variation of the old question men reputedly ask prostitutes "What's a nice girl like you doing in a place like this?" she obviously applied a heightened female sensitivity to the experience (as discussed by Dr. Brannon) and wasn't comfortable with the situation.

It appears that, apart from going to male striptease shows, very few women cheat via commercial sex. However, I was contacted by one extraordinary case, Jennifer, a woman of the future. Jennifer, a married woman of forty-five, with two children, *keeps* a male lover. Chuck, who plays the "mistress" role, telephoned me first. This is his side of the story.

I am in a relationship now where I am the male counterpart of a mistress. Jennifer is wealthy and she pays all my bills. She wants to have all my time so she pays all my bills and gives me charge accounts which she pays. I met her in Florida. I was already an up-market hooker (I've seen about a hundred women) and I was getting one hundred dollars a time. The other women were all career women, about twenty-four to thirty-five and they were seeing me because they wanted fantasies that their husbands wouldn't do. Jennifer and her husband are very wealthy—serious wealth with constant traveling, a home in Palm Beach, an estate in New York. Her husband is always on the move; he goes away to Europe all the time. So she decided she wanted me to be constantly available to her. She got me an apartment in New York. She is not concerned with my fidelity. She has all rights but when she is out of town, I am not restricted to just seeing her.

A lot of it is power. Jennifer is clearly into the power trip. I am submissive to her. Just as she is submissive to her husband, I am submissive to her. It's role reversal. Everyone needs to get out of the bag they are in. I'm giving her value for money. I'm her sex object. I'm a legend in certain circles because I give women great head. They love to lie back and enjoy themselves while I give them head. One of the reasons women come to me is that they are not having enough sex from their husbands.

Jennifer wants control over my fidelity in a way. She gave me to one of her girlfriends as a divorce present. I have a certain reputation and I think she wanted to show her friend what she owned. It's part of her fantasy. I think she likes to know that she has this good-looking guy at her disposal whenever she wants.

Jennifer's story provides another perspective on the female heater and commercial sex.

My husband is forty-nine. I am sure he cheats, he's the type. I do love him, but I like variety and that's why I cheat. My husband travels on business, so it is never much of a problem. I like the idea of cheating, and I've never fallen in love.

I knew what Chuck was when I met him. It was exciting for me and I liked the idea that I could buy a man. I think everyone should have a male mistress. Why not? If a man can do it, why not a woman? A lot of my friends know and they all like it, except one who says, "Why don't you go out and have a regular affair," but I don't want that.

Once in a while I go out with Chuck, but that's not what I'm interested in. He gives great head. My husband does give head, but not like this. I do know, though, that I'll reach a point when I get bored with him. I just like the feeling he is there because of my money. I pay his rent (six hundred a month) and his odds and ends, his clothes and charge cards. It feels incredibly powerful. I went to see Chuck a week ago. I walked in, he gave me some bills and the rent check. I sat in a chair and told him to mix me a drink. I didn't like the idea that the first thing he did was to hand me the bills. I wasn't wearing any underpants and I took my dress off. I was looking over the bills when he brought me the drink. I told him to do his thing, to earn his money. The feeling was very exciting. It put everything into perspective. There he was, kneeling, giving me oral sex. I'm paying the bills—so what I say goes. After all, it's like that in my marriage.

Chuck and Jennifer: an exception to the rule. Yet perhaps their relationship is a futuristic example of male/female role reversal which may one day be the result of female emancipation. Then married women will perhaps be financially able to indulge in the safety valve of commercial cheating in the same way as men. Commercial cheating may not be desirable, but it could be argued that one of the logical results of equality might be that commercial sex be equally available to male and female.

Overall, however, commercial sex is a male market. And one of the primary ways in which the safety valve operates via commercial sex is sex fantasies. If the average woman has a bizarre sex fantasy, she either has to reveal it to her husband and risk alienating him, or she has to suppress it and let it simmer. But a man can fulfill his sexual fantasies outside the framework of his marriage (without endangering the marriage) by paying a prostitute to enact fantasies which might be shocking to his wife. The fantasies might in fact appeal to the wife, but the husband may be unwilling to view his wife in a very sexual light, preferring to seek strong sexual satisfaction outside of marriage and restrict his wife to a madonna role.

Marilyn is a call girl who works in New Jersey. She advertises in *Screw* under "Silken lips, satin hips will visit your office. $50-$100." She says that the main reason men visit her is because their wives won't participate in anal sex, oral sex, and sex fantasies.

> If the average man gets sex at home four times a week he won't fool around. It is really a lot of trouble. Fooling around is also very expensive. But if a man can't get it up with his wife, he will go somewhere else. If I were married again, I would screw my husband as much as he wanted me to and do any kinky things he wanted that weren't harmful to my mental and physical health.

Sherri, who ran a brothel, Sherri's Ranch, in Nevada, told me that the majority of men who patronized her place did so because their wives refused to give them oral sex. However, there are other men with more extreme desires, who use commercial sex as a way of acting out their fantasies.

Alan, a thirty-five-year-old marketing executive, typifies the man who feels he has sexual needs best taken care of outside his marriage.

> I'm very submissive but I don't want my wife to lose respect for me. I'm a professional with multiple college degrees, I play the society game and I don't know how to tell my wife that my desires are left-of-center. In my business I'm very aggressive and very successful. I've eight people working for me and I don't want to be exposed in terms of my sex life.
>
> My parents were divorced when I was very young and I was raised by my mom. I don't know my father at all. When I was

fifteen, I visited my aunt for the summer. She caught me masturbating while I was wearing her underwear. I was embarrassed and I ended up getting lectured then and there. It lasted an hour and I was questioned in detail about my sexual feelings. My aunt was thirty-six at the time.

That evening after dinner she called me into her room, sat down and said I was going to be punished for that afternoon with spanking. I was so embarrassed and confused. I was willing to be spanked rather than have her tell my mother. She spanked me over her lap. She was wearing a housedress and stockings. The spanking was supposed to be painful but I got turned on and there was no way to hide it. The more she paddled me, the more turned on I got. I came and she was furious. The next morning she walked into the room as if nothing had happened.

I carried on my affair with my aunt from when I was fifteen to when I was thirty-two and she was killed in an airplane crash. She was in her fifties by then and not married. I was very much in love with her and I'd see her once a week. I've often looked for a woman like my aunt. But when you get out of college you are supposed to get married, according to U.S. society. I married a lovely girl, but we grew apart and divorced. I fantasized about marrying a dominant woman, but they are far and few between. Also, the woman has to be fifteen-to-twenty years older than me, which according to society isn't the age group of women I was supposed to marry.

I married again five years ago, but never felt comfortable telling my wife about my sexual preferences. So I went to hookers. I am into infantilism (being dressed up as a baby) and the nastier the woman is, the more I enjoy it. I put all the dominant women up on a pedestal, almost to the point of worship. It really is more of a verbal humiliation experience.

My wife hasn't got a dominant personality, but we have a good sex life. I consider myself monogamous in so far as I have a steady relationship with my wife. I care for her and she cares for me. I have other needs best taken care of outside the marriage.

Commercial sex enables men like Alan to cheat without endangering their marriages, and without suffering the pangs of guilt. Infidelity with a prostitute is relegated to a strictly financial transaction aimed at providing momentary sexual relief without guilt or the danger of discovery. Commercial cheating also allows men to compartmentalize their sexual experiences into madonna and whore, leaving their wives unsullied by the more perverse aspects of their fantasy lives.

Ken, a forty-three-year-old married commercial artist, exhibits the madonna/whore complex and the way in which going to a prostitute allows it to operate.

> I cheated a year after marriage. Cheating is purely a physical thing and sometimes it is fun that I am getting away with it. I definitely believe in monogamy. But I like variety; I eat different foods and I like different women. I make sure I never fall in love, by going to hookers. That way I know it is going to remain a short-term encounter without any emotional complications. And I can ask hookers to do things I would never dream of asking my wife.
>
> My wife has a lower sex drive than me. I couldn't ask her to do the things I do with other women. All my life I read about golden showers (urinating on someone) and sadomasochism, but I had never tried them. Finally I did. I also wanted to have anal sex with hookers. Anal sex would degrade my wife if I did it to her. Also anal sex is painful and I wouldn't do that to my wife.
>
> If my wife did sadomasochism and golden showers I would probably be faithful to her. Then again I don't know if I would want to be married to a woman who did that. Maybe I wouldn't value her.

Ken also demonstrates the male cheater's lack of introspection about his wife's reaction to his infidelity. "I don't know if she suspects I cheat. If I were to ask her, I think she would say she didn't know. She wouldn't leave me if she found out."

When I asked Ken about his wife's possible reaction to his affairs it was obvious he had never considered the subject.

Robert, a thirty-four-year-old married executive, also has a madonna/whore complex which he satisfies by going to prostitutes.

> I wanted to be faithful to my wife when I got married. I cheated the first year of the marriage. I don't look at it as unfaithful, though, but as an enrichment to my life. I've got a strong libido. I had my first affair at thirteen with a woman of fifty.
>
> I didn't know, when I was married to my wife, that she wasn't sexually more active. She wasn't as aggressive as I wanted her to be. She doesn't ever initiate the lovemaking. She is not into fantasies either because of her upbringing.
>
> I go to hookers because I want someone who is enticing and cute, who will wear sexy lingerie. I am into lots of different kinds of role playing. Sex with hookers is a way of fulfilling my fantasies. But sex with my wife is duty, marital obligation.

Robert highlights another frequent characteristic of the male cheater who has casual sex; he believes passionately in his wife's frigidity. Again and again male cheaters earnestly assured me that their wives had low sex drives, that their wives were frigid. Perhaps for many men, sexual frigidity in their wives is a strong enough rationale to justify their own cheating.

The commercial sex cheater of today has another outlet available to him, which may not even be termed true infidelity. The latest commercial sex innovation is "phone sex." Advertising in nationwide newspapers, hookers provide a phone number which men can phone, give their credit card numbers, and then have an hour's "hot chat," centering on their favorite fantasies. Phone sex is relatively new but magazines like *Penthouse,* featuring stories on the phone-sex phenomenon report that business is flourishing. Perhaps phone sex is the ultimate development in commercial sex infidelity, a foolproof way of attaining orgasm without involvement.

Another commercial sex outlet is the male prostitute, patronized by married (and single) male homosexuals. The gay world is set up to accommodate the desires of married homosexuals. The *male* gay world, that is. The same facilities for anonymous commercial sex don't exist in the female gay world. Although in certain parts of the country the homosexual male has come out of the closet, complete with aggressive uniforms and color-coded handkerchiefs advertising his sexual preferences, the female lesbian has kept a lower profile and rarely dresses blatantly in order to proclaim her sexual proclivities. Female prostitutes for married lesbians are a rarity, but male prostitutes for men ply their trade quite openly in many of America's major cities.

Richard is a car salesman in his thirties who has been married for seven years. His story illustrates the world of homosexual commercial sex which is available to the married homosexual cheater.

I've never talked to anyone about this before. I believe in monogamy and I want to keep my marriage and family life intact. But I have other needs and requirements. No one would know or suspect that I am gay. I don't know what would happen if my wife found out. I never want to divorce her because I love her very much. My relationship is very deep and committed and we have been together since high school. My wife has no idea that I am gay. My sex life with her is very good and I don't think that she could handle my homosexuality. She would probably end up in Bellevue if she found out.

I cheated in the first year of my marriage. I felt guilty as hell, but that didn't stop me from doing it. I go to male hookers I meet in gay movie houses or in gay baths. I go to a gay bath at least once a week. I make no excuses and I am home when I should be. It is like going to an adult fantasy world, like Disneyworld for adults. Like a gay Plato's Retreat. You pay an annual membership and you rent a private room eight feet wide and ten feet long with a chair and a platform bed. They have a pool and a sauna and a steam room.

I'm passive and I sit in my room and leave the door open. Men come in and take charge. Not all of them are hookers, some are also married gay men. I have two or three men at a time. Many rooms have glory holes, holes in the wall where men put their penises to be sucked off. It is so easy to cheat in a gay environment, so safe and anonymous. Being gay is something that I have grown to accept. It's a physical and an emotional need, but I am still a good parent and provider. I just feel completely different when I am at the gay baths or with a gay hooker. I'm living out a secret part of myself that is allowed to exist just for that time.

The ease with which married homosexuals can cheat has been thoroughly documented. In "The Marital Liaisons of Gay Men" sociologist Joseph Harry writes in *Family Coordinator* that "Gagnon and Simon (1973) have suggested that the liaisons of gay men are characterized by much infidelity because of the sexual socialization of men generally, both heterosexual and homosexual. Males are socialized to place a greater emphasis on sex than on affection than are women and to partly separate sex and affection. As a result, liaisons between males should be more sexual than affectional relationships, liaisons between females should be more affectional than sexual relationships, while those between a man and a woman should be a compromise between the two with the woman restraining the man's tendencies toward infidelity. Consistent with this hypothesis, the liaisons of gay men (with each other) have the least fidelity, those with lesbians have the most, and heterosexual husbands are less faithful than their wives."[17]

Harry's statement that gay men have very sexual relationships has bearing on the extramarital affairs of married homosexuals; because of the easy availability of male prostitutes and other sexual partners, and the casual quality of homosexual sex, it is easier for them to cheat than for any other cheater profiled in the book.

At the same time, to be fair to male homosexuals, they do sometimes relate on a more emotional level. The story of John, a married homosexual of fifty-seven, illustrates both the emotional quality of homosexual love and the dilemma faced by the married homosexual.

> I was married for thirty-six years and led two lives during that time. My wife never knew that I was gay. But all the time I was married I had sex with other men. I also had sex with my wife but I would often avoid it by telling her I had been working too hard and was too tired for sex. She never knew I was gay and had no idea that while she was having two or three orgasms, I was fantasizing I was with a guy.
>
> I felt so guilty. I tried suicide three times. I never told my wife I was gay. She only found out three months after I had left her. Everyone knows now that I am gay. I am a grandfather and I'm not ashamed of my life. I've been living with a man for two years and we have sex twice a day, seven days a week. I'm faithful to him and I love him. I don't think there is a married couple who is so happy.

Before dealing with the one-night-stand infidelity, it is important to stress that some men are resistant to the convenience of sex with a prostitute. At one extreme there is the cheater who said, "I find having sex with a prostitute is a challenge. With an average woman the goal is always to undress her. But with a prostitute I want to dress her, to form a relationship with her."

On the other is the seasoned cheater who confided to me, "If you brought me the most desirable, beautiful prostitute, I could not be sexually aroused by her. I wish I were like a lot of guys I know and could go to a prostitute, take care of business, then shower and go home. But I can't. In my sick head I want to be loved for myself. And I can't feel that way if the woman is faking it."

The Hit-and-Run Cheater

Midway between brief commercial extramarital sex and the sustained long-term extramarital affair is what I term the hit-and-run affair. The one-night stand. Like commercial infidelity, the hit-and-run affair is mostly the perogative of the male. Despite the women's movement, the majority of women seem to prefer sustained affairs to quick hit-and-run casual sex. The 1970 *Psychology Today* survey showed that of the men who report extramarital sex 14 percent surveyed claim to have had more than six partners while only 7 percent of the women reported as many.[18] The hit-and-run affair is usually casual, unpremeditated, and mostly done for the sake of sex. In general, the hit-and-run cheater says he doesn't cheat because there is anything wrong with his marriage, but because he enjoys the game of infidelity. A usual comment on hit-and-run cheating is "My wife is wonderful, my marriage is perfect, but even if I were married to the most wonderful woman in the world, I would still be unfaithful." The majority of these male cheaters don't think twice about their infidelity nor (as we have seen) do they bother to speculate on the effect of their extramarital affair on their partners. Dr. Brannon has commented on the differences between female and male capacity for introspection, and it may well be that part of the reason why women don't generally tend toward having casual extramarital affairs is that they are too aware of the possible consequences of the affairs, too conscious of their partner's possible negative reactions. This factor, along with society's disapproval of women having multiple partners, and the dangers of picking up strangers for sex, make the one-night stand less attractive to women than it is for men.

Most of the men I talked to seemed able to brush aside the one-night stand. It was, they told me, just sex. The "just sex" excuse seems to vindicate infidelity in the eyes of male cheaters, whether commercial or hit-and-run. Even Dr. Strean (the psychoanalyst I interviewed) says, "A one-night stand can be a harmless regression at times. I see a great difference between the one-night stand and needing someone quite consistently as an extramarital partner." The one-night stand does indeed seem a tidy way of compartmentalizing extramarital sex. However, again and again, I've encountered the cheater who started out on a hit-and-run fling, only to fall in love and develop a sustained secondary relationship affair. Although the average hit-and-run cheater is arrogantly confident that he can control the outcome of his affair, I've found that whereas in the past, love sometimes led to sex, today, sex often leads to love.

Male hit-and-run cheating crystallizes all the elements of infidelity mentioned in the book so far: peer pressure; the image of masculinity in today's society; the tendency of the man to make his wife into a mother figure and see how far he can test her; the male's lack of introspection (which naturally minimizes guilt); the availability of single women prepared to have affairs with married men; and the belief that men are biologically polygamous so that male infidelity is justifiable.

David is a classic hit-and-run cheater, unfaithful for infidelity's sake, totally convinced that his wife (a mother figure), will never leave him. He is a twenty-five-year-old stockbroker and was so proud of his cheating prowess that he even gave me his telephone number in case I had further questions about his exploits.

> I cheated six months after I got married, with someone at work. In three years of marriage, I've been with six or seven women. My marriage is fine and I love my wife. I don't think my cheating has

anything to do with my wife or my marriage. Sex is like a sport to me. I find life empty if I don't experience other people sexually. I don't feel I am even married at all when I pick a girl up.

I never get involved. I'm not looking for involvement, I'm just looking for sex. I don't think I would fall in love with another woman. One way I make sure I won't fall in love is to have sex with ugly girls. That way I *know* I won't fall in love. The other night I had sex with a very fat girl. I think she might fall in love with me because I didn't tell her I was married. I usually do but in her case who knows if I would have got what I wanted? I'm terrible, aren't I?

My wife and I have a good sex life and she has no idea I cheat. She thinks I am kidding around when I look at girls in the street. I don't feel guilty. After all, I don't feel guilty when my wife wants to watch a TV movie and I put on a hockey game instead. If you have meatloaf every night, sometimes you need chicken and other times you need veal. My wife doesn't cheat. No way. I'm the only man she's ever been with. Her sex drive is lower than mine. I'd like to get a hooker to have sex with me without paying her. I'm only twenty-five and I can't wait to see what I am like when I'm thirty-five.

David's story illustrates two of the strongest qualities of the hit-and-run cheater; he is convinced he can compartmentalize his infidelity into casual sex and that it will never impinge on his marriage. He believes he is so powerful that he can control his relationships. He will never fall in love with another woman and he can always manipulate his pickups so they remain mere hit-and-run encounters. He is also totally sure his wife would never cheat on him. He is convinced that her sex drive is far lower than his and that he is the only man she has ever been to bed with. Every hit-and-run cheater I talked to maintains the same story (when compelled to analyze their emotions about their wives); their wives will never be unfaithful and their sex drives are very low.

Warren is a policeman of thirty-nine. His story illustrates

the hit-and-run cheater's unformulated attempts to justify his cheating.

In the police department we meet a lot of women. I've been married twenty years and I cheated from the first year. My wife doesn't suspect I'm a hypocrite. I go to church with the family. I'm active in the Boy Scouts, in the Little League and I look like a typical family man. I don't think she cheats. She is always at home with the children. In fact, if I were a betting man, I would bet a month's salary that she doesn't cheat.

I guess I cheat because I'm out to prove I'm a man. Cheating proves I'm still a man. I am bald and putting on weight, but cheating proves I am still attractive. My wife is thirty-six now—she's put on weight. When I first married her she looked like Samantha Eggar; I suppose it is too much to ask her to be beautiful like when I met her. I'm not an Adonis anymore either. I'm not Mr. America myself. I guess I cheat because I am not what I was when I met my wife.

Considering that Warren first cheated only a year after his marriage, his remark "I guess I cheat because I am not what I was when I met my wife" really doesn't ring true. Warren, I felt, was improvizing, casting around for answers when I asked him why he cheated because basically he had never before considered the subject. Most hit-and-run cheaters don't feel compelled to provide any explanation of their infidelity, even to themselves. They cheat because they cheat. And Warren, like David, is also adamant that his wife doesn't cheat. Some hit-and-run cheaters, though, do have a sense of irony about their blind faith in their wives' fidelity, given their own rampant cheating. My advertisement in *The New York Review of Books* produced one cheater who telephoned and said, "I'm chronically unfaithful, but my wife doesn't know. C'est la vie. I know my wife is faithful to me. I can tell by her voice and her mannerisms. Then again, I wonder if she is saying the same thing about me. Have you had a call from a female named Jean?" I hadn't but at least this particular gentleman could laugh at his own double standards. Most male cheaters aren't even aware of them.

Bill's story is a typical example of the classic one-night stand cheater he cheats for excitement, has had sex with his wife's sister, and sees his wife as the madonna, while the other women are the whores, open to all types of sexual practices.

> Without cheating I don't think I'd have a very full life. I do it for the excitement of doing something I am not supposed to be doing. I tell the other women I am married. I don't think my wife knows. I say I am with the guys or at a meeting.
>
> One of the most exciting experiences was when I had the chance to sleep with my wife's younger sister. My wife went out for an hour to see one of her friends. The sister was fifteen, and her being so young excited me. I never felt guilty and I think it would be nice if it happened again. I don't know what my wife would do if she found out. She would be very unforgiving about her sister.
>
> I do sexual things with the other women I won't do with my wife. With her, it is straight sex and a little bit of French. With other women it is straight, French, Greek and I like to see them touch themselves with vibrators. I don't like to see my wife do that. I'm afraid she wouldn't. I would also like her to exhibit herself to other people. I've told her to dress more sexy. But she is a little cold. I think I really love her and I like having her around. I don't know what I would do without her.

Joe's story is an example of Dr. Strean's contention that compulsive cheaters will be unfaithful no matter who they are married to: "I would say that if a cheater divorces his wife and marries again, he will probably cheat again. The idea of marriage is frightening to him and he can't sustain a marital relationship so he will cheat again." As Joe says,

If I were to change my wife I would still be in the same position again; of having another woman to cheat on. I just want to find that kick of variety, that zipless fuck, that irresponsible relationship. The perfect stranger who is perfect because she remains a stranger.

Marriage isn't about sex. Marriage is about companionship, being with a woman and creating a whole world for yourself. I'm a very good cheater because I'm so weak in the face of my strong sex drive. I know I'm not going to get involved with anyone.

Joe's remarks focus on the dilemma of familiarity with which many married men and women have to grapple. The closer someone gets to you, the less strange they become. The less strange they are, the less easy it becomes to fantasize about them sexually. There may not be any answers except to make the choice between intimacy and fantasy.

Jack is a thirty-five-year-old executive who has been married for twelve years and has a five-year-old daughter.

I believe in monogamy. Then I don't. There are reasons why I cheat. The excitement isn't there after a while, no matter how many games you play. I don't like the word *unfaithful.* If you are physically involved with someone, it doesn't necessarily mean a thing, it's just sex. In a way, it is exciting because it is taboo. There is stimulation there. On the other hand, there is a little feeling of guilt because you are cheating. I never get involved with cheatees, though. I have a commitment to my child and I am loyal to that.

Jack is one of the few hit-and-run cheaters who mentioned his child in the course of the interviews. When the majority of male cheaters do manage to focus on the possible consequences of their affairs, they rarely go as far as to consider the children. Generally they all believe that their infidelity won't lead to divorce. I asked every male cheater—hit-and-run, secondary and commercial—whether he thought his wife would leave him if she found out about the affair. Ninety-five percent were convinced that their wives would never leave them, come hell or high water.

Cliff, a married cheater in his fifties has been unfaithful for twenty-eight years of his marriage. He is the archetypal male hit-and-run cheater.

> I always cheated. I do it for ego and conquest. For the satisfaction of meeting an attractive woman who finds me attractive. It's the mystery. I could be married to the most exciting woman in the world and I would still cheat on her. There is nothing my wife could do to stop me. She is a very lovely woman whom I love today maybe more than when I married her. No matter what she would change, I would still cheat. I believe in monogamy and would never get divorced or leave my wife. Cheating has nothing to do with love. The way I see it, it is a separate need I have, like food.
>
> I don't have any guilt about being unfaithful. But I will tell my sons to be faithful. Absolutely. I think monogamy is a better way of life. More secure. I don't cheat just for sex. I like the intimacy and the touching. I tell my wife I am busy at work. I don't think she knows I cheat, and if she does, she has never said anything. She is asexual so she would never cheat on me. If I didn't do what I do—if I didn't cheat—I would have been divorced by now. I would have felt like I was in prison, chained to a conventional way of life and that I was missing something.

Cliff touches on the issue of guilt and most cheaters bandied the word around. But when I asked them to define guilt, very few definitions emerged. Instead I asked the cheaters what they most disliked about cheating. Guilt was rarely mentioned. There is, however, a marked discrepancy in male and female answers. The majority of male cheaters say they most dislike the fear of discovery. It is likely that this comment is related again to the male image of wife as mother. This then would lead to the feeling that if the infidelity is discovered, the game might be stopped.

Women, in contrast, mostly say that they dislike not being able to see their lovers when they want. This might well be related to the fact that the majority of female affairs (as opposed to male affairs) are emotional, so that as women are more involved with their cheatees they would naturally tend to dislike not being able to see them whenever they want. Presumably, though, the same factor applies to men in love. Glass has pointed out that "when male affairs are emotional, the effects appear similar to female affairs."

The guilty male cheater's fear of getting caught is almost childlike and is related, I believe, to the process by which many cheaters transform their wives into a mother figure. The cheater is worried about getting caught, but at the same time he isn't evolved enough, or introspective enough, to probe the workings of his wife's mind. Harry, a thirty-three-year-old accountant reveals the spirit of the guilty male cheater.

> Sometimes I believe in monogamy, sometimes I don't. When I got married I believed in it, but I've been unfaithful three times in three years. I don't think I cheat because of my wife. It really has nothing to do with her, nothing at all. But now and again I do feel guilty. How does guilt feel to me? The first time I cheated I felt terrible. I didn't know whether I looked different, felt different, or was different. But I don't think she noticed. The night passed. We didn't have sex. I wouldn't take the chance. I thought, "If I've caught something, I don't want to pass it on."

Harry is virtually cheating out of habit. Some male hit-and-run cheaters, however, cheat out of hostility. Burt is a forty-six-year-old Chicago executive who has been married for twenty years.

> I go through stages. I have the desire to cheat and if it happens, it happens. Sometimes, if my wife is tired and doesn't want to have

sex with me I think to myself, If she ever knew what went on in my mind, that she isn't the only woman in the world . . . I still don't think that she would believe I cheat. She wouldn't think, after nearly twenty years of marriage, that I would look at anyone else. She thinks I am too innocent. She couldn't cheat. Absolutely not. If she found out that I was cheating on her she would never leave, she needs my money.

The interview with Burt was done in 1982, but reading it one would think it took place in the world of the sixties.

One of the most publicized repercussions of extramarital sex—most particularly the hit-and-run affair—is herpes. However, very few of the cheaters I interviewed mentioned the virus and even then didn't seem at all deterred by the sexual revolution's most deadly spawn. Ralph is a twenty-five-year-old married cheater.

I enjoy the married way of life and I also enjoy the cheating way of life. I love it because I like different types of women. I try and avoid being caught, I am very careful about lipstick and all that. But I'm frightened about the herpes epidemic, herpes is a scare for a cheating man. It really scares me. I don't know how I could explain it to my wife. But I don't want to stop cheating.

Despite Ralph's fear of herpes, nothing will prevent him from cheating. He is typical of the cheating man in general in that he is convinced he will get away with infidelity, no matter what. He feels he is powerful enough to overcome any obstacles to his pleasure, even as tangible an obstacle as herpes.

Pete, a thirty-six-year-old salesman who has been married for twelve years, sums up the typical hit-and-run cheater.

I first cheated eight weeks after our wedding. I cheated with an old girlfriend. Since then I've had about one hundred affairs. I feel bad and guilty about lying because my wife is so good to me. But when I go on business trips I cheat all the time. Men find it difficult to be faithful. I meet a lot of women on the road. I don't think monogamy is natural for men—all my friends cheat. I have a desire to be with other women. It's in me.

I cheat because I like it. I like to be with as many women as I can. I get a lot of enjoyment when I'm with another woman. I get a little kinkier when I cheat. I might go with a woman and a man, or do a quickie in the car. When I'm with another woman I'm a much more energetic lover and my penis always gets at least an inch longer and is always harder.

I never think of leaving my wife. I love her dearly. I just like cheating. I wish she would make appointments for her girlfriends to come over and let me make love to them. Once I asked her if she would go for a threesome, but she took it that I was kidding. Her sex drive is quite high, but she doesn't cheat on me. She's deeply in love with me. I satisfy her totally.

My marriage is perfect. My wife is good for me. I don't love the other women the way I love my wife. With my wife I love her more as a person. I respect her, well I suppose I really can't say "respect" when I cheat on her. But I do respect her steadiness. She's a good organizer. She takes care of my daughter and she takes care of the checkbook. She's always there when I come home and my dinner is always on the table.

I'd never get caught cheating. I'm too sly. I never cheat near home. I tell my wife I'm going out with the boys and she doesn't question anything I do. She doesn't suspect a thing. She's never said anything, she's always loving. She says, "Have you been faithful?" sometimes, and I say, "Of course." If I really believed she would leave me if she found out about my cheating, I would stop. But she wouldn't leave. I can convince her of anything. I can sell anything and I do.

Pete is the total hit-and-run cheater. He sees his wife as a mother figure and even talks about her as if he were a schoolboy praising his mother. He compliments his wife on her organizing ability, the fact that she is always there when he comes home and that his dinner is always ready for him. And like a schoolboy he wistfully wants "mother" to find him other little playmates to bring home now and again. However, to do Pete some justice, he does note the irony of proclaiming one minute that he respects his wife and that he cheats on her the next. But that is the full extent of his perspective on his own cheating. Otherwise Pete brazenly views infidelity as his right and sees no need to justify what amounts to his favorite sport.

In contrast to male hit-and-run cheaters, the majority of women I talked to who cheat on a hit-and-run basis usually have a well-thought out explanation for their infidelity. This may be due to a combination of factors; first there is Dr. Brannon's observation that women tend to be introspective about relationships, because traditionally relationships were their bread and butter; then there is the theory that women cheat reactively, because of a flaw in the marriage. I have also found that a large number of women cheat in retaliation, that men usually cheat first in the marriage and that one of the ways women respond to their infidelity is to cheat in revenge. Kinsey (1953) found that women were more likely to stray in their thirties,[19] which is consistent with Athanasiou's findings that men cheat earlier than women in a marriage.[20] Therefore, the man usually cheats first, whereupon the woman (who is often in her thirties) retaliates by cheating herself.

There is also another reason why women have lucid explanations for their infidelity. Society, as we have seen, still judges the female cheater more harshly than the male cheater (because of the children, because of tradition). Therefore, it may well be that women feel pressured to justify their infidelity to themselves, whereas men do not.

Barbara is a forty-five-year-old housewife who has been married for twenty years. On the surface, her motivations for having one-night stands seem no different from those of male cheaters—not enough sex. However, it is obvious that Barbara's attitude toward her flings is introspective, considerate of her husband's response, and in general less casual even though her cheating is, indeed, one-night-stand.

> My husband is twenty years older than me. I married him at fifteen and he took care of me. My parents died and my husband was like my father and my friend. He took care of me. All my life I was so used to him but when I got older I realized that I had made a mistake. I needed my husband when I was younger—he taught me everything I knew about sex and I had never had sex with anyone else.
>
> I cheat because I need sex and my husband can't or won't have any. I first had an affair fifteen years ago. I told my husband that I was going to pottery classes and I asked another girl to cover for me. I picked up a younger man at a bar. I had never done anything like that before, it was playful. I need sex. Usually I go away on weekends with girlfriends and then I meet someone. I think my husband knows. He never mentions it but I think he does know. I think he is hurt. A lot of times I want to confess and I feel bad about it.
>
> I try not to feel guilty about cheating, but it is difficult. I try to tell myself that I deserve it because my husband has given up on sex. He says he is too old for it. I asked him to go for help and he said he wouldn't. He says he will do anything in the world for me—except have sex. If he had sex with me again I would stop cheating.

Barbara's refrain was continually repeated, a female litany of guilt and concern about the husband's reaction.

Pat, a thirty-six-year-old saleswoman who has been married for eighteen years, has sex with her husband twice a month.

> I've been cheating for two years and I've had eighteen cheating affairs since I started. My husband is very busy with his own life and is generally happy with me and our twice a month sex life.

He doesn't question what I do and where I go. He loves me.

I first cheated with a family friend. I used shopping, friends, spa, and work as an excuse and asked friends to cover for me. My friend was better in bed than my husband. He took more time, was truly interested in me sexually and didn't treat me as just somewhere to put it. He could go on for hours just holding and touching me. In some ways my sex life with my husband was better after the first time I cheated. I felt so guilty that I tried to make it up to him, tried desperately to please him. I felt guilty and rotten, low and selfish. I tried to be a better wife in every area possible.

I don't like the deception and the fear, the knowledge that I will hurt my husband someday when he finds out about my cheating. I've had one-night stands and afternoon events since the first time I cheated. I've enjoyed every one of them. I completely love the abandonment that comes with a purely sexual relationship. I can be aggressive or passive, depending on my mood and that of my partner. I can be raunchy as hell and not ever see the man again. I can play the sweet little thing—out for my first fling—and let the man "teach me." I enjoy the men and they enjoy me. I come home relaxed, nonfrustrated. And I think I am a better mother and a more loving wife because all my aggression and pent-up sexual aggression is gone.

Pat has developed a casual approach to her affairs similar to that of hit-and-run cheating men, but at the same time she is clearly worried about the effect of her affair on her husband. The next women profiled are extremely close in attitude and behavior to the male hit-and-run cheater, are all in their twenties, and are perhaps examples of a new breed of woman created by the sexual revolution of the seventies, which taught them to give free rein to their fantasies and their wildness. These women may be exceptions to the norm but their cases do illustrate a new trend in female infidelity.

Janet is twenty-three and has been married for three years.

I cheated two years after marriage. I picked someone up at a disco and used work as the excuse. I wasn't satisfied with my sex life at home and I needed variety. Our sex life was boring and I wanted something exciting. My husband is very gentle and loving, but when I cheat it is always raw sex with lots of lust.

I don't think my husband could ever stop me from cheating. But if I really thought he would leave me, I wouldn't cheat anymore. The first time I had sex with someone else, I wanted to confess to my husband because I felt so guilty. But I didn't. I came home after making love to the other man and my husband wanted to make love to me. I told him I was hot and sticky and wanted to take a shower first. So he didn't find out.

I don't know if I will ever stop having affairs. I even had one with an obscene phone caller. He phoned up to say he was horny and I said he had a sexy voice so we went out together. I do love my husband and I depend on him. But I have a wandering eye. I think other women do too, but are afraid to admit the truth.

Sharon is a twenty-five-year-old woman who also is brazenly proud of her wandering eye.

I've been married for two years and I had an affair right the first year. I missed something when I got married. I wanted some kind of adventure, or fun. Infidelity was a rejection of respectability to me. I married my husband because I love him so much but sometimes I think life would be more exciting for me if I were single again. I was brought up in a respectable Southern home and I envied the girls who were loose. Now I like being treated like that by my lovers, not like a little housewife. On one-night stands I can dress in flashy costumes and make out in public places and cheap hotels, doing the kinds of things that at sixteen I thought were wicked and adult.

I miss the image of being very fast and free. I don't think I am capable of monogamy. I do feel a little guilty when I cheat and I don't want to be found out, though I don't think my husband can stop me from cheating. Although if he treated me like my lovers do, I would be faithful to him. If he didn't treat me so respectably, if I were more sexy in his eyes, I wouldn't feel the need to go out.

I meet men to cheat with in singles bars. I did fall in love once. The man was wonderful. But then suddenly things weren't fun anymore and I realized that the whole thing could change into another monogamous relationship and stop being so exciting. So I stopped the affair. I would stop cheating altogether if I had children. I don't think it is good for children to have parents who divorce. So I would stop cheating.

Sharon is a female equivalent to men with a madonna/whore complex. Her husband is too much of a madonna to her, so she goes elsewhere to find sexual enjoyment with whores.

Leigh, a twenty-seven-year-old graduate student at Yale, is a female Don Juan, or perhaps a more apt term would be Donna Juanita. It is interesting to note that like Sharon (whose interview precedes hers), and Jamie (the final female hit-and-run cheater in the chapter), Leigh has no children.

I love my husband very deeply, but I cheat because I have unfulfilled sex fantasies left over from when I was younger. If I read something erotic, I want to do it. I love the *Emmanuelle* films and try to live them out. So casual pickup infidelities are erotic for me. I cheat for the thrill of doing something forbidden. To me cheating is adventurous and exciting. I do it for the thrill and the need for variety in my sex life.

I felt guilty the first time I cheated. But it was like living out a childish fantasy. I feel more like a bored housewife. I wouldn't be unfaithful if my husband were more aggressively physical and wanted to play more sexual games. But he doesn't. So I get a thrill out of casual bar pickups, out of the feeling and the thrill that the next person I make love to is adultery. It has a delicious cinematic quality about it. I never fall in love with the men.

I usually tell my husband that I am in the library. If he found out about my cheating I think he would be very violent. I can even imagine him challenging the other man to a duel. I don't think, though, that my husband would leave me. If I thought he would it might stop me from cheating. The trouble is that there is no thrill of the forbidden with him. We are passionate but there is no spice to our sex life. And I need that.

Jamie, a thirty-year-old computer programmer, takes Leigh's hit-and-run affairs further. Sometimes, in pursuit of her fantasies, she even cheated for money. Her infidelity led ultimately to divorce.

I planned to be sexually faithful when I got married. I believed in monogamy, but I didn't have much sexual experience. My husband had a stronger sex drive than I did. At the beginning, at any rate. He was only the third person I ever had sex with. But as time went on I began to think about sex more. I had a lot of sex fantasies that were building up and had nowhere to go. I told my husband a lot of them, but some things I couldn't tell him. They involved having sex with a stranger.

I think a lot of my cheating is related to my sister. We grew up in a suburb of Dallas and went to private school. I was very turned on by what my sister was doing. She was very self-assured and in control. Once she even went down on the whole basketball team. When I was about thirteen I would have liked to have sex with my sister. I fantasized about it but never did it. But in many ways I would have liked to be my sister sexually.

I envied my sister, being so sexually active. So two years after my marriage I had a one-night stand. I felt odd. Suddenly all those thoughts came true. It took my breath away. I never fell in love. I created a new girl. I picked up older, married guys and even did it for money a couple of times. A guy said, "You've got really nice

> legs, I want to get into your pants." I was wet, as it was the best sexual fantasy I had ever had. So I had sex with him for a hundred dollars. I know I am pretty, but if a guy offers you one hundred dollars then you have a value.
>
> I tried to act the slut. I was very blatant and my husband found out the truth and divorced me. Really, I didn't hide what I was doing—the woman I had created wouldn't hide anything. I didn't wear underwear to work, I did my hair real slutty, and I had sexual tastes that the married me shouldn't have had; being felt up in public, doing a lot of anal sex. I think I slept with more men than my sister ever did.

Jamie's story is extreme, her hit-and-run affair turning into prostitution, but it illustrates that rare cheater—the *female* hit-and-run cheater. Hit-and-run cheating as a way of life, seems alien to the majority of women I interviewed. Most of them tend to engage in what I call the secondary relationship, sustained extramarital infidelity with one partner.

Profile of the Secondary Relationship Cheater

The secondary relationship may begin as a quick hit-and-run fling; the fact that it often blossoms into love, perhaps carries with it a subtle message about human emotions and the inability of man to control his destiny or contain his emotions. Perhaps too, on a more prosaic level, it may say something about the law of averages and the roulette wheel of relationship chance; it may happen with the first fling, or the ninety-second, but there is always a possibility that the quick hit-and-run affair can escalate into an enduring secondary relationship based on emotion and caring.

In Europe, the secondary relationship is often conducted openly and elegantly by those with money. Suzy, the society columnist, comments, "I think a mistress is accepted in many

European capitals. There it is just run-of-the-mill. A wife is one thing and a mistress is another. A wife is in a separate compartment and a mistress is in a separate compartment. It exists in America too, but it is not accepted. It is viewed with a raised eyebrow when it occurs."

The secondary relationship in which a married man supports a mistress is still a primarily European phenomenon, although in the case of the super rich of America there are secondary relationships like that of Alfred Bloomingdale, who allegedly conducted a twelve-year affair with Vicki Morgan, keeping her to the tune of $18,000 a month.

In England, the aristocrat often has a wife safely tucked away in the country, while he frolics with his mistress in town. He has the time and the money to support and satisfy both women and both life-styles. He also has the approval of the society in which he travels.

The French are so sophisticated about the secondary relationship that they have even set aside a specific time and name for it; *cinq à sept* (five to seven), the hours in which the philandering Frenchman visits his mistress. The structured way in which the Frenchman conducts his extramarital relationships was evident to me when I talked to a Parisian mistress who had been involved with a married man for fifteen years. He visits her every day, pays her rent, introduces her to his business colleagues, and goes on vacation with her. Yet she doesn't even know his wife's name. After fifteen years, the man has never once discussed his wife with his mistress, or even mentioned her name. When he is with his mistress his wife doesn't exist and vice versa.

The Italian also exhibits a similar attitude. Prince Egon Von Furstenberg told me, "Italian men always have two mistresses to demonstrate their power." Marcello Mastrioanni, the Italian film actor, who had two well publicized affairs with Faye Dunaway and Catherine Deneuve (by whom he has a son) still remained married to his wife, Flora Carabella, who suffered through it all, telling *Quick*, "He is a notorious cheater. I can only warn every woman who lets herself get involved in a deep relationship with Marcello Mastrioanni."[21]

European movie stars, princes, and millionaires may flaunt their secondary relationships, but in America, the secondary relationship is maintained on a more secretive level. In many cases, the secondary-relationship cheater keeps his motivations for having a sustained affair a secret from even himself. Analyst Dr. Strean explains, "I think a lot of people rationalize their activity. They might say to themselves, "There is nothing wrong with my marriage. But I feel compelled to have a girlfriend." Or they say, "I was lured into it." But in order to be led away from a marriage, one has to have a readiness to do so."

The majority of male secondary-relationship cheaters I interviewed, exhibited an inability to be introspective about their motivations for having the affair. Women, in contrast, were as usual, introspective about their extramarital activities.

Otherwise, men and women in sustained secondary relationships respond similarly (echoing Glass's claim that male emotional affairs are similar to female emotional affairs).[22] The only difference is that initially men are more surprised than women if a hit-and-run fling develops into love. Perhaps this is due to differing expectations, with men expecting relationships to remain purely sexual and women more prepared for relationships to evolve into love. The secondary relationship is obviously the enemy of the casual hit-and-run sexual encounter and has been the downfall of many a hit-and-run cheater who believed he could control his infidelity without getting involved. If infidelity is considered playing with fire, the secondary relationship is often the burn the player receives. The secondary relationship is, in many ways, the triumph of love over casual sex. The cheater may start out on a brief fling, then fall in love. Dr. Neubauer relates the birth of the secondary relationship, in many cases, to young marriages: "A man may have married his wife in another stage of his development and she stayed at that stage. He on the other hand, knows what he is looking for now (which he didn't when he got married) and all of a sudden he has this new relationship, then he is in trouble."

For both sexes, the secondary extramarital relationship seems to exist in a twilight no-man's-land between a happy marriage and an acrimonious divorce. The long-term secondary-relationship cheater, his spouse, and the cheatee are in perpetual limbo. The secondary relationship triangle is sometimes maintained for years without resolution.

The secondary relationship often acts as Band-Aid for the cheater's marriage. The extramarital affair prevents cheaters from confronting the deficiencies in their primary relationship. Instead of confronting what is wrong in the marriage and dealing with it, or divorcing, the long-term secondary-relationship cheater sidesteps the failings in his or her marriage by going elsewhere. The secondary relationship is often a substitute for divorce—the cheater's sole outlet and escape from the realities of the marriage.

The secondary relationship can become an ersatz marriage, existing to avoid the problems and guilt of divorce. Sometimes the secondary-relationship cheater refuses to make the connection between his sustained extramarital affair and the health of his or her marriage.

Barry is a forty-three-year-old teacher who has been married for eighteen years.

> My marriage is strong, but I was weak. I got involved. When I met Karen, all I wanted to do was to go to bed with her. She was sexy and cute and I didn't think a quick fling would hurt my wife or my family. After all, I'd been cheating for most of my married life and it didn't have anything to do with my marriage.
>
> Sex with Karen is fantastic. But other things have crept in as well. We discovered that we had similar interests and the same

way of looking at life. We laughed at the same jokes, enjoyed the same books and never stopped talking. I found myself telling Karen things I had never told my wife. Of course, my wife is marvelous and I am sure she doesn't suspect a thing. Karen and I have been together for five years now, we see each other every day and I love her. I love my wife too. One relationship doesn't detract from the other. My marriage is perfect. I feel as if I have known my wife all my life. I suppose I have two wives. I know there is nothing wrong with my marriage. The two relationships have nothing to do with each other.

Barry is the classic male refusing to confront. He also typifies the secondary-relationship cheater who started out having a casual extramarital affair, but then fell in love.

Cliff, the fifty-seven-year-old hit-and-run cheater in the last section, once, despite himself, fell in love with his cheatee.

I've never been close to leaving my wife. Absolutely never. Nor would I. I like to control my extramarital involvements. Of course, I'm not a robot. I like some emotional involvement but I do like to control it. I am not happy if I don't have any involvement. I want to call her, to talk to her, to tell her that I miss her but if the involvement is too strong, I end the affair. But the trouble is, I don't have the power of God to say "I'll take ten percent involvement but no more," and once I fell in love.

I met her six years ago. She was twenty-six, single, and lived in Philadelphia and used to come to New York each week for the evening. She was a real traffic stopper, a Susan Anton lookalike. She was the daughter of a general and used to come into my business. I would say, "Hello, you army brat," and kid around with her. One day my salesman said to me, "Why don't you invite Penny out to dinner?" I said, "Are you crazy?" He said, "She is waiting for you to ask her out." It was a hell of an unexpected ego trip for me.

She called. We had instantaneous chemistry. I told her about me. We had drinks and went to dinner. She called me a week later and we went out. I guess by the third time, she was the only thing on my mind. I ended up going to bed with her. It was beautiful and spontaneous. After that she came to New York every Thursday and I told my wife I had to go out of town on Thursdays, for a production meeting every week.

I would go to dinner and stay with her. It was unbelievable. We were very happy, laughed all the time, and called each other every day. I was with her for two years. She was on my mind constantly. But she was very insecure and eventually we had a tremendous fight. She was always prodding me to leave my family. I would wake up in the middle of the night and look at my wife sleeping, or look at my kids and I'd think, How can I leave my kids, how can I leave my wife? Finally I told her that I wasn't going to ruin my life because of her insecurity and constant bickering. I said, "I'm not going to move out from my family and live with you because in six months I'll kill you. I'll realize that you have ruined my life and I'll blame myself and stick a knife in you." I didn't want the pain anymore. My mother and father were divorced when I was young.

Cliff extradited himself from his extramarital relationship and resumed his pattern of quick extramarital flings. However, some extramarital secondary relationships which happen accidentally do lead ultimately to divorce; Edith is a fifty-one-year-old teacher who was married for twenty-eight years.

I was a virgin when I got married and I definitely believed in monogamy. I was faithful to my husband for twenty-three years. We met in college. I really wanted to succeed in marriage. My mother and father were divorced and in many ways I think I wanted to be superior to my mother and be successful in my marriage while she had failed in hers. I think I stayed in the marriage longer than I should have done. I never wanted my two children to live in a broken home like I had, but basically my husband was making me suppress my individuality.

I went back to college after twenty-three years of marriage and I felt freer. At college I met a professor I was attracted to who also had marital problems. Except, though, at the time, I didn't think I had marital problems. I didn't plan to leave my husband. I thought I had a terrific marriage. Funnily enough my husband was better in bed than my lover, who was impotent the first time we had sex.

Before I had sex with my lover, I told my husband about what I was planning to do. Five years before, he had said he thought it would be nice if we had other sexual partners. I think it was a fantasy because I am sure he never cheated, as we had a lot of trust. Anyway, the professor and I were friends for five months, then he asked me if I would like to get involved. I was thrilled at the idea, but at the same time felt very guilty. I only wanted to go to bed with him. I told my husband I was planning to do it—because we had wonderful trust. At first my husband thought it was a great opportunity for me. But in a couple of days, he changed his mind and said he didn't want me to do it. He said he felt insecure. After he told me, my husband thought that was the end of it all and felt relieved. But I went ahead and had sex with the professor at a motel. I felt a little bit strange and guilty. I told my husband and he hit me. I never thought he would react that way. After all, he had wanted an open marriage so I thought he would approve of my fling.

The man and I got involved, but I absolutely denied our affair to my husband. I went out of the way to avoid any kind of confrontation. But he realized the truth and I think he was surprised that I was unfaithful. The affair went on for three-and-a-half years. I think it freed me. I was really in love with the other man; I think it is difficult to separate sex from love. I wanted something to come of the relationship.

My husband and I separated and divorced as a result of the affair. I am still with the other man. His divorce is now final but I don't know whether or not we will get married.

Edith's story illustrates the case of a woman who started a relationship casually, then got involved. The divorce was initiated by her husband, but Edith admits that she wanted the relationship to lead somewhere. I have found that very few female secondary-relationship cheaters want the triangle situation to be sustained indefinitely. Most of them want some sort of resolution—either a change in the marital circumstances that led them to cheat in the first place, or divorce and remarriage to the other man. Men, on the other hand, seem more comfortable with sustaining the long-term secondary relationship for as long as it lasts.

Joe is a thirty-one-year-old post office worker who has been married for six years. He has also been involved in a secondary relationship with another woman, Betty, for the same amount of time.

> Men find it difficult to be faithful. Anyway, I think you can love two people at once. I love my wife and I don't want to leave her. She is very strong. She is a hard worker. I never think of my wife as being unfaithful. I don't think she would be. She doesn't seem the type. She is too much in love with me. Then again, I could be wrong.
>
> I cheated on my wife within a couple of weeks of our marriage. Betty was a close friend of ours and we cheated in a hotel. I fell in love with her. Betty is beautiful and she has got a great body. She knows how to make love really well and is open to anything sexually. I am deeply attached to her. She is twenty-nine.
>
> Sometimes I spend the night with Betty and I tell my wife I am working on a double shift. I see Betty at least twice a week. I don't think my wife knows about Betty. I think if she did she wouldn't say anything. If she does know, she doesn't want to lose me, so she is making like she doesn't know. I don't think she would leave me if she caught me. She loves me too much. I guess I am cheating on my wife because of sex. Her sex drive is low.
>
> Betty and I swing with other couples, do orgies, anal sex, and

she's a lot better than my wife at oral sex. I never ask my wife if she would do those things, I guess because I have got Betty. It doesn't bother me if Betty goes out with other men. I know she isn't faithful to me. She likes sex too much. I don't mind, it excites me. If I were married to Betty, I probably wouldn't be faithful because I like some variety myself. Also I think I would be too jealous if I were married to Betty and we invited another man over for her.

I love Betty, I take care of her needs and I do nice things for her. She is a lot of fun. But if my wife said "Pick me or Betty," I would have to pick my wife. I feel more secure with her. She isn't as wild as Betty, she is more stable. The thing I love Betty for, her sexuality, frightens me. If Betty and my wife were drowning I would try and save both of them. If I could only save one, I would save Betty as I get the most pleasure out of her. With Betty there are other things too. Our interests are more alike. Did I marry the wrong woman? Maybe.

Joe has sustained his secondary relationship with Betty for six years. At first sight, it seems that Betty is the whore, and Joe's wife the madonna. Yet, as an afterthought, Joe mentions their mutuality of interest. Joe's speculations on his wife's knowledge of the affair raises a theme which will be explored in depth in the victim section; it is likely that Joe's wife knows about the affair, yet remains silent. Her silence is, in effect, a form of collusion. And countless married men are able to maintain their secondary relationships because (for motivations which will be explored) their wives allow them to.

Patrick is a twenty-four-year-old garage mechanic who has been married for five years.

I got married at eighteen and I started having affairs then. My wife doesn't really want me to mess around but it is all right as long as I come home at night. My wife knows about my girlfriend and my girlfriend knows about my marriage. My girlfriend wants me to leave my wife, but I won't leave my wife for my girlfriend.

I love my girlfriend too and I am not going to give her up either. I'm one of those guys who thinks he should have two women. I'll keep it going for as long as it lasts. I was very pampered by my mother and I am used to being pampered by women.

Patrick may have articulated the prime reason for his long-term secondary-relationship cheating. He was very pampered by his mother. Now he has succeeded in finding two women who are prepared to pamper him further by sharing him. On the surface, it appears that Patrick must be capable of a high level of love and commitment if he is able to love and commit to both. Or, conversely, the truth may be that by committing to both women, Patrick is, in reality, committing to neither. The long-term secondary-relationship cheater avoids putting all his ego into one basket, as it were. And by having two lovers, he ensures that both will be trying hard to please him, and that he is increasing his chances of never being alone; if one partner leaves, he has the other as backup.

Patrick exhibits the simplistic attitude of many male secondary-relationship cheaters. He assumes that he can cheat without endangering the stability of the marriage. His experience has proved him correct; the double marriage situation has persisted because his wife hasn't made waves or demands. Patrick's story profiles the calculated secondary-relationship cheater, the cheater who deliberately sets out to get involved in a long-term secondary relationship.

Marie, a twenty-seven-year-old advertising executive with no children, set out to compensate for the failings in her marriage by starting an extramarital secondary relationship.

I had been married to my husband for six years before I cheated. I strongly believe in monogamy. But I felt my husband and I were drifting apart. I felt taken for granted and I felt that if he let the relationship deteriorate to the point it had got to, I ought to look for someone else to give me the attention I was lacking. I once wrote a poem that expressed how I felt:

I feel like a couch that needs a new cover.
What's the alternative? I'll take a lover.

I picked someone I had known for years. He came to visit me at my office and started paying a lot of attention to me. I cheated at his house. At first it felt good. I thought, I am desirable, other men do find me attractive. It wasn't all my fault. There must be something wrong with my husband. The guy came on so strong about being in love with me. I didn't love him. I was attracted to the fact that he was attracted to me. I wasn't interested in a relationship. I decided I didn't want to see him anymore and I picked someone else instead with whom I did want a relationship. There is so much about my new man which is more in tune with me than my husband is. And now I am in love with him.

I don't like cheating. First of all, I feel very angry with myself, angry at my husband, it is a very uncomfortable thing. I feel angry with my husband because I want the marriage to work. It is the lack of attraction sexually and the lack of attention that makes me cheat. I don't always want to be in the aggressive role. I want to be wined and dined once in a while. But I feel so bad about having cheated, when I got married I thought it was forever. I haven't worn my wedding band since I began my affair. Somehow I feel I've crossed a line I held for years and somehow in crossing that line I am almost afraid that I can't go home anymore.

Marie may have cheated calculatingly and has deliberately formed a secondary relationship, but, unlike the majority of male secondary-relationship cheaters, she makes the connection between the state of her marriage and her infidelity. To most women an affair is a signal that something is wrong with the marriage; men, in contrast, don't seem to feel the same way.

Al, a forty-eight-year-old salesman has transformed the secondary relationship into a way of life. He has been married for twenty years and has conducted four secondary relationships during that time.

I don't believe in monogamy for myself. I think men find it more difficult to be faithful because they can handle a wider range of activities and responsibilities without falling between the cracks. My parents were faithful to each other. When they married back in the twenties that is how it was. My father was almost six feet tall and three hundred pounds of muscle. My mother was five feet and weighed about ninety-two pounds. He spoke, she jumped. Really I didn't like the relationship because it was like a dictator/peasant relationship.

My wife knows without saying that I have stepped outside the bonds of marriage many times. She has complained for years of headaches. We have sought medical help and doctors say there is nothing wrong with her. In frustration, I said, "If it isn't available at home, then it must be available elsewhere.

I first cheated with a bookkeeper whose age was in the late twenties. Her husband only had sex with her once in four or eight weeks. And then only out of duty. She felt rejected and we were talking one day while waiting for lunch. I said to her, "What do you want?" She quickly responded, looking me straight in the eye, "I would like to have you for lunch." We had lunch together many times for months and months before her husband transferred to another assignment. How I miss those wonderful lunches.

My longest cheating relationship lasted for six years. She was our babysitter. She was married too. We met her through our social outings with friends. She was a very open and warmhearted person. I mentioned something to her about my wife's puritanical ethics and the conversation became very adult in no time flat.

Soon we were doing some of the things our mates would never dream of doing because of their boring habits about sex and their unwillingness to change.

We had no plans to break up the marriages. I would go shopping or for a ride with her. Plans were easy and very open and changeable. Once I indicated to my wife that I was going for a ride (I had the intention of meeting my lover) and she said she would like to go too. When we got to the shopping center, my wife saw my girlfriend and invited her to go for a ride with us. I never admitted to cheating—that is my guilt and not my wife's.

Another long-term relationship I had was with a single woman I met at the library. She was nice. We had certain books in common. I like sci-fi, and so did she. I like Hesse, and so did she. We ended up in bed. I didn't feel as guilty as the first time I cheated. Maybe because I got used to it or because I didn't get caught the other times. I felt for her. I did love her, but not like I love my wife. She knew I was married and she wanted me to leave my wife. From the beginning I told her that my affairs had nothing to do with my wife. It's just me. I don't know what it is. And I don't know why I do it.

Now I have a relationship with a woman which is moving towards greater importance than anything I have ever been involved with before. She is a good lover and has a good mind to go with it. We offer each other little things that our mates have long forgotten to say or share with us. I don't think, though, that my relationships have changed my marriage or my love for my wife. They have just helped me vent some of my built-up frustrations at my marriage.

Al uses his secondary relationship as a way of venting his frustrations at the marriage and presumably his wife. He has no plans to divorce. Few male secondary-relationship cheaters have.

Sometimes the reasons for a secondary relationship are clearly defined by both the man and the woman. John cheats on his wife because she only has sex with him once a month. Mary cheats on her husband because he has Altzheimer's disease. John and Mary (their names are clichés but those are the ones they themselves picked for the interview) phoned me from a motel in Connecticut. John is a sixty-five-year-old teacher who has been married for forty years.

I cheated five years after my marriage with someone I picked up. My marriage is very good except that my wife isn't sexual enough. She says that my interest in sex is abnormal, but we only have sex once a month. When I talk to her about the situation she says, "If you can find a woman who will lay you two or three times a week, then be my guest." She can't conceive of someone like that. I didn't know she was the way she is when I married her. You see a woman who is attractive and you hope things will work out.

I love my wife and I feel guilty about cheating. I wish my life were different, I am not really happy the way it is. My life would be very dull if I didn't have an intimate relationship with a woman. I put an ad in *The New York Review of Books:* "Married schoolteacher, 64 seeks a white woman who wants an occasional warm man in her bed." I didn't know if anyone would answer. But three people did. One of them was scary, in that the woman wanted to know how big my penis is and sent me a nude picture of herself.

Mary was the first answer. She wrote, "I too am married and I am interested in your offer." I called her and we met in a parking lot. We see each other once a week now. If I were married to Mary, I would never stray. But I can't leave my wife. I wouldn't be able to. I can't picture myself leaving her, it would be against everything I was brought up to.

Mary is a sixty-year-old schoolteacher who has been married for thirty-five years.

I was absolutely happy till my husband got the disease. We had a marvelous relationship and I never cheated. When he got the disease he became a vegetable. He couldn't speak unless he repeated himself. I couldn't even read because he would interrupt and I couldn't go out of his vision without him going crazy. I don't want to break up John's marriage. But if I were married to him I would be faithful.

Angela, a twenty-one-year-old artist with two children, cheated on her husband because she discovered he was unfaithful to her when she was pregnant.

I felt so ugly when I was pregnant, then I found out my husband had cheated on me. He denied the affair, then admitted it. I was hurt. But it was hard to feel anything for him because I was eight months pregnant. But I guess I will never forgive him.

I cheated so that I would feel better about myself. I used to feel I shouldn't stray because of the way I was brought up. But I've changed my mind after what my husband did. I cheated with a friend of my husband, and since I did that I realized that there are a lot of men interested in me. Now I have a long-term relationship with one of my husband's friends. He is very gentle sexually whereas my husband is rough. My sex life with my husband is worse because I think of my lover.

My husband hasn't worked for six months and I am the breadwinner. I have been solely supporting my husband since we got married. I feel like a husband at times, so to feel like a woman I turned to another man. But the main reason I cheated was because my husband had the affair when I was pregnant.

Evidence points to the fact that the majority of women cheat reactively, after their husbands have done so. Often, like Angela, the affair has destroyed their self-esteem, or, like Linda, who also had a secondary extramarital relationship, because they wanted revenge. Linda is a twenty-seven-year-old secretary.

The reason I first cheated was because I found out my husband was having affairs. He promised he would stop doing it and I believed him. But two years later I asked him if he had been unfaithful to me and he told me he had quite a few lovers. He even told me what he did with them and how highly sexed one girl was. At the time, I had two young babies and I felt I had to get revenge on my husband. I had never looked at another man and the idea of being unfaithful to my husband was very bad. I felt rejected, numb, sick, drained, and then violent. I decided that I was going to play him at his own game and that the very worst thing I could do to my husband was to go to bed with his best friend.

I didn't tell my husband, but I got involved with his best friend, John. We had a long affair. Then he married another girl. I had the wedding at our home and I felt like dying inside. Neither John's wife nor my husband has any idea about the affair. I tried to break up with John and get him out of my system, but for a long time I couldn't. I compared every other man with John.

By that time my husband was drinking heavily and I knew that the marriage was over. We had no interest in each other at all and I asked my husband for a divorce. Now I am married to another man and I am very happy at last. He is kind, very thoughtful, a wonderful lover and a good friend. I would never cheat on him as I have too much respect for him. If you cheat things can never be the same again and it leaves a space in you that can never be filled again.

Linda's story illustrates the revenge motive, the woman who has an affair as a reaction to her husband's. But the cheating epidemic can only be fully analyzed by examining the motivations, reactions, and emotions of the victim of an extramarital affair and of the third party.

THREE

Profile of the Cheatee

Why the Cheatee Had an Affair with Someone Who Was Committed to Someone Else

The increase in infidelity indicates that many men and women are ready and willing to become enmeshed in the intricacies of the eternal triangle. And given the availability and participation of the cheatee, the extramarital affair is easier than ever to arrange.

The availability of the cheatee is related to a chicken and egg syndrome. The increase of female cheaters supplies male cheaters with a new source of cheatees, because many cheaters prefer to cheat with married cheatees. They feel that if both cheaters are married, the illicit affair will be less dangerous because both parties risk destroying their marriages if the affair is discovered. The result is that more cheaters become cheatees.

Another change in the modus operandi and motivations of the eighties cheatee is that both men and women feel less guilt about being the cheatee, because many of them grew up with stepparents who were once the cheatee but were eventually fully accepted as family members. Observing the lack of stigma associated with being a third party naturally leads to less guilt about assuming that role oneself. Even without being part of a fractured family, scruples about being the other man or woman may also have lessened as the institution of marriage has fallen into disrepute. "Because I can't ultimately take marriage seriously, I am not concerned with the morality of going to bed with a married person," writes actress Shirley Maclaine. That quote (from the New York *Daily News,* June 5, 1983, taken from Shirley's book *Out on a Limb*) provides the reason why many people today are readier than ever to become the third party in an extramarital affair. If marriage is no longer viewed as sacred, then jeopardizing a marriage will not be considered wrong.

Cheatees are also more available today because society no longer condemns the other man or woman, and consequently they feel far less guilty about their role in an extramarital relationship. The fact that society doesn't frown on the cheatee is evident in the way in which (as we have seen) married men no longer feel compelled to lie about their marital status. Even though they are now blatant about being married, they find plenty of women willing and eager to play the part of the other woman. During my research I only encountered one woman who was adamant in her refusal to date married men.

The other man role has changed less in recent years than the other woman role. Having an affair with a married woman is a time-honored sexual initiation rite for a young boy. However, some men are unable to make the transition from perennial other man to commitment in a one-to-one relationship. The Duke of Windsor, for example, was a celebrated other man and had relationships with two married women, Freda Dudley-Ward and Thelma Furness, before finally wooing Mrs. Simpson away from her long-suffering husband. The other man may deliberately pick his role because he fears a long-term relationship and only wants part-time love.

The same lack of commitment may also propel a woman

into the part of the other woman. Career pressure in today's competitive market also can have the same effect. During my research I repeatedly encountered women who proudly proclaimed, "I want my relationship to be the way it is. I would rather have a married man who won't make demands on me and who will help me with my career and leave me time to pursue it."

A major change in the role of the other woman today has been generated by the male/female ratio. The current shortage of men compels many women to either share someone else's husband or remain alone. And despite the doctrine of women's liberation, many women today still prefer having half a man to being totally alone.

Debbie is a twenty-five-year-old nurse. For the past four years she has been having an affair with a married man, Andy. Andy's wife accepts his excuses for coming home late without protest.

> Andy and I have the perfect relationship. We never get bored with each other because every time we see each other it is like the first time. I don't have to do his laundry or worry about his work problems. I do enough caring and worrying in my job, so all I want from Andy is tenderness, relaxation, and sex. I do love him, but I don't know how long it would last if we were married.
>
> Of course, I date other people, and Andy hates it, but it's really none of his business. He is married; he doesn't own me, so I think if he minds me going out he ought to marry me. As things are, we see each other five nights a week for three hours and I feel like we are semimarried.
>
> All my friends think I am crazy. I've only got one third of a husband, but I don't care. I love the excitement of being with Andy, of knowing that I will always be the woman that he wants to be with while his wife is just the woman he has to put up with. I don't hate her though, I get the cream and she is just left with the milk, the everyday run-of-the-mill stuff.

At first all Andy and I used to do was make love, but now that has changed. We have mutual friends, and he even comes with me to visit my mother. My family don't really like me being so involved with a married man. But I know Andy's the right man for me. We have so much in common, we love each other so much that it makes up for him being married.

Sometimes people say that I protest too much about being happy with Andy, but I am. He's the best friend I have, the hottest lover in the world, and the only man I'll ever love. Now and again I wish I was with him all the time. But deep down, I am scared it will never work. Perhaps Andy wouldn't like me if he saw me every day. This way we can keep the magic.

Because I am not with Andy all the time, I know that in his eyes I'm really glamorous and sexy. I know that he fantasizes about me and longs to see me, just because he can't be with me every day. I think he loves me more because he isn't with me. And I am afraid that if we were together twenty-four hours a day, he wouldn't love me anymore.

Anne is a thirty-four-year-old executive secretary who has never married.

I started working in television when I was twenty-nine and on the first day I met David. Of course he was married, but I tried to push that fact out of my mind. I also tried to forget something I'd written in my diary when I was sixteen: "Resolution—never go out with a married man." My mother had been badly hurt, you see, by my father having an affair with another woman. And I always thought it would be terrible if I ever hurt someone's wife that way. But when I met David I suddenly didn't care.

I had just broken up after a seven-year relationship. Bobby and I had been in love since college and breaking up with him was traumatic. So when I found David, who was so sympathetic and eager to help me, I just fell right in love with him. Of course I know he will never leave his wife. But I still want to be with him.

After I lost Bobby I never thought I would ever find someone else again. But I found David. I feel, in a way, that he is my last chance, that if I lose him, no one else will ever love me again. I know that I am settling for less than most women, but I suppose it is because I feel less is all I can get.

Psychologists have said that many men and women who knowingly become the third party in an extramarital affair, do so because they have very low self-esteem. Anne's story demonstrates that point. She is also a far more classic example of the other woman than the kept temptress of mythology.

In *All the Good Ones Are Married* Marion Zola writes, "Approximately fifteen percent of the women I interviewed, were at least partially kept by wealthy men, often in an atmosphere of affection and tenderness."[1] The other woman is no longer fallen and as a result, the married man no longer needs to compensate her financially for her disgrace. It is far more likely that she jumped right in, rather than fell and is totally prepared to take responsibility for her own role in her lover's extramarital relationships.

Yet the cheatee only has half of a relationship, is often alone and has (in most cases) to live with the underlying knowledge that he or she must take second place in the emotions of the person he loves. Why, then, does a man or woman become a cheatee?

Dr. Strean explains the motivations some men and women have for assuming the role of cheatee: "I think many people are very excited by competition. It goes back to the old Oedipal thing of being fascinated by 'the man who belongs to my mother' or 'the woman who belongs to my father.' Many people are attracted to and can only be interested in a situation where there is a triangle."

Scott is a single man of thirty-two. He had a two-year affair with Laura, a married woman of thirty-eight. His story illustrates the cheatee who becomes enmeshed in the extramarital affair because he is afraid of commitment.

I loved Laura a lot, but when she left her husband for me I panicked. We had planned it for so long but at the last minute I couldn't deal with the situation. Laura and I were so close, and I really believed that I wanted to marry her. But I couldn't. I never got emotionally involved with a woman until I met Laura. I used to find them, go to bed with them, then forget them. I don't know why I was the way I was. I don't really want to talk about it.

Laura and I met when I took a class she was teaching. Having an affair with a teacher always turned me on. I used to fantasize about it when I was a kid. We had coffee after school, and one thing led to another. I took her to a local motel and it was incredible. Laura was unhappy with her husband. All he could ever do was talk about his job, and Laura also thought that he was screwing around on the side. So that is how it started.

I couldn't get enough of Laura. Not just sexually, but in every way. She had traveled all over the world, knew all about classical music and was so dynamic. Quite different from all the other girls I dated. A real woman. She had so much to give me. And I wanted to take care of her, to give her all the attention that her husband hadn't. It was always so intense. Such passion. The summer we met, 1975, the song "Feelings" was popular and it really summed up the way we felt about each other.

Often Laura was too tired and we couldn't have sex, but that didn't matter. I loved holding her in my arms. We began spending more and more time together. And then she managed to get away on a vacation. The vacation was a dream and we felt more in love. I began to see a possibility of a future together. Eventually I asked her to leave her husband and marry me. I figured that everything would be paradise. Then she moved in with me.

Everything changed. Laura had a child and the guilt about leaving him made her difficult to live with. Before, we had never

> had any fights and every moment had been perfect and intense. But we started fighting and everything went bad. I should have walked away right there, but I didn't have a choice.
>
> Half of me wanted to stay with Laura, the other half wanted to run. Suddenly I didn't have any privacy, I didn't have any time to myself, and I realized that I didn't like living with Laura. But I really didn't have a choice. She'd left her husband and kid for me. So I had a responsibility. But the trouble is that I didn't want any responsibility. I tried to be nice to her, I tried to be her friend. But I couldn't live with her. I did love Laura, but I just couldn't go through with anything serious. Stolen moments seemed to suit me far better than mundane life with Laura. I suppose you could say that I only wanted Laura when I couldn't have her. I don't like to think that I was that way, but I suppose it is true.

Scott's story demonstrates both the lure of being the cheatee and the psychological makeup which exists among many people who play the other man or other woman role. The secret, romantic, despairing quality of an extramarital affair is often far more preferable to the cheatee than is the cold light of reality.

What Dr. Strean terms "the old Oedipal thing" is sometimes expressed by aggression. Joseph, a forty-five-year-old male cheatee gleefully boasted to me, "I really get a kick out of dating married women. I laugh at the idea of their husbands slaving to make money all day while I am at home having fun with their wives." However, it is probably true that the Oedipus conflict has always been the overall impetus prompting single men and women to become the cheatee in an extramarital affair.

Whether or Not the Experience Was Pleasant

In an interview for my first book, Glenda Jackson observed, "I think women can be infinitely kinder, gentler, more loving and more hopeful. They always believe in tomorrow; they don't stay with the situation they are in; they always believe that there will be something better; they are essentially optimistic."[2]

Glenda Jackson's comments typify the mental attitude of the average other woman. The majority of female cheatees I talked to admit that although the experience of being the other woman was unpleasant at the time, they still willingly endured the clichéd hardships—the long weekends alone, the holidays feeling rejected. I found that very few categorically insisted that their mistress existence was unequivocably pleasant. Of course, every relationship had its fiery beginnings, with the passion of forbidden pleasures; "I'll never forget the first time Richard touched me," remembers Maria, an eighteen-year-old secretary who had an affair with a married older man. "He had seemed so remote, then suddenly I was in his arms. It was like being kissed by a god. I almost felt blessed."

Maria's relationship finally broke up when he moved to another job and she was left feeling hurt and bitter.

The closest I came to finding a cheatee who experienced the affair as being completely pleasant was Don, a director now in his late thirties, who looks back on his affair with an older married woman as "fantastic. We both knew it wouldn't lead anywhere. I learned all about love and sex from Katherine. And just because I didn't spend too much time with her, I had all the time I needed to concentrate on my career. I don't think

I would have been nearly as successful as I am, if it hadn't been for my affair with Katherine."

Becky is another woman who believes that her affair with an older married man enriched her life. It is important to note that the majority of unmarried cheatees are younger than the men or women they cheat with.

> I was twenty-one when I went to work with Paul. I didn't work directly for him, of course, he was the boss of the newspaper. I knew I was talented, I knew I had drive, but really it was Paul who taught me everything I know today. On the very first day at the office, he made it clear that he wasn't going to help me too much and that I had to prove myself to him professionally.
>
> After a few weeks, I was doing quite well, but I was disturbed by Paul because I was so attracted to him. The office was full of gossip about his bad marriage and how he and his wife were practically divorced. Some mornings he'd come in with scratch marks on his face and we were all warned by his private secretary that he was in a terrible mood. He came in, started a fight with one of the editors, then threw a table at him. Everyone said that it was disgusting, but really I felt sorry for Paul.
>
> A few weeks later I was covering a political event and Paul turned up in the pressroom. At first he seemed really remote, but then after a while I felt as if I had known him my whole life. Paul drove me home and when we got there kissed me. I knew I couldn't resist and we had sex right there in the car. I don't even like to call it sex because it was beyond sex. And the beginning of love.
>
> I didn't think about him being married at all. After all, everyone in the office knew how unhappy Paul was. At first I did wonder what kept him with his wife. Then he told me about his father. His father, you see, was a salesman and used to travel around the country having affairs. When Paul was six his father ran off with another woman. Paul says it ruined his life. In a way,

I would have thought that the whole experience should have stopped Paul from cheating in the first place. But it didn't. It just made him feel that however bad the marriage was he'd never leave his kids.

After two years, Paul and I broke up and I got another job. We broke up because I wanted to go out with other men and Paul didn't want me to. He acted almost as if he created me, as if I were someone he was molding. Really though, it all came down to possessiveness and after two years I wanted to be independent.

I suppose I was heartless having an affair with a married man, but I knew all along that his wife didn't care what he did as long as he paid the bills every month. So I never felt guilty. I did mind a bit when I saw Paul's daughter Sarah because I felt sorry for her. She seemed so helpless and I really pitied her, after all, what if my father was having an affair? But I never hurt any one. Paul's wife didn't find out about the affair. I never wanted to split them up because I always knew that if it hadn't have been me he was having the affair with, it would have been someone else.

I don't regret my affair with Paul at all. We had fun and I learned a lot about reporting from him. When I started my new job, I got involved with another man, more my age, and we are planning to get married next year. I hope he won't cheat on *me*. . . .

Valerie, a thirty-five-year-old New York executive also enjoyed her affair with a married man and seemed able to control the situation.

I still went on with my social life even though he was someone I loved. I told him from the start that I would be going out with other people and he didn't like it. He got upset but I told him that he had no right to get jealous about me going out with other men. But whenever I did, he gave me little presents. I did love him. The relationship was for real, but it never got into my real life.

Valerie may have been able to control her affair, but she still wasn't able to control the emotional repercussions of being the other woman and said, "I've always had trouble with the idea of being a wife and the ability of two people to stay together forever. I am not sure what I am going to do about marriage when I do it. I do want it to be monogamous, but sometimes I think I won't be able to maintain a monogamous marriage."

Whether or Not the Cheatee Trusts the Cheater

The majority of the cheatees I interviewed did. The typical response comes again from Valerie: "I trusted him not to cheat with a third person. He had too many problems. He had problems with guilt. I knew I was the first one." Most cheatees rely on the glamor of their illicit situation to sustain their relationship and keep it relatively monogamous. On the other hand, a few male cheaters boasted to me that they maintain two cheatees simultaneously and that neither know of the other's existence, but those cases are an exception to the rule.

The Cheatee's Attitude to the Cheater Having Sex with the Victim

Just as the victim is able to successfully delude himself that the cheater is faithful, the cheatee is usually equally successful in deluding himself that the cheater only has marital sex under the most stressful, pressured circumstances. But the majority of cheatees resign themselves to the fact that they have no control over the marital sex of their lovers and ignore the subject altogether. I did encounter two female cheatees who fantasized about having a ménage à trois with the cheater and his wife, and one who actually did so, but male cheatees don't ever exhibit the fantasy of simultaneously going to bed with the cheater and her husband. All in all, the cheatee's attitude to the cheater having sex with the victim is predominantly ostrich politics.

Whether or Not the Cheater Wants the Cheatee to Leave the Victim

According to my findings, most cheatees start out without planning to marry the cheater. But as the relationship becomes more intense, the increased involvement does lead to the cheatee wanting the cheater to leave the victim. The stronger the involvement becomes, the greater the pressure for the cheater to leave the victim.

FOUR

Profile of the Victim

I was being interviewed on a radio show in New York and the host was laughing hysterically at the intricate antics of a cheater who had just called in to confide the secrets of his successful cheating. I laughed loudly along with the host, every bit as amused as he was. Then another caller came on the air.

> I've been married six years. In the beginning I had a small period where I cheated. I felt so terribly bad about it. I don't know if I made a mistake, or if I was right, but I told my wife. Then I stopped doing it. But two years ago I found out that my wife was cheating with another man. She used to work from eight to twelve. I would call at work to see if she was there, but she wasn't. My wife and I kept fighting and it all escalated. Then she left with my six-year-old daughter.
>
> I don't know where they are. I don't know where my daughter is. My wife took my daughter's birth certificate and all the personal property. All I want is my daughter back. The bonding between us was tremendous. For the past two years I've bathed her, ironed her clothes, taken her out all the time. The marriage is gone but that child was my heart. I want everyone to know that cheating isn't really worth it. If you are in a relationship with

somebody you feel like cheating on, get out of it before you have children. There is too much pain involved.

The man was crying, sobbing heartrendingly over the air. The talk-show host and I looked at each other, not knowing what to say next or how to help the suffering man on the phone. We had been confronted by the agonizing reality of infidelity—the victim.

It happened again in Florida, this time on a television show with a live studio audience. A sixty-eight-year-old woman in the audience stood up and told the following story.

> I think it is really sad if you have a good marriage and all of a sudden one of the partners cheats. I don't care what happens afterwards. Even if they say they are never going to do it again, the marriage is never the same.
>
> My husband traveled a lot because he is a photographer. He would be gone for three or four months at a time. One day, his best friend called me and told me that my husband was sick and that I should come right away. When I got to the hotel room, I found my husband with another woman. I could have died. We didn't divorce and now we've been married for forty-four years. But it isn't the same. I still like him. And I love him, but not like before. It isn't all open trust. I don't think he has cheated again, but still, the feeling is always there. I used to feel as if I would do anything in the world for him. I used to feel that I would lay down my life for him. But I don't have that feeling anymore. Not since he cheated.

Infidelity may be exhilarating and exciting just as long as you are the one doing it and it isn't being done to you. Infidelity takes on quite another aspect when it is being viewed from the perspective of victim.

While doing the book, I've found many people are prepared to laugh at infidelity, to smile patronizingly and knowingly at the tales of cheaters and cheating. And underneath that reaction lies the assumption, "It could never happen to me. Perhaps I might become a cheater, but I would never ever be a victim." Infidelity is virtually treated like a serious illness, a cancer. Although we are all aware that no one is immune and that the statistics are staggering, we prefer to ignore our fears and say "It could never happen to me."

Yet we all know that 50 percent of married men and women today are victims of infidelity. And perhaps it is true that people today, more than ever, are vulnerable to the hurt and disillusionment of discovering that their partner has been unfaithful to them. Today's world isolates people, forces them inward into a stronger reliance on their intimate relationships. The pressure of life in the eighties, the struggle for economic survival, has become so intense that many people crave the security of being able to believe unquestioningly in the honesty of their partners. And infidelity undermines that security.

In the late seventies, Gordon Clanton and Lynn G. Smith also defined why infidelity may be more terrifying to us now than it was in the past. They begin by addressing their comments to the victims of infidelity.

> But perhaps you fear more than loss of face. Perhaps you fear you are losing control; control of your spouse, control of the relationship, control of the future, control of yourself. You cannot predict your partner's behaviour. You are reluctant to voice complaints because you don't know how your partner will react. You don't trust the third party. Your anxiety breeds tension which corrodes your relationship.
>
> This fear of loss of control, rooted in insecurity, is a specific form of neurosis quite common today. As we lose control of other sectors of our lives or discover we never really had control, we wish all the more to be secure in our intimate relationships and our family life. If things are chaotic at work, if the crime rate is

> going up, if the country's government seems to be corrupt or incompetent, the security and stability of the home becomes more important.[1]

By investigating the emotions and actions of the victim, I believe we will come face to face with the repercussions of infidelity.

Expectations of Fidelity

The victim's reaction to his partner's infidelity is colored by his initial expectations of fidelity. I've found that many women start out their marriages by almost expecting the man to cheat. In contrast, men start out expecting women not to.

Janice Francis in her article, "Toward the Management of Heterosexual Jealousy," in *The Journal of Marriage and Family Counselling* confirms my findings when she writes, "Despite reports indicating that males and females are equally likely to become involved in extradyadic interactions, males are much less likely to suspect females than are females to suspect their male counterparts of those involvements."[2]

Women, even today, still expect male infidelity. This again relates to Alan Gross's remark (quoted before), "The belief that men have a stronger sex drive than women persists with no compelling evidence to support it." The alley-cat image of the male still remains, creating in many women the expectation that men will stray.

However, the expectations of men regarding the fidelity of their wives, are totally opposite. The majority of male cheaters and victims I talked to, confessed that they have always been convinced that their wives will never be unfaithful. There are two primary reasons for this male conviction. First, men have different standards of behavior for women than for themselves; and second, even now, many men still believe that women are unable to separate love from sex.

Dealing with double standards first, almost 60 percent of the men I talked to said, "She would *never* cheat on me, she loves me too much." But those same men were nevertheless quite content to cheat on their wives while at the same time maintaining, "Even though I cheat, I really love my wife." It seems that men set idealistic standards of behavior for their wives, that they don't set for themselves. The way in which men evaluate the quality of female love seems to include a belief that if a woman loves she would never cheat. But in contrast, they don't seem to think that a man's love need preclude infidelity.

The consequences in regard to fidelity are that many men expect their wives' love to preclude hurting them, while their love is permitted to include infidelity (which could hurt the person they profess to love). Men have seen that their mothers often loved unconditionally, and expect the same quality of emotion from their wives. Although they can cheat and still "love" their wives, many men cling to the idea that their wife's love will never include a similar contradiction between behavior and professed emotion.

The other major male assumption is that women who become wives are unable to separate love from sex. However much information and publicity there is about women having their own sexual desires, I have found that men don't really believe this to be true. Many men in America still believe that while *they* are biologically polygamous, women are by nature monogamous. This again is partially related to the image of mother many men grew up with—the virgin on a pedestal. Women, on the other hand, often find out that their father is cheating and expect men to be promiscuous.

It seems incredible that men still believe women can't separate love from sex, but my findings startlingly confirm this. Richard, a thirty-four-year-old salesman who has been married for ten years, says that he is convinced his wife can't have sex without love.

She has only ever had sex with me. She knows that I cheat and that I answer ads in *The Voice*. I suggested that we explore swinging together, but I don't think she could do that. She is more interested in a candlelight romantic affair. I don't like it. I think I would be angry as I wouldn't want her to get involved. It would take her from me. But I think most women look for romance. Women can't separate love from sex.

Michael is a thirty-year-old construction worker who has been married for four years.

Yes, I believe in monogamy. I'm somewhat faithful. I've been unfaithful ten times. My wife and I only have sex every two weeks. We have talked about it and she says, "What do you want me to do?" In a way, she is a good all-round deal; a good housekeeper, a good companion. But sexually, forget it. I don't think she would ever cheat on me. Sex and love don't have to coincide, but I don't think my wife could have sex without love.

Bill is a married cheater who married his wife Sherry when they were both in their mid-thirties.

I know Sherry had a lot of boyfriends before she met me, but I am sure she was emotionally involved with them. I can't imagine her having sex for just the sake of it. I know she is very sexual, but I really believe that for Sherry, sex and love have to go together.

I feel bad cheating on her, but I know that I can compartmentalize my cheating so that it doesn't touch my marriage. I have always fooled around. First on my girlfriends and now on Sherry. I don't care about the girls I go to bed with and I never will. If Sherry cheated on me I know it wouldn't be fooling around like the way I fool around. It would be serious. Maybe not love but definitely emotional. I know sex is different for men than it is for women. I don't pay any attention to what those women's libbers

> say; women aren't the same as men. They don't handle love and sex like we do. They need romance and flowers and all that sort of thing. I don't know why they are that way—they just are.

The female interviews, for the main part, bear those judgments out. But that may be due to socialization. However, many men still attribute female monogamy to biology. Pete, a thirty-seven-year-old salesman, a habitual cheater, says,

> Men find it much more difficult to be faithful. My wife would never cheat on me. She's deeply in love with me. She would never cheat on me. I'd kill her. I satisfy her totally. I think it is all right for me to cheat, but not her. Women aren't made that way.

Harry, a thirty-three-year-old accountant, says,

> I've been unfaithful many times. Sometimes I believe in monogamy. Other times I don't. The fact is that you can love someone and still cheat without ruining that love. But my wife can't separate love from sex. For her somehow the one enhances the other.

Discussions of Infidelity Between Husband and Wife

The expectations of fidelity, as previously explored, don't seem conducive to discussions of fidelity. Men don't expect infidelity from their wives, so they don't discuss it. Women, however, usually accept male infidelity as inevitable, therefore also failing to discuss it at the start of a marriage. And by not discussing fidelity, both men and women make it easier for their partners to cheat without guilt.

Occasionally men and women do discuss fidelity, but it is usually the man who makes his feelings about infidelity patently clear.

When Sylvester Stallone left his wife Sasha for another

woman, she was asked by writer Marilyn Laron Funt if she dated other men during the separation: "No, Sly would be a hard act to follow. Also, he would have punched another man in the nose. He came right out and said he didn't want me to date anyone else. He couldn't handle it."[3] Stallone may have exhibited male double standards (he was with another woman, but didn't want his wife to be with another man), but unlike the majority of women I surveyed, he openly came out and said so. Perhaps again, his honesty was partly due to a feeling of power which many men still feel they have over their wives. Their role in relationships makes it possible for them to demand fidelity, but women who lack that same power are forced to either ignore the situation or accept the infidelity.

If men worry about their wives being unfaithful to them, they tend to tell them in advance how they will react if they have an affair. A woman wrote to Abigail Van Buren saying, "I asked him what he would do if I got involved with another man and he said he'd break my neck. Is that fair? He thinks he is being fair with me because he is telling me in advance." Many men make it totally clear to their wives what they would do if they found them cheating. However, women rarely employ that same tactic.

I found that most women I talked to hadn't discussed their feelings about fidelity with their mates. Very few of them stated in advance how they would react if they discovered that their partners had been unfaithful to them. And because their wives don't discuss their feelings about infidelity, many men feel they have a license to cheat. After all, their wives have never actually said they minded. Nor what they would do if they found out the truth.

Bob was married for four years and cheated with his wife's tacit consent.

> We never discussed infidelity. I just knew I wouldn't remain content with just my wife. I assumed my wife understood my

needs, which really are the needs of any male. So she always handled my cheating really well, never asking any questions or worrying if I came home late. I always assumed that she knew the score.

At one point we took the situation very far and had a threesome with another woman. We were a bit drunk. I know she did it to make me feel nice and not out of desire and interest. Then afterwards things weren't the same between us sexually. When I am fully erect I am eleven inches, and my wife has always been enamoured by that. I think perhaps when she had to share it with someone it became less hers.

I realized by her reaction that she would never accept me cheating. Until then I had assumed that she didn't mind, that she knew and put up with it. Perhaps she did, but after the threesome, I knew that she minded. I don't know what to do. I can't give up cheating, but I don't know where it will lead.

By ignoring their suspicions and giving the cheater the impression that they don't really care about the infidelity, the female victim contributes to making an extramarital affair pleasant for her mate. I was surprised that many women maintain this attitude even when the details of the affair become impossible to ignore.

The Victim's Reaction to Suspicions That the Cheater Is Cheating

Just as expectations of marriage and monogamy are formed partially by what the child sees in the parental marriage, so I believe, is the reaction to being a victim of infidelity.

Again, it is likely that the child, watching a parent become a victim of infidelity, almost sits in judgment on his reaction. Then the child's behavior pattern (as an adult in the same circumstances) is influenced by that judgment. My own case is an apt example. I saw my mother leave my father because of his repeated infidelities. I believed that her decision was right. Consequently, that belief formed my reaction to infidelity in my own relationships, so that I have always made it patently clear to any man I'm involved with that if he cheats on me, I will leave him. I may not be able to prevent him from being unfaithful, but at least he is totally aware how I will react if ever I become a victim of infidelity.

On the other hand, if I had disapproved of my mother's actions, perhaps I would instead be prepared to put up with infidelity in my own relationships. Conversely, if my mother had been unfaithful and my father had found out and done nothing, I would probably have expected to cheat without consequences in my own relationships. Perhaps the case of the late President Kennedy reflects the same pattern. He saw his mother, Rose, tolerate his father's infidelity and so, perhaps, expected the same behavior from his own wife.

Differences Between Male and Female Victims' Reactions to the Infidelity of Their Partners

People's expectations of fidelity set the stage for the way in which they deal with infidelity in their marriages. As we have seen, many women expect their mates to cheat, and most men don't expect their mates to. These expectations determine subsequent reactions to infidelity. My overall finding is that when women discover their partner has cheated on them, they tend to avoid confronting the situation as long as possible, ignoring the evidence. And if they are compelled to deal with the infidelity they try to dismiss it as a sexual fling and minimize the importance of the other woman. Men, on the other hand, tend to confront the situation, are totally devastated by the infidelity and sometimes threaten the other man with violence. I have also found that the male reaction to infidelity often puts an end to the extramarital affair while the female reaction invariably encourages it.

I have to admit that I began interviewing female victims with a prejudiced preconception. I expected to find that they reacted in the same way as my mother had. Obviously, that expectation was not rational and objective, but emotional and subjective; after the first few interviews I revised it, expecting female victims to be divided equally between women who uncomplainingly endured male infidelity and those who rebelled. But I was wrong. The majority of women not only ignore their husbands' infidelities but even sometimes help cause them to happen, by making it clear that no matter how strong their suspicions of infidelity might be, they will ignore the evidence.

The Female Victim: Ignoring the Evidence of Infidelity

The media may try and promote the image of the strong, confident, liberated woman who doesn't put up with unequal treatment, but I rarely encountered her. Instead I found many women who are prepared to sublimate suspicions of their husbands' infidelity, unwilling or unable to confront them.

Abigail Van Buren's column is full of accounts of female victims not confronting their suspicions of infidelity, despite what seems like obvious evidence. There was the woman who found pierced earrings on the bedside table and listened uncomplainingly as her husband assured her that he had never seen them before and had no idea how they got there. A classic victim's letter read:

> Dear Abby,
>
> I've been married to a good-looking cross-country truck driver for ten years. I'm not the suspicious type, but Friday night he came off the road with two long scratches, yet neither his shorts nor his trousers were ripped.
>
> When I asked him where he got the scratches, he said they were probably from a feather in the bed. Now, Abby, I'd like to believe him, but do they still have feather-bedding in modern motels? And could anybody get scratched like this from a feather?[4]

The letter was signed "Not Dumb." And perhaps she isn't, because after all she is only part of a pattern I've found typical—the female victim who prefers to bury her suspicions that her husband is being unfaithful. This pattern, as the section on male victims will confirm, is more common to women than it is to men.

Detective Johnston says that many of his female clients don't want to believe the initial proof of infidelity that he provides them with.

> More than fifty percent of our clients who catch their partner at infidelity, try again a second time. And many women don't want to believe the initial proof that we provide them with. Sometimes they just don't want to accept the truth. A woman hired us to follow her husband. I took pictures of the husband kissing and hugging the other woman. His wife confronted him with the pictures and the husband said, "That isn't me." Of course it *was* him, but his wife brought the pictures back to us and said, "You know, it really doesn't look like him." But it was him.
>
> The same woman hired us a few weeks later. That time we took a picture of the husband meeting the girl. It was a great picture. They were in front of their own cars, embracing. We had a picture of the two cars with the number plates showing. The wife took the pictures to the husband. Two days later she called me and said, "He says it isn't him." I said, incredulously, "But the car is

his car." She said, "He says it is a coincidence, and I tend to believe him." I told her that she was wasting her time and her money because she didn't want to know the truth.

It seems unbelievable that in 1984 there still exists a real-life parallel to the old joke about the man whose wife finds him in bed with another woman. As she starts screaming, the husband turns around and says, "Nothing is wrong. Who are you going to believe, me or your own eyes?" The joke may be old, but judging by Detective Johnston's case history the reaction still occurs. Perhaps part of its basis lies in Glenda Jackson's remarks about women forever remaining optimistic.

Playing ostrich politics in the face of a husband's infidelity is a classic female pattern.

Joanne is divorced and in her early forties.

I never imagined my husband would cheat on me. Never in a million years. We were always so happy together. He did come home late sometimes, but I figured it was work. I didn't ask him where he had been or who he had been with. I'd have felt like a spy or a detective if I'd asked those sorts of questions.

Of course I know that there is a lot of cheating going on, but I never expected it to touch my life, to be a part of our marriage. No way. Looking back, I suppose I was very naive. But at the time I really believed in my husband. It wasn't just him I believed in, it was our marriage. I suppose if you had held a gun to my head and forced me to say if I thought he had gone to bed with another woman since we got married, I'd have said yes. A prostitute or something, but no one he would have spent time with. No one who mattered like I did.

Looking back, the first sign was the way in which he altered towards me. He started having more sex with me. Well, I didn't mind that, I enjoyed it. Then there was the car seat. I am very small and so the passenger seat is always quite far forward. But all of a sudden it was always pushed back. I didn't make a connection at the time, but now I know it was because my husband's girlfriend, Bobby, had really long legs. He started coming home later and later, always with another excuse: entertaining clients; the car broke down; the boss wanted him to work late. And all through it, I didn't question anything.

In the end, my husband confessed everything because he wanted a divorce. I suppose I would have let the whole thing go on for years if he had not said anything. I did love him, but then again, I let love make me into a fool. I truly did. I was shattered by the whole thing. You never think your husband will actually fall in love with another woman and leave you. I felt so useless, such a failure. Bobby isn't much younger than me, but she has obviously got something I haven't. Looking back, I wish I had known about her from the start. Then I could have seen what I was up against.

Now I am divorced I date a lot of men, but I don't expect them to be faithful to me. I suppose men are just like that. I don't know why. I did believe in my husband, but I was wrong. And I am never going to believe in another man again.

Again and again the female victim's initial reaction to suspicions of infidelity is choosing to ignore the truth. Valerie (an other woman in the preceding chapter) remembers meeting her cheater's wife.

She didn't know that we were having an affair and I felt sorry for her. I was a waitress while I was at college and he was the bartender. He would stay out all night with me about four times a week, but his wife never said a thing.

Then when she came into the bar one day, we started talking. I felt sorry for her. She acted as if she didn't know anything. We were talking and she said, "Well, I expect that people who work in bars go out after hours and then in the morning go to the beach and hang out with each other." They had only been married for two years, but she obviously didn't want to find out what he was really up to. She supplied all the excuses for him.

Baseball ex-wives Bobbie Bouton and Nancy Marshall told *People* magazine in a June 1983 interview that they had avoided dealing with their suspicions that their husbands Jim Bouton and Mike Marshall were unfaithful. "Mike would say things like 'I think it's really stupid that these guys are risking their marriages by going out with these really dumb broads,' and you think that if he is telling you this, then he certainly isn't one of them," says Nancy Marshall. Bobbie Bouton added, "I had a nagging suspicion from time to time, but never any real proof, so I never had to confront it. But when *Ball Four* came out [former New York Yankee] Joe Pepitone called Jim 'the horniest bleep in baseball.' That's got to give you a few doubts."

The Female Victim: Playing Mother in the Face of Evidence of Infidelity

If the female victim of an affair fails to confront the situation, the cheater often casts her into the role of an all-forgiving mother. This, naturally, makes it easier for the cheater to stray without feeling guilty.

Bill is a forty-year-old data processor who has been married for seventeen years.

> I believe in monogamy—partially. I love my wife, she loves me and she knows I fool around. At least, I think she does. I have my own business so I tell my wife that I am out with a client. She could control me more than she does, but she never once says anything about my cheating, so in a way she is giving me permission to cheat.
>
> Once, though, she did ask me about cheating. We had just had sex and we started discussing infidelity. She lit up a cigarette and asked point blank if I had ever had sex with another woman. I said yes. The cigarette nearly fell out of her mouth and she said,

"Don't ever let me catch you with another woman. And don't let anything happen, don't get serious." She never really shows that she minds infidelity. I don't think she does mind deep down. She says, "What I don't know, won't ever hurt me."

I cheated after ten years through a radio interview program called "Dial a Date." Since then I've had twelve affairs. I once fell in love with a woman but she moved to California. Since then I don't get involved with the other women. If I were married to a hot-blooded woman I wouldn't cheat on her.

In Bill's interview, the wife again seems to have taken on the role of the mother to a naughty little boy. She says "Don't ever let me catch you" and the implication is that Bill is a child who has to be indulged, who must be allowed to play in the mud now and again just as long as he comes home and takes a bath afterward. The victim-as-mother syndrome (also highlighted in the Cheater chapter) makes it simple for the cheater to cheat without too much remorse. After all, a mother forgives all.

Some women willingly conspire to take up the role of mother to their cheating husbands. And some women even enjoy the role. In *Elizabeth Taylor, the Last Star,* Kitty Kelley quotes Sybil Burton (who ignored her husband's affairs), "You do become an absolute nursemaid because your husband has to face the public every day. You worry about his sleep and his health, the way you do with a child."

The late Bill Lear, whom his widow Moya Lear admitted on *60 Minutes* was a cheater, even called his long-suffering wife, Mom.

In *Cousin Bette,* Balzac pinpoints the victim-as-mother syndrome.

Madame Hulot dated her Hector's first infidelities from the final dissolution of the Empire. The Baroness then, had held for a dozen years of her married life the position of prima donna absoluta, unchallenged. She still continued to enjoy the inveterate old affection that husbands bear to wives who have resigned themselves to playing the part of good kind companions. She knew that no rival would stand for two hours among one word of reproach from her, but she shut her eyes, she stopped her ears, her wish was to know nothing of her husband's conduct outside his home. In the end, she came to treat her Hector as a mother treats a spoiled child.

Cathy is a female victim in her fifties.

I married Bob after high school. You could say we were childhood sweethearts. We sort of grew up together. I can't even begin to describe what we have been through together. A lifetime really.

Of course I know Bob cheats. I am aware of it from the time he goes out in the morning. There is something about the way he walks, the clothes he picks, the trouble he takes in tying his tie. And he is extra sweet to me when he leaves. Of course I don't know who he is with or what he is doing with her. I don't know who *she* is. In my opinion he's probably with different girls each time.

If cheating makes him happy, then I don't care. If that's what Bob needs to feel young then I am not going to stand in his way. Just so long as he comes home after. And he always does. He is a bit like a naughty child when he gets home. He has a funny look on his face, as if he expects to be told off. But I don't say anything. I let him get away with it. As long as I love him and he loves me, nothing else matters.

If some women play mother and give their husbands permission to cheat by not dealing with their suspicions, there are plenty of husbands who are prepared to play son and accept. The bargain is rarely made out in the open. It is merely that the excuses become lamer and lamer while the victim continues to ignore the affair.

The Female Victim: Acceptance of Infidelity, Powerlessness, and the "Just Sex" Excuse

Once a husband's infidelity is impossible to ignore, many wives persist in refusing to confront the affair and, instead, accept it. This is a Miami-based woman talking to me about her husband's unfaithful behavior.

> Whenever we go shopping, my husband just wanders off and looks for any chick available. It seems that every time we go out, he is whistling at women. I am so embarrassed.
>
> He comes home at twelve o'clock at night, or even at two or three in the morning and I know he's cheated. But I act real normally when he comes home late at night. I don't ask anything like, Where were you? I play along with his little charade and he doesn't think that I know. I figure that if I start getting suspicious, he might get mad with me and then he would want a divorce.

The Miami woman didn't go on to explain exactly why she is afraid of her husband divorcing her, but whatever the reasons, she is speaking in the voice of the powerless. The average female income is still far lower than that of the male, leaving many women economically helpless in the face of divorce. Many women feel they have no choice, despite their husband's infidelity, but to remain married, because they are economically vulnerable.

Dr. Strean says that sometimes female patients respond to their husbands affairs by saying, "I had nowhere else to go." Detective Johnston adds, "What most women want is to have their husband back. They don't want their marriages to break up. We are still in a society in this country where you have two or three children and a mortgage. If a wife finds out her husband is involved with another woman, she very often thinks, If I lose him, I lose the home. How am I going to support the children? I can't support three children. We find that most women will try and put their marriages together again."

Economic desperation may be the cause of many women accepting their husband's infidelity. There is also another reason: Society still tells women that male infidelity is understandable and that being a female victim of infidelity is virtually woman's fate. There is a prevalent attitude that being the female victim of infidelity isn't as demeaning as being the male victim. After all, there is no female word equivalent to *cuckold.* The female victim may be pitied, but she isn't scorned. When society views a female victim, the reaction is diluted by the feeling that, Oh well, we all know what men are like. And while the woman who puts up with her cheating husband may be patronized, she isn't really laughed at and is, in many ways, regarded as noble. When Mrs. Bill Lear talked about her husband's infidelities on *60 Minutes* and revealed how she loved him throughout, many people told me that they admired her.

Mrs. Lear accepted her husband's affairs throughout the entire marriage. She was questioned on *60 Minutes* (May 23, 1982) about her late husband Bill Lear's extramarital relationships. Ed Bradley asked her about her husband's affairs. The transcript of the show reads as follows:

ED BRADLEY: I don't want to be impolite, but if—if half the stories that I've heard about Bill Lear are true, he had—he had a lot of ladies on the side.

MOYA LEAR: (Laughing) Yes, he did. He'd wake up in the

	morning and say, "Damn it, I did it again, didn't I?" (Laughing)
BRADLEY:	And that didn't bother you?
MOYA LEAR:	Well, you—Oh, I can't say that. Sure it did. But I loved him so much and understood him, and it never meant that much. You know, okay, if it mattered and I say, "Okay, I'm going to get a divorce, I can't stand this any longer," I wouldn't have him anymore. You've got to figure out what means the most to you. And he meant the most to me.

Mrs. Lear expanded on her thoughts about her husband's infidelity in a *People* magazine interview with Nancy Farber on November 30, 1980. "How can girls think they can marry an attractive, fabulous guy and be the only one? Sure, I was hurt at times, and at other times we laughed about it. He was always very, very sweet to me when he came home. I was always secure in Bill's love. He was my first and last."

Mrs. Lear's attitude may be touchingly stoical, but it also provides insight into the wife who accepts her husband's infidelity with resignation. She reveals both the female's high standard of behavior she sets for herself and the lower one she sets for her husband. There is an inevitability about Mrs. Lear's resignation to the infidelities, a belief that it was either she put up with her husband's affairs or lose him. Again we hear the voice of the powerless wife, unable to prevent her husband straying.

In 1967, Dr. Robert Seidenberg, a clinical professor of psychiatry, analyzed the dynamics of infidelity, and his analysis, surprisingly enough, can still be applied to many women of the eighties.

> One generally hears of loyal servants or subjects, rarely of loyal masters or rulers. This can be applied to aspects of faithfulness in marriage where the rules of conduct as far as infidelity are concerned are much more stringent and condemnatory for the relatively powerless woman than the man. In the male dominant-society, the infidelity of the man is generally excused whereas the woman's lapse has severe consequences. This well-known double standard has been rationalized and vindicated in the fiction that the male of the species is basically polygamous, and therefore his transgressions are part of his basic nature; whereas the woman's is a moral fault. This is another instance where power can write its own favorable rules supported by an on-going mythology. We might have to agree with the cynic when he says that if one is powerful enough one does not have to be sexually faithful, and yet at the same time can demand unswerving loyalty from another. The best safeguard for marital fidelity may be a healthy balance of power.[5]

Many women today still feel powerless to control their husband's infidelity and consequently cope by either ignoring it, accepting it, or dismissing it as "just sex." They minimize the deception and dishonesty inherent in cheating and say, "Oh, well, men are just like that," and dismiss the infidelity as "just sex." "Just sex" in the view of many women is a male preogative, one that is rarely challenged. Therefore women are often more accepting of the possibility of infidelity because they have grown up with the idea, "It's different for men because it's just sex." And if it is just sex it is more easily dismissed. However intellectually aware women are that men really aren't more polygamous than women, they still don't believe it on an emotional level. And with it comes the idea that men are biologically destined to suffer stronger sexual urges which make infidelity unavoidable. It is almost as if some female victims view men as helpless animals unable to control their own sexuality.

Rachel, a New York hairdresser, encountered the same situation when she discussed infidelity with her future husband just before they planned to marry.

> Tony and I had gone out for three years when we decided to get married. A few weeks before the wedding we sat down and talked about fidelity. I wasn't really comfortable with the conversation, but Tony started it by asking what I would do if he cheated on me. I didn't want to think about it, but I knew I hated the idea. I tried to change the subject, really because I thought Tony wouldn't marry me if I told him how I really thought.
>
> I didn't like him bringing the subject up, but it preyed on my mind for a few weeks. I thought about it for a long time and decided to tell Tony exactly how I felt. But really it seemed awful to be talking about it.
>
> At first I told him I didn't want him to cheat. Then Tony (who is fantastic looking) said, "Well what if I am really tempted and can't help myself?" I asked him if he had ever heard of self-control. Because really I think that's what it's really all about. I told him it was difficult for me to be faithful and that I would also be tempted.
>
> Then Tony asked me what I would do if I caught him cheating. I said that I would go out and cheat twice as much myself. Which I would do. Tony looked shocked and then said, "If you cheat on me, I'll kill you." So I said, "Yes, but you would have started the whole thing by cheating yourself in the first place."

The whole concept of male sexuality still dictates that men, as in the Marlene Dietrich song "Falling in Love Again" just can't help it. And all the phrases like "animal instincts," and the romantic novel portraits of males simmering with unbridled passion contribute to the concept that sexuality is an elemental force peculiar to men. Female sexuality even today is still considered far milder and more manageable than male sexuality.

The Female Victim: Her Relationship with the Cheatee

The only weapon female victims who accept their husbands' affairs seem to employ is that of derision, minimizing the importance or stature of the other woman. Moya Lear, according to *People,* stitched a needlepoint with the heading of "Ah, L'Amour," followed by the names of Bill Lear's girlfriends and ex-wives, ending with the observation "Some I've forgotten, some I didn't know." Nancy Marshall employed the same approach when dealing with her husband's extramarital affairs. She was asked (in the June 1983 *People* magazine article) if most baseball wives accepted road-trip affairs as just part of the game. "If you are a sensible person you know they are. But if wives get asked about it, they'll give a flip answer instead of expressing their feelings. I did accept it, but I didn't like it and it had a very negative effect on our marriage."

Jean Harris (who was virtually a wife to Dr. Tarnower), initially dealt with his affair with Lynne Tryforos by trying to laugh it off. When asked about her reactions to the affair in court, Mrs. Harris told prosecutor Aurnou that she conveyed her feelings about the affair to Dr. Tarnower but "always in a very light vein." When Mrs. Harris saw the advertisement Lynne Tryforos had placed in *The New York Times,* wishing the doctor a Happy New Year, Mrs. Harris coped with the situation by quipping, "Herman, why don't you suggest that she use the Good Year Blimp next year? I think it's available." Mrs. Harris strove desperately to dismiss the other woman, and in doing so, the infidelity itself.

Judging by an account by the White House kennel keeper, Traphes Bryant, Jacqueline Kennedy used the same tactics in dealing with President Kennedy's infidelities. Bryant says that Jackie once found a woman's undergarment tucked in a pillowcase in Jack's room. She deliberately held it out for him to see, saying, "Will you please shop around and see who these belong to. They are not my size."[6]

Minimizing the extent of the affair as well as totally dismissing the other woman is another way the female victim copes. When Betsy Bloomingdale discovered that her husband Alfred had conducted a twelve-year affair with Vicki Morgan, she reacted by saying that she and Alfred had a wonderful marriage and that she wasn't going to let the affair bother her. Debbie Reynolds also resorted to the same type of reaction when she found out about her husband's affair with Elizabeth Taylor. "I'm still very much in love with Eddie. I just hope this separation will iron out the difficulties so that we can get together and be happy again. We were never happier than we have been in the last year. Don't blame Eddie for this, though. It's not his fault. He's a wonderful guy."[7]

Some female victims do deal with the situation and confront both parties in the affair. Annie is a Chicago-based woman who discovered that her husband had been having an affair after twelve years of marriage.

> I had a feeling that my husband was having an affair. There were too many occasions when he couldn't account for his time and there were a couple of times when he told me he was somewhere but when I checked he wasn't there. I asked him about it and he told me he had picked up a strange girl and had gone to bed with her.
>
> Then, last week, he came home intoxicated and told me that it really was my best friend. She's been a family friend for twenty years. I am forty-four, my husband is forty-five and she is fifty-nine. I felt doubly betrayed because she was my best friend and she went out to stab me. The fact that she went out to get me

bothers me more than his cheating. I am never going to see her again, no way.

We had a three-way conversation on the phone, my husband, the woman, and me. It started out with them saying, "It just happened." Then the story got into two versions. He told me that she had promised to buy him a boat and take care of him. She is quite well-off. She denied it and said she never had any intention of buying him a boat. Her reason was that she was afraid of him and she couldn't get rid of him. He said that when he realized she wasn't going to buy him a boat, he came home and blew the whistle on her. I believe it just happened.

He's acting as though nothing happened now. And I am supposed to accept it and go on as though nothing had happened as well. But I can't. He's promised that he will never call her or speak to her again. But I don't think I love him any more. I'm kind of looking at him as if he were an alien.

Another, more radical way of reacting to both victim and cheatee, is violence. Unlike men, the majority of women attack the cheater, and not the cheatee. They are more logical than men (who attack the other man) and go after the person who has betrayed them, as in the case of Jean Harris who killed Dr. Tarnower rather than attacking Lynne Tryforos. Women do indeed commit crimes of passion, but mostly by attacking the cheater. After all, it is the cheater, not the other woman, who owes her loyalty and who has betrayed her trust.

The majority of female victims ignore their suspicions of their husbands' infidelity. They either accept the affair, dismiss it as just sex or cheat in retaliation themselves. There is very often a form of collusion between husband and wife. By failing to confront an extramarital affair, both husband and wife are sometimes using the infidelity as a Band-Aid, a distraction designed to cover up the inadequacies of the relationship. And as we have seen, the sexual fling which the victim is so studiously ignoring, may lead to a meaningful secondary

-nship. The victim, or the cheater, who dismisses the infidelity as "just sex" may well be deluding himself because "just sex" could eventually evolve into love.

Of course, some female victims do confront and vanquish the infidelity. Detective Johnston tells of a female victim who specifically requested that he video tape her husband when he caught the husband with his girlfriends.

> We followed the man, a successful doctor. We found he was with a number of girls and we video taped them together. Then we gave his wife the video tape. Later that year there was a big family gathering, with the children, aunts and uncles present. The woman played them movies of past family parties, then included the pictures of her husband with the other women. The man was a saint in everyone's eyes and she did this to show him up. She loved it. And the husband promised that he would never cheat again, as he was totally embarrassed.

But in general, I've found that when a female victim suspects her husband's infidelity, she fails to confront or discuss it, and so gives him tacit permission to carry on cheating. However, male victims react in a dramatically different way.

The Male Victim's Reaction to Infidelity: Shock and Surprise

The initial male reaction to suspicions of infidelity is one of shocked surprise. Every one of the male victims I talked to admits that they had never expected their partner to cheat on them. Even the most inveterate cheater seems unable to countenance the possibility of his wife being unfaithful to him.

As I noted before, the majority of men don't expect their wives to be unfaithful because they don't believe women can separate love from sex. Consequently, when they do discover that their wives have been unfaithful to them, they are unable (as women are) to dismiss the affair as "just sex."

The fact that men believe that women can't have sex without love gives them license to apply the double standard to their own advantage; as a male cheater said to me, "I can cheat without falling in love but she can't." At the same time, this attitude creates a situation whereby the male victim is totally devastated if he finds out his wife is unfaithful. By believing that women can't have sex without love, he doesn't have access to the "just sex" excuse. And even if his wife's infidelity was indeed a quick sexual fling, he can't react to it as such. Given that he believes women can't separate love from sex, he naturally assumes that if his wife has had an affair it must automatically entail love; so the male victim's first shocked reaction is often that his wife's affair must inevitably involve love.

Danny is a thirty-two-year-old musician who was a rampant cheater. He not only cheated with various women, but also had an affair with his wife's sister.

> She lived upstate and my wife and I went to see her a couple of times. Even though I was with my wife, I started to fall in love with her sister. We got extremely affectionate, but without sex. Eventually that is what happened. I was in love with her. Really I wanted to have my wife and her sister at the same time. To have both of them live with me.
>
> I told my wife that I really loved her sister. I felt a little guilty. The sex was different with her than with my wife. It was a lot more erotic and more open. It didn't affect my sex life with my wife. Our sex life continued to be exciting and pleasurable.
>
> Eventually my wife admitted that she was cheating on me. I was really hurt and upset and couldn't believe she would do that to me. I felt I could handle myself cheating but that she couldn't. I thought I could handle it and not get involved. Even when I was in love with her sister I still wouldn't have wanted to leave my

wife. I think she would have been a lot more emotionally affected by her affair. She told me that she didn't have sexual intercourse with her lover, but just oral sex. That made me feel really bad, it was more emotional. I couldn't stand it. The idea of my wife having hot sex with someone else. I couldn't stand it.

Most men who believe their wives can't cheat without falling in love take refuge in the concept of entrapment and cling to the idea that the other man has lured her away from him. That scenario then prepares the ground for him to absolve his wife from responsibility, places her in the category of property which can be owned (and stolen) and also sets the stage for a violent confrontation with the other man.

Pete, an ace cheater, says that he can't envisage his wife cheating, but that if she did, it wouldn't be her fault.

I just don't see her cheating. She is very vulnerable, very petite, I can see her being taken in by a very sharp talker who might persuade her. But I know she would never cheat of her own free will.

When Ingrid Bergman left her husband Petter for another man, Roberto Rossellini, her husband was quoted by a newsperson as saying Ingrid must have been under the influence of drugs and therefore didn't know what she was doing. Ingrid denied that, and said Roberto never took drugs but the inference of the seduced woman had still been made.

Even today some men still believe in the old concept of entrapment and fix on the image of the innocent woman being seduced. Don, a thirty-two-year-old data processing assistant who says he cheated three months after the marriage ("The sex came to me, rather than me coming to the sex."), says that he would be jealous if his wife cheated on him: "I would hate it if the man wanted to dominate her or feel superior to her. I would feel jealous that she was being used against her will."

Again, the male attitude is that women can't have sex without love. So if they do, the other man must have trapped them into it.

Men are also more surprised when women cheat on them because (as Dr. Robert Brannon has pointed out) they are far less introspective than women and have, in many cases, failed to consider the possibility.

The Male Victim's Reaction to Infidelity: Violence and Confrontation with the Other Man

According to my findings, men, unlike women, rarely put up with their wives' infidelity. There are no male Mrs. Lears and it would be difficult to imagine a man appearing on CBS-TV and proudly announcing that his wife was unfaithful to him, but that he loved her enough to stay with her.

Martyrdom isn't considered a desirable male quality and the male who accepts his wife's infidelity isn't admired or considered masculine. The prevalent attitude is that the male victim is a figure of scorn—a cuckold—and that because of the mythology that women don't cheat easily, her infidelity is a reflection on the husband's sexual prowess. If a man cheats, society regards his infidelity as a male characteristic and blames male sexuality in general. Yet if a woman cheats, the cheating is regarded as evidence of her husband's failure to satisfy her. All in all, the image of the male cuckold in society's eyes (and his own) contributes to his confronting his wife's extramarital affair and dealing with it.

There is also the question of the male biological heritage.

The biological heritage of men in the pre-birth-control era does justify a greater fear of female infidelity due to paternity. As anthropologist Lionel Tiger pointed out to me,

> You are dealing with an animal who is fourteen-million-years old. Women find it mystifying why men get so jealous if they are unfaithful and have no comprehension as to why it is such a big issue for men. When you consider what it will cost to have an offspring in time and money, the man wants to be certain that the child is his. Some birds will hover around the female until she gives birth and even sit on the egg. That way, no one will mess around with his offspring.

The issue of paternity as exhibited in the animal kingdom was discussed by anthropologist Dr. Beer in an interview with me. "There is always a risk that he is putting his energies into someone else's genes so it matters if the female has another mate. A man called Bertram has said that when one lion takes over the harem of another, he kills all the young of the previous owner so that he doesn't invest his energy in raising someone else's genes. The same has been claimed by Hardy for a breed of monkeys in India."

The male victim's desire to confront infidelity is often expressed by violence to the other man, a violence which is implied but isn't always carried out. Detective Johnston recalls that many of his clients have said, "I will kill him, I will beat him up, I will make sure he never does business again in this city."

Resorting to violence, verbally or in reality, does seem to be a stereotypical reaction for the male victim. In an article in *Psychology Today,* "Getting at the Heart of Jealous Love" (May 1980), Virginia Adams quoted a 1976 survey which showed that out of 143 murders committed in jealous rage only 20 of the perpetrators were women. Violence does seem to be male territory, whether by instinct or because society expects it of the man, even today.

In an article on "The Male Role: Definitions, Problems and Sources of Changes," Joseph H. Pleck of the University of Michigan writes,

> Males are expected to show greater emotional control than women and are often described as being more alienated from their feelings; but at the same time, men appear to become angry or violent more easily than women and are often rewarded for doing so, covertly, if not directly.[8]

I talked to Dr. Robert Brannon about the differences in the way in which men and women cope as victims of an extramarital affair.

> The concept of confrontation fits in with the whole issue of masculinity and the male role. Infidelity is a bigger insult to male masculinity. Men weren't raised with the image of women having affairs.
>
> Men are more able than women to confront. If you find a man's car bumps into their car, men are more likely to bang on the man's car door. Men are physically bigger and so they get practice in physical confrontations. They are not invariably the victim. So men are better able to carry off a hostile confrontation because they are more practiced and ready for it.
>
> Also there are a lot of things that men do which they don't do because they think they would turn out well, but because they think they would be a coward not to do them. The issue of cowardice is a big issue with a lot of men. They will do things so as not to be cowardly. And if you are abused by another man, you can't let him get away with it.

It seems incredible, but it is, according to my findings, undeniably true, that male victims attack the other man and treat him as if he is a thief who has stolen their property. In these situations, the macho man comes to the fore—the cowboy of mythology who has a shootout at dawn and fights for "my woman."

Dr. Neubauer says, "There is a lot of society approval involved. Society says a man can shoot another man and there are still countries where men don't even get punished for that if their wives have been unfaithful to them." While women tend to make light of the other woman and ignore the affair, men are prone to attacking the other man and confronting the affair.

Frank's story is a classic one of the male victim who becomes violent to the other man whom he considers has taken his property.

I cheated a couple of times in my marriage. But when *you* are the one doing it, you never label it as cheating. You justify it in a million ways. You don't say, I am going to cheat on my wife. I told myself that things were going so badly that it didn't make any difference and that I had no choice.

Five years after I got married I found out that my wife had cheated on me. A friend told me. He didn't know how to break it to me. I didn't believe it. I didn't expect it from her. You never expect it. You always figure your wife will not go out, no matter how rough things are. Especially on someone she knows to be so tough. I thought she would be afraid to gamble on me finding out. I never expected it of her. She loved me.

Things were starting to go wrong. I checked it out. I never thought it was possible. I went to a restaurant where I had heard she was with the man. Sure enough, she was there. Knowing me, she became almost comatose. My first reaction was to go after him. I controlled myself for a moment and asked him if he knew she was married. I thought maybe she had said she was single and the guy was innocent. But the dummy said that he knew she was married. No one who knew me would have done that. When he admitted it, I went bananas. I hit him. I'm surprised that I didn't overreact and kill him. In five minutes there were cops. I broke his nose and it was very messy. It didn't bother me at all, it felt good.

Why did beating the shit out of him give me satisfaction? I'm very protective of what is mine and if anyone touches it . . . That's my woman and she can't cheat. She's my property and if you are with me, you are with me. I had to hit him. I needed the satisfaction. You could say it was primitive, not being able to control myself. But if I hadn't hit him, I couldn't have been able to face myself. He was sitting there with *my* wife and if I hadn't gone after him I wouldn't have been able to face myself ever again.

Frank's reaction was indeed primitive. As he told me his story, an anonymous voice over the phone, I knew I was in touch with the most primeval of male reactions to infidelity: violence. Frank's anguished cry, "I couldn't have faced myself" if he hadn't been violent to the man who was with his wife, harks back to Dr. Brannon's comments about male role pressure.

John, another male victim of thirty-two, found his wife with another man and his cry of pain may sound primitive and simplistic but really expresses the way in which many men feel when they find their wives have been unfaithful to them.

> She told me she was in love with him. I never discovered the full story. I asked her who the guy was and she said it was none of my business. I was mad. I was going to kill him. Why not kill her? I was in love with her. It was instinct. He had *my* wife. And nobody is supposed to have my wife but me.

Elvis Presley, at the height of his career, acted in a similar way when he discovered that his wife Priscilla was having an affair with Mike Stone, a karate instructor. In *Elvis* Albert Goldman describes Elvis's behavior when he found he was a victim of infidelity.

> Then he would call Priscilla and tell her he was coming down to the Marina that night. He was going to be carrying his M16 automatic rifle and he would have all the guys with him armed to the teeth. She would see Mike Stone down on his knees vomiting with fear, begging for his life.

At another point Goldman comments,

> Sometimes he would pour abuse on Mike Stone, calling him obscene names and suggesting that he was just a pimp living off Priscilla's money. Eventually he would always work around to the thought that obsessed him; the threat to kill or maim Mike Stone while Priscilla was forced to stand by helplessly watching the hideous scene.

Goldman defines Elvis's behavior in a way that perfectly describes the attitude of other male victims I have observed: "According to the macho code which Elvis embraced, women are possessions that can be stolen by another man. Elvis was furious at Stone because he was a thief."[9]

Once a female cheater becomes aware of her husband's propensity toward violence, she may stop cheating. Male rage and violence then has its desired effect; it seems unfortunate proof that a show of power (in the form of violence) can, indeed, enforce fidelity.

Ellie is a thirty-two-year-old artist who left her first husband because of her extramarital affair.

> Things weren't good with my husband sexually and I cheated with my teacher. It went on for a year. I felt very guilty and I confessed to my husband. I thought he would be hurt, but I didn't expect him to get violent. I knew he wasn't a violent man. I decided to try and make the marriage work, but a while later things were bad sexually and we divorced.
>
> Now I am living with another man and I know he is violent. He has thrown things at me. And because he is violent, I am less likely to be unfaithful. He is very possessive and if he found out that I had cheated, he would kill the other man. My first husband was too passive and if he had been more forceful and possessive maybe I wouldn't have cheated.

Ellie's reaction to her boyfriend's threats of violence is one that many men are fully aware of; they are conscious that they have an built-in weapon, calculated to prevent infidelity. Many men assume that the threat of violence implied if not stated, will prevent their wives from cheating. One reaction from a bemused male victim was "I was so surprised that she cheated, I thought she would be too afraid of me to be unfaithful." Many women are afraid of the consequences of male jealousy. A London woman wrote to me because she was terrified that her husband wrongfully suspected her of infidelity and she wondered if I knew where she could have a chastity belt made for herself to pacify him. The power of the jealous male frightens some women and prevents them from cheating. And perhaps if women had a similar power over men, men wouldn't cheat so lightly. The dynamics of infidelity, once again, are stacked in favor of the male.

Male violence to the other man may also be partially promoted by a fear that the other man will outdo them sexually. This fear is rooted in the competitive quality of male sexuality. In adolescence, males compare penis size, and then compete with one another in scoring sex with women, so that many male victims feel that they have lost a sexual competition if their wives have sex with another man. This response is sometimes reflected by the victim obsessively questioning the cheater about the other man's sexual prowess, or by the victim judging the worthiness of the victor.

Dick accepted his wife's infidelity but complained,

> My wife got involved with a really ugly guy. It upset me, because she was very la-di-da, country club, perfect lady, perfect to be seen with. But this guy was so ugly that I couldn't imagine her going out with him. I felt she mistreated herself by going with him and it made it worse.

There is, however, another syndrome sometimes exhibited by the male victim. I call it the love trophy syndrome. These are the male victims who demand details about their wives' cheatees and are sexually excited if the men are either attractive or prestigious.

Janice, a stewardess, told me that her husband was outraged when he discovered that she had cheated with a passenger, then demanded details of his sexual performance and finally was mollified when Janice revealed that her cheatee was in fact a minor celebrity in his own right.

I was terrified when my husband first found out that I wasn't with my girlfriend on the night that I was out with Joe. Joe isn't his real name, but I have to call him that for the interview. He is a talk-show host, and I met him when I was on duty in the first-class section of the plane. At the time, I was going through a rough patch with my husband. His father had come to live with us and I was feeling neglected and taken for granted. So when Joe started phoning me up and paying me attention and asking to take me away on vacations and to buy me gifts, I just melted and played along.

Joe and I weren't in the least bit serious. It was really just a sexual fling and because I was flattered. We went out a few times, then went to bed, but the sex wasn't really worth writing home about. There was, though, of course, the whole idea that Joe was so famous. I didn't want to be a groupie but at the same time, I couldn't help getting a thrill everytime I looked at his famous face in bed beside me.

My husband found out about the affair the third time that I went to bed with Joe. I had asked a girlfriend to cover and it all went wrong, so my husband realized the truth. After he yelled at me for ages, he calmed down for a few hours and then really began to grill me. I couldn't believe the questions he asked. He wanted to know every detail about Joe's sexual performance. At that point, he didn't even know who Joe was. All he knew was that

I had been to bed with another man. He asked about what Joe did, what I did, what positions we used, how long it all went on for. I didn't know what to say, I wasn't prepared for his reaction and just didn't know how to cope at all.

In the end I burst into tears and told him everything. That Joe hadn't been sexually that great, that I hadn't really enjoyed myself. At first he wouldn't believe me. When he finally did, he asked me for Joe's name. I didn't want to give it to him but in the end I did. I knew he wouldn't let it drop if I didn't. So I told him Joe's name. He just seemed so stunned. The look on his face was incredible. And once he knew, I had to tell him even more details. Not just sexual ones this time, but details about where we went, what we did, what we ate, who we saw and who saw us. Especially what Joe said. I couldn't believe my husband's attitude. He seemed almost proud that I had gone to bed with Joe. All his jealousy disappeared and he even asked if there were any similarities between him and Joe.

That night my husband made love to me three times, and he usually only does it once. And all through it he kept on asking if he was as good as Joe. Since then he has told all his friends that Joe and I used to go out. Of course he says it was before we got married. But no matter which way he puts it, I know that my affair with Joe excited my husband.

Janice's story is an overstatement of the love trophy syndrome: men who tend to regard women as objects and to value them more if they are coveted by other men whom they admire. One is reminded of tribesmen who offer their wives to honored guests to symbolize their importance. Being excited by the prestige of a wife's cheatee is primarily a male phenomenon; I never encountered a woman who felt the same way.

Palimony lawyer, Marvin Mitchelson reflecting on infidelity, commented in an interview with me, "Let's face it, if your wife came to you tonight and said, 'I'm having an affair with Prince Charles,' you might hate him and it might hurt you. But by God, you could understand it. But if she said, 'I just knocked off the plumber,' it is worse." Again, we are back with the macho concept of property—the husband owns the wife so her taste in a lover must, in his eyes, be worthy of him.

Bart, an accountant, articulated that viewpoint in no uncertain terms.

> I have been married for thirteen years and my wife cheated on me after nine years. I was surprised. I didn't mind too much, though, because she was away on a business trip and it was only a one-night stand. But then things changed. She got involved with someone in the office. I told her not to and I prefer her not to. She sees him every day and I thought the relationship would be too close. I didn't like him.
>
> I thought he was lower-class. He was Italian. I found it insulting, because if your wife takes up with someone, it puts him above you. And I don't want any greasy Italian to be put above me. The next man was even worse though. I thought he was unsporting because he declined a second chance. It was bad enough he went to bed with my wife the first time, but by refusing to go to bed with her a second time he was criticizing *my* taste.

The proprietary attitude of many men to their wives still persists, despite the women's movement.

Pete, the cheater mentioned in the entrapment section of this chapter commented, "I don't think I would like all those men depositing their sperm inside *my* wife. It would turn me off. I don't want to put my face down there and find another man's sperm."

The Male Victim's Reaction to Infidelity: Devastation and Destruction of Trust

Many men initially react to their wives' infidelity with threats of violence, or violence itself; ultimately, they are devastated by the affair and often, I have found, feel that they will never again trust another woman. Dr. Neubauer verified my findings: "Men who find out that a woman has been unfaithful to them are hostile to women they meet afterwards, even though they themselves have been unfaithful all over the place." And many men find that they are unable to continue the marriage. This is supported by Kinsey's 1953 findings, which showed that twice as many husbands as wives felt that their mate's extramarital affairs were destructive of the marriage.

Long-term reactions of male victims range from never again wearing the wedding ring to never again having sex with the cheater. The story of Chris, a twenty-eight-year-old teacher, illustrates the whole gamut of emotions felt by a male victim, from thoughts of violence to trust destroyed.

> I sensed that my wife had something hidden in her behavior, like a child with a secret. For a while I did nothing. I didn't want to think that she was seeing someone else. I just watched and tried to see what was happening. She began to be more strident about going out with no excuse. Her whole style changed and she became more younger and more aggressively sexy. It became a challenge, she began to flaunt it.
>
> A hundred years before I would have issued a challenge and been out there on the dueling field. I would rather have been in white silk and sabre, shooting someone in a romantic setting,

rather than in a sleazy bar. Finally I followed her. I am not a violent person and I wasn't going to slap her around. But I followed her. I saw her go into a single's bar and watched her pick someone up. It was like watching a film, I could have confronted her, but I didn't.

I sat there and remembered how she had been when I met her. It was like watching another person. They left and I went home. I waited forty-eight hours and saw some friends for a couple of days. I didn't want to do it in hot blood. It was the feeling you get when something you have counted on evaporates. Like being fired.

I came home and she was by herself, I said, "This isn't the prelude to a fight. This is a decision. I saw you out. I know you are having an affair with at least one person." She said she enjoyed picking people up, not being faithful. I asked if I had failed her as a lover and a companion. She said I hadn't, but that she liked to have cheap unknown sex with a stranger. It bothers me that I was making love to her after she had made love with another man.

We divorced. I was good to her, good for her, but I was a given in her life. I regret losing her and I miss her opinions and her company. But she could no longer be the person I married and the other new person wasn't for me. I don't know if I forgive her. And I don't know if I will ever trust another woman again.

Steve, a man in his fifties, never married because of his pain after a woman was unfaithful to him.

I once had a girlfriend who cheated on me and I was so hurt that I never married. I think that what stopped me from getting married was that I have yet to find a woman I could trust and would want to spend the rest of my life with. Once a woman has cheated on you, it is difficult to ever trust another one. People tell me all of them are not the same. But I am afraid.

One of the strangest male victim reactions I encountered during my research was when I appeared on a New York radio show. A thirty-four-year-old male victim telephoned and over the air told me how he was dealing with his mistrust of women which had developed after he had been a victim of infidelity.

> I believe in monogamy. But I'm scared. When I was young, a girlfriend cheated on me. I was in love with her. I asked her why she had done it and she never gave me a reason. I was very upset. Since then I have been scared that if I am with a girl and we have an argument she will say, "Well, there is always someone else." Even the thought of that upsets me. If I got married and my wife cheated on me, I would be very upset.
>
> I don't know how to keep a woman faithful. I am seriously thinking of buying a wife. They have marriage brokers in East Africa and I have been doing some research on them. I would like to find a woman who is chaste and has never known a man. If she is a virgin she might be faithful. I've tried the romantic route and it doesn't work. If she comes from another country and she doesn't know the language here well or the environment, I may have more control over her. I've found out that women only understand power and that there is no equality in any relationship. There is always the stronger and the weaker. And if I buy a wife I will be able to control her.

My first reaction to the man explaining his plan to buy a wife was shocked amazement. But then I realized that his story really demonstrates many men's deepest fears and desires: the fear that a woman will be unfaithful to them, and the desire to control her. As we have seen, the fear is related to biological heritage (in case the man brings up another man's child), the disgrace in the eyes of society of being a cuckold, and the fear of being unfavorably compared sexually with another man. Men seem terrified of that, whereas the majority of women don't. Again, the reasons seem to lie in the basic makeup of male and female sexuality.

Male sexual performance can be measured in terms of penis size, staying power, a number of "sexual performances." The boundaries of super-male sexual "performance" are very clearly defined. However, female sexual competitive instincts are usually aroused *before* bed. Women tend to compete with each other in outward appearance but not sexually. When a woman discovers that a man has been unfaithful to her, her first remark, according to Detective Johnston, is, "Is she prettier than me?" A man tends to ask if a cheatee was better in bed.

The wife buyer's story illustrates a common male desire: to control women. He wants to find a woman who is totally dependent on him so he can control her. His story may be extreme but perhaps his basic desire for control magnifies an element which is at the very heart of many men's desires. Again, perhaps, the male desire for control may be based on differences between male and female sexuality.

Despite all the mythology about uncontrollable, rampant male sexuality, it is, of course, the woman who is capable of sexual insatiability, who is physically capable of having sex with countless men without tiring. Perhaps it is male fear of female sexual insatiability that causes men to want to control women, to play up masculine sexuality while attempting to control female sexuality. It is incredible that despite the women's movement's attempts to educate men about women, in this day and age, a man still exists who wants to buy a wife so that he can control her. Perhaps it is male feelings of impotence that cause male victims to be devastated by their wives' infidelity.

FIVE

The Consequences of Infidelity

Confessing to an Affair

Both men and women often confess their infidelity, either as a way of ending the marriage or to hurt the victim.

Bob is a male cheater, a fifty-five-year-old doctor. After thirty years of marriage he fell in love with his cheatee.

> Men have the most opportunity to cheat. I first cheated because I was bored and then because I was unhappy. I fell in love with my cheatee and I no longer loved my wife. The relationship was exciting because of the planning and the fear of getting caught.
>
> I wanted to marry my cheatee. My wife found out about the affair because she found a Valentine's card and I confessed. We got divorced, but I think we would have anyway.

Dr. Strean observes that many cheaters try to be found out.

> I doubt very much if there is an individual involved in an extramarital affair who isn't feeling very guilty. He may rationalize the guilt, give a million and one reasons, but it is very difficult to if there is always guilt. If the person is rebelling and fighting the spouse, there is a lot of guilt. Then confession is easier. If I've

strayed and I feel guilty every time I look at you, every time we have dinner, I'm upset. Sometimes living with the guilt is so upsetting that I confess.

Another rationale for confessing to an affair according to Dr. Neubauer, is to test whether the confession causes jealousy in the partner. However, while confessing to infidelity may be a relief to the cheater, it can cause great emotional pain to the victim. Psychotherapist Fredlee Kaplan points out, "Once an affair is revealed, it is a very difficult thing to resolve because the person who hasn't had the affair has to cope. The person who has the affair has to find out why they revealed it, because of guilt or wanting to hurt the other person."

Forgiveness and Improved Marriages

Women tend to accept extramarital affairs, but men don't. It follows that women are more prone than men to forgive infidelity. Detective Johnston bears this out: "More women forgive cheating husbands than vice versa and very few men accept their wives' extramarital affairs and allow them to continue."

The male victim is rarely forgiving or accepting. A Miami-based woman phoned me with the following story.

My husband and I were fighting a great deal and I had no attention at home. I felt I was being taken for granted and being used to take care of the kids and clean up. My husband and I separated, and a couple of weeks after that I went out with someone. He knew the problems that I had been having with my husband and gave me the attention I needed, and talked to me in the way I need to be talked to.

Then my husband and I got back together again. I told him that I was sorry I went out because I felt bad and guilty. I figured that if I confessed, he would forgive me. Then he told me that he had been cheating on me for thirteen years. I never knew it, and I told him about my affair first, but he won't forgive me. He said he won't *ever* forgive me. Even though we've been together again for two years, he still won't forgive me. He keeps reminding me of it and says that it is much worse for a woman to cheat than for a man. With a man, cheating is natural, but for a woman it isn't.

Some cheaters, however, believe that infidelity has strengthened their marriage. Not all extramarital affairs that are revealed destroy the marriage. Dr. Strean observes that he has seen some affairs have positive effects on the marriage.

I've seen some couples start to say, "Well, there aren't that many differences between my girlfriend and my wife or my husband and my lover—so that they appreciate their partner more. I've also seen a man or a woman routinely who have been very depressed for various reasons, get involved in an affair and feel a kind of high for a little while. Then they cope better. But it's like a drink. Initially, there is a euphoric feeling, but it only leads to a hangover.

Dr. Neubauer adds,

If infidelity isn't a way of life but happens once or twice, then perhaps it can be forgiven. If, on the other hand, you find out that your partner has had a long extramarital relationship, perhaps for twenty years, it can be very hurtful. It would hurt the victim because all of a sudden they find out they have only had half a husband or wife or just a fraction. But it all depends on how you look at the situation. You can say that if the other woman/man was so attractive that he/she stayed with her/him for twenty years but still didn't give the husband/wife up, then the husband/wife must also have something he/she needs.

Joan is a thirty-one-year-old female cheater.

Monogamy is loving one man. I need to love one man and I need to be the only one he loves. One must work at a good marriage, but men find it easy to be unfaithful. It is expected of them. I had one cheating relationship for three hours, after I had been married for a year. He was my husband's so-called best friend. I couldn't believe that he would do that to his best friend. But he did. I felt very uncomfortable. I was very naive and I was seduced by pretty words. I felt stupid and weak-willed but I was confused and needed physical release. He didn't really care and he took advantage of me. It was really just a zipless fuck. My husband was much better in bed and put my needs first.

I had an intuition that my husband had been unfaithful to me. I asked him and he admitted the truth. I forgave him. It made our sex life a lot more exciting, especially when I told him about my affair. We have always had great sex, but our affairs made it greater.

Vicky is a thirty-seven-year-old female victim who discovered her husband was cheating. Vicky believes that the experience brought her and her husband together.

At first I didn't want to accept the truth. Jerry was always on about one of the women he worked with, Marge. Because they worked together, they went away on business trips. I didn't think anything of it. But then I decided to surprise Jerry in Buffalo and found him with Marge. I nearly died. I was so hurt. Jerry and I went home together and he told me all about Marge. She deliberately went out to get him. Ran after him for years. Then she almost raped him one night while they were away on a trip. After that, Marge did everything to make him love her, to undermine him and make him dependent on her.

Jerry told me that he realized that he didn't love Marge at all, that she trapped him into a situation that he didn't want or need.

And he began to hate her. She nearly destroyed his life. Jerry left his job, but before he did, he took the boss aside and told him how manipulative and evil Marge really is. I also know some of her friends and I did the same thing. If Jerry and I could have, we would have made sure that Marge lost her job. It is funny, though, our hatred of Marge brought us closer than we have been for years. It seems strange that hating the other woman can unite a husband and wife, but that's what it did for us.

Susie is a twenty-three-year-old aerobic instructor. While her husband was in the service in Germany, she was raped; then she turned to another man for comfort and got involved with him.

I believe in monogamy, in one man and one woman together in love. My husband has fulfilled my ideal as a man, the dominant husband, and I believe a wife should take care of a man. Sexist, I guess, but I believe it is perfectly natural. God gave woman to man to serve him.

I cheated on my husband when he was overseas. I was raped and the man who comforted me started out as a friend. Because of what happened [the rape], I assumed that my husband wouldn't want me anymore. And there was this friend offering me love. I told him I was married and that I loved my husband. He was someone I worked with and he didn't listen. I fell in love with him and he really cared for me. By the time we slept together we were both emotionally involved. I cheated because of the unhappiness of feeling unwanted, being away from my husband and not knowing how he felt about the rape. I wanted to be wanted.

My husband came back. I told him the truth because I felt too guilty to hide it. He was angry and hurt and that made me feel more guilty. But he helped me and helped relieve me of my guilt. He was always a much better lover than the other man is—perhaps because I love my husband with my whole self and didn't feel good about myself when I had the affair.

I asked my husband if he had been faithful to me. He lied to me and said he had because it was so soon after the rape and he didn't want to upset me. But later he told me the truth. I wasn't upset that he had been with another woman but that he had lied to me. I felt it was my fault because of the rape and the affair and we discussed it all. I love my husband even more now because he told me about his affair. I forgave him immediately. If anything, we have sex in more different positions and more often. I love him even more now that he has cheated on me.

If anything, now I want to be more faithful to my husband, no matter how horny I feel. I won't ever cheat again because the hurt is too heavy to deal with. I regret ever having started the affair because I not only hurt my husband but I hurt my friend as well. Now no other man has a chance with me, and I trust my husband not to cheat either. When I put my wedding ring on my husband's finger I said, "I give this ring to you as the symbol of my love and fidelity." But what good is the symbol without the truth? When my husband gets out of the army we are getting married again to renew our vows of fidelity. I think the infidelity was a good experience for us both because we learned how important we are to each other and how to talk to each other.

Sometimes, the discovery of an extramarital affair can actually stimulate the sex life of the husband and wife. Dr. Strean explains why this may be the result.

Sometimes the husband/wife can be turned on by discovering a spouse's affair. Even though on the surface they may hate the other man/woman, they are still thinking about them all the time and may even be stimulated by those thoughts. In those cases the victim is probably a latent homosexual.

I've found evidence of the process Dr. Strean describes: Diana, a female victim in her thirties, confessed to me that she was sexually excited by her husband giving her graphic details of his affairs; Mack, a male victim (who had had a certain number of homosexual experiences) said that he was excited by walking in on his wife while she was making love to another man; Marie, a female victim, said that her only complaint about her husband cheating on her was that she herself was bisexual and so she deeply resented not taking part in the sexual side of the affair. Naturally, these reactions are not common, but they are still worth noting, as they all make up the intricate mosaic of infidelity.

Damaged Relationships

Sometimes infidelity doesn't lead directly to divorce but suspends the marriage in limbo, damaging the relationship.

John is a thirty-six-year-old clerical worker who found out that his wife was unfaithful to him.

> I suspected that my wife was unfaithful when she started telling me about women's rights, bringing home *Playgirl.* She became more sexually aggressive and made advances to me and compared me to the pictures in *Playgirl.* At first I didn't think of infidelity and thought that the whole thing was a phase. But then she started going for a drink with the girls. After four months I found out by accident that she wasn't with who she said she was with. At that point, it hit me like a ton of bricks.
>
> I asked her who she was with and she told me she was seeing a co-worker in the office. I didn't want to know about him. I was surprised that she cheated. I was also surprised that she wasn't scared of me and said "this is the way it is." I'd never hurt her before so she wasn't afraid. I've more or less forgiven her for the affair and our sex life is the same as before. I still love her, but the edge is off the love, the special part and the trust.

Sandy is a forty-five-year-old female cheater.

My husband never realized how unhappy I was in the marriage. We never really talked to each other. So when Rick came along and really talked to me and listened to me and cared about me I fell in love with him. We had a beautifully romantic affair, met every Wednesday night when Jack, my husband, thought I was at Chinese cookery classes.

After a while, though, I began to get really confused. There were times when I nearly called Jack, Rick, and vice versa. I was so close to blowing everything by doing that that I coped by calling both of them, Darling. Sometimes in the morning I'd wake up in Jack's arms thinking of Rick and other times I'd look at Rick and feel desperately guilty about Jack. You see, I was brought up to believe in marriage and monogamy, but plenty of my friends were having affairs so finally I did the same thing.

After two and a half years I couldn't stand the strain of all that deception. I broke up with Rick and Jack never knew what had happened. In a way, the fact that I was able to deceive Jack so easily made me lose respect for him. I almost wanted him to find out about the affair so he would take more notice of me. But he didn't. I don't know what's going to happen to our marriage now.

Robert is a thirty-year-old chef who found his wife cheating a year after marriage.

I came into the apartment one night and she was having sex with another man. I got real mad and left. He was a business associate of hers. I had a long talk with her and asked her if she was still in love with me and if she was, what she was doing in bed with another man. She said she still was. But how can you tell? I decided that the only way I could tell was by time.

She still fools around. I found out through friends. She doesn't really hide it from me either, but I don't feel like making love to her after she's been with another man. It is like having used merchandise. It is different for a guy to go and fool around than for a girl. I am unfaithful to her once a year, but she doesn't ask about it.

She doesn't get involved with the men but I am still hurt and surprised that she would cheat on me. I used to trust her but I don't trust her anymore. I used to trust her tremendously. I don't think I love her as much as I did, either. Infidelity takes something away. I don't know how long I will put up with it. I cheat now because it looks good.

It seems that once infidelity is out in the open the other partner is often tempted to cheat as well, and the downward spiral toward divorce begins.

Rick, a thirty-two-year-old Wall Street broker, has been married for ten years and discovered that his wife was cheating on him.

I found out that she was seeing someone in the building where we live. I was hurt. When I found out who it was, my reaction was to kill the other man. I felt like I got kicked in the face. I wanted to kill him. He took something from me that was precious.

When I married my wife she was a virgin. She said she didn't cheat for sex, she said she needed the attention and that she was confused. She told me that she didn't want to tell me because she was afraid of my temper. At first I wanted to know details of his sexual performance. I don't hate my wife, but I am not sure if I still love her. I still don't forgive her for what she did. I am still hurt and I don't see my wife as the same person as before this happened. It was so tacky. I don't know why I haven't left but a part of me still wants the marriage to work.

Clint is a forty-two-year-old cheater.

I always believed that no woman in the world was equal in anything to my wife Louise. Sexually she was fantastic, a great cook, thoughtful wife, and perfect mother to our children. Of course I still fooled around with other women, just for the hell of it. I never thought that what I did would damage our marriage, but now I realize that it has.

The whole problem was when I met Nancy. I really thought we'd have a quick fling and that would be it. But it wasn't. Nancy was a psychologist and we talked for hours about life and people and everything under the sun. Being with Nancy helped me to realize all the different sides of myself that were being stifled by my marriage. At first I didn't want to admit that I was having doubts about the marriage. It was just that when I went home at night I suddenly found that I was bored with Chris my wife. I tried not to admit how I felt but I knew that I couldn't wait to be with Nancy again. When I saw a TV program I enjoyed or read a book that I liked it was Nancy I wanted to discuss them with, and not Chris.

Things now are very bad with Chris. She is aware that something is wrong between us, but she doesn't know what. I can't really explain how I feel. I expect it is all to do with the fact that I had Chris up on a pedestal. But now my relationship with Nancy has toppled her off. I don't know what I am going to do. I still love Chris but it's Nancy I need. I have no idea where any of this is going to end. All I know is that my marriage will never be the same again.

Anna is a thirty-five-year-old female victim, whose husband's affair led to an uneasy truce in their stormy marriage.

I met Jim when I was thirty-two. By that time I was convinced that I would never get married, but I didn't care. I enjoyed being single. I enjoyed having a life of my own and not answering to anyone. But Jim was bright and funny and sexy and successful, so when he wanted to marry me I said yes.

The trouble was that soon after we first got married Jim began coming home late from work. I guessed he was with other women, and I'd tease him about it. That was my only way of dealing with things. I didn't want to fence him in you see, because I'd valued my own freedom and didn't want to take Jim's away. The situation became ludicrous. Jim and I had always fought like cat and dog, but our fights used to end with the most tremendous, passionate lovemaking. But after months of Jim coming in late our fights would just be fights with no making up and no making love afterwards. Then things took a turn that was even worse. Jim began to come home and tell me about all his women. He'd give me every detail, who they were, how they looked, and what they did with him in bed. Part of me was slightly excited, but the other part of me was bitterly jealous. I also thought that if Jim was telling me about his flings they couldn't mean much to him. I figured that I was almost sharing them with him by listening to the details. I know it sounds sick, but that's what happened.

After a while, I couldn't take any more stories from Jim and I told him to either stop fooling around or get out. Now Jim comes home on time, is very nice to me, but deep inside I know it is just a matter of time. It's like he's a child who isn't allowed to go and play with his friends, so he is stuck at home. And all he can do is look out of the window and wait for playtime again.

When I think about it I know I should never have indulged Jim by listening to details of his affairs. Some of the problem was because I hated the idea of being his conventional wife. Things were fine until I got the label *wife.* I just didn't want to be a textbook wife, so perhaps that's why I went along with him when all the time he was hurting me.

This is Susan, a thirty-one-year-old female victim.

Nine months after I got married I started suspecting that my husband was cheating with his superior at work. He is very materialistic and I think he felt that cheating was his right if he was building a power base. It was really a power play to get what he wanted in his career, but I didn't realize that at the time.

There was always an excuse to be with her. I suppose I knew inside what was going on, but I always ignored the situation. I strongly hoped that if I ignored it, it would go away.

Finally one of my best friends broke down and said that I ought to find out what was really going on. So I did. Finding out damaged my love irrevocably. When I found out the truth, my husband admitted that he didn't think fidelity was a necessary part of marriage. For me, though, there was no going back. I got very hurt badly and the marriage will never be the same. Once you break the bond of trust there is no way to keep things together. It becomes a total breakdown. And I ignored the truth for as long as I could. Now we are talking about getting a divorce.

Open Marriage and Swinging

According to my research, open marriage and swinging sometimes are the bridge between infidelity and divorce.

I have found that once infidelity is discovered in a relationship, the discovery often leads to open marriage or swinging, which in turn often leads to divorce. As sociologists Clanton and Smith have said, "Many open marriages are (conscious or unconscious) strategies for ending the marriage and/or for smoothing the trail to the next relationship." This is from "Co-Marital Sex and the Sexual Freedom Movement" in the *Journal of Sex Research*.

Open marriage and swinging are often not defined as infidelity because both partners are aware of the situation. But usually the same emotions come into play: fear of loss; jealousy; fear of being unfavorably compared with someone else; and the feeling that one is not unique. The infidelity may be organized and controlled, but ultimately, the human emotions are not.

The majority of open marriages assume that structure only after infidelity has been discovered; however, some couples begin married life with an open-marriage agreement. In either case, though, the boundaries of the open marriage usually become blurred so that what begins in an organized fashion often ends in chaos and confusion. Bruce's story illustrates this phenomenon.

Bruce is a thirty-three-year-old manager of a health club and began his married life five years ago with an open marriage.

When I married my wife I told her that I wanted to carry on seeing other women. I don't want to mislead anyone. When we started to live together I told her that I wanted to see other girls. She said, "Fine, we will both be free." I encouraged her to see other guys because I felt so confident in myself. I loved her and thought she wasn't going to meet anyone she liked better. I was seeing other girls, but I didn't tell her. She had been cold to me for a few weeks and I asked her if she liked any of the other men more than she liked me. She said, "With Mike there is something about those blue eyes . . ." I started to cry. She said I wasn't a man because I was crying. I left her and tried to stay away from her. The only way she would have me back was if I married her.

I cheated within a few months of our marriage. Since then I haven't gone a week without seeing another woman. I don't consider it cheating because I don't get involved emotionally. If I went somewhere with my wife, I would make eyes at other women and I would get their phone numbers while she was in the ladies room. It's not that I don't love her. I can't give up other women. I am still a man. I try not to lie to her, but I can't give up living.

The worst was when I said I would be back in fifteen minutes because I was going to the store. I met a girl and stayed with her for three days. When I came home, my wife was very mad. She wrecked the house. She didn't know where I was. I couldn't help it, I felt guilty, but I couldn't get to a phone.

No matter how attracted to a woman I am, I still want to be with another person. Hannah, my wife, once said to me in a fight, "Why don't you screw another girl?" So I did. I met a girl I was in college with, and took her home to bed. I thought Hannah would like it so I told her. She went crazy. Then we had a threesome with another girl. I don't want her to go out with other men, but with the girl in the first threesome it was O.K. because it wasn't love. We still have threesomes. Hannah likes other women. She had an affair with her best friend and I thought I was going to lose Hannah to her. They were once alone together and I didn't hear from her for a day. I felt I was losing her to this girl and I was jealous. I had enjoyed the situation, but I was still jealous.

If I had a child, I wouldn't cheat. I don't want them to grow up with divorced parents. I wouldn't want them to see anything like that, or they would think I was a bad person. If I thought Hannah would leave me, then I wouldn't cheat.

Bruce's story is confusing and classic. He is the open-marriage cheater who is more open than married.

John has been married for twenty years and was unfaithful to his wife Sylvia for all that time. Finally, on the verge of divorce he confessed everything to Sylvia.

I expected Sylvia to kick me out, but she didn't. She stuck by me and even said that she would go along with my cheating. So now I go out with other women whenever I want and Sylvia doesn't mind. I know she never does the same, but I still feel strange about the situation.

Somehow, now that Sylvia knows what I am doing, the edge is off the cheating, the fun and the thrill. I almost feel like I have been deprived of a game or something. I even wonder if Sylvia goes along with our arrangement because she doesn't care about me.

I go to hookers, have one-night stands, and even swing clubs where I take other women. But none of it excites me anymore. I can't understand the reason but I know I was happier when I was cheating behind Sylvia's back.

Some so-called open marriages are also open in name only—open at one end that is. In these marriages the man usually has been discovered cheating and continues to do so with his wife's consent.

Simon, the lawyer quoted before, openly cheats on his wife.

I don't answer if my wife asks where I am going. If anything, I just say "Out." I sit in the den, and I lock my door if I am at home. I know she knows that I cheat and she puts up with it. I don't hit her and I support her well. I am discreet and I never think of my wife divorcing me, though I wouldn't want to be married to me.

As things are, I plan to carry on with my open marriage. Perhaps it isn't perfect but love and marriage are like a bit of velvet. When you drop it on the floor, you may pick it up, but it isn't quite clean. Once it is tainted, then it is tainted.

Sometimes, the marriage is open only as far as the woman is concerned.

Bob, a thirty-seven-year-old mechanic with three children, had an open marriage with a difference—a ménage à trois with his wife and her girlfriend.

I did believe in monogamy. I didn't think people should cheat. I came home when I wasn't supposed to and I found my wife having sex with another woman. I was really shocked. I thought the girl was just a friend. My wife was thirty-four and the other girl was twenty-eight. They told me that it had been going on for six months. My wife and I had been married for four years at the time.

I had no idea that my wife had lesbian inclinations. She acted as if it was nothing and that she really enjoyed it. I felt put-off. But eventually I started to accept the affair. I didn't want to divorce her and I still loved her. The affair improved our sex life. It became a turn-on. I gave my wife more oral sex because she had it from the other woman. She said she really enjoyed it and that only another woman knew how to do it well. All of a sudden I competed. Eventually, I went to bed with my wife and the other woman. I had sex with the other woman and I enjoyed it. For one and a half years we had a threesome. I wasn't jealous of the other woman. I thought the whole affair would pass, and it did.

Mark, a teacher, has been in an open marriage for two of the ten years of his marriage. His interview expresses the viewpoint of the open marriage participant who is uneasy about his marital arrangement.

I believed in monogamy when I was younger and more idealistic. But as you get older, your values change and you realize that you are here for a limited time and there are other experiences you should have.

Now my wife and I have our own separate lives. I never try and find out about her cheating and she never tries to find out about mine. We just know we are both doing it. It all started two years ago when my wife told me she had cheated on me. I felt as if my trust had been violated. She felt I had a right to know. I guess I was angry with myself. I wasn't providing what she needed. I was pretty straight and I wasn't having sex with her enough. She wanted to try other things. She wanted men and women and S and M. I rebelled and instead of giving her what she wanted, I looked for things on the outside.

Now I have a goal of five women a week. I meet them in bars and parks and I tell them I am married. My wife and I don't explain anything to each other. I am sure she still cheats. I never try and find out about it. I guess she may fall in love with someone, but I'll cross that bridge when I come to it. I don't want to get involved with anyone. I don't feel guilty, but I am bothered that she wants to have sex with other women. I can't compete with that.

John is a forty-year-old lawyer who has been married for twelve years.

Yes, I basically believe in monogamy, but I think you should be able to explore other areas. I believe in marriage to one person, but I don't believe that you should stick to that one person. I believe that the same goes for my wife.

I was unfaithful to my wife after a year of marriage. My girlfriend was another attorney. Our paths crossed constantly. A lunch led to a dinner, and another dinner, and a weekend. I told my wife it was another business trip. It went on for a year. I planned to stay with my wife and I did. It didn't do us any harm. But later on, I did fall in love. I had a partner and I fell in love with her. My wife realized that I was spending a lot of time traveling with my partner and asked me about it. She saw me in town one day with her and also heard me talking to her on the phone. I admitted to her that there had been other people, but nothing of any consequence. I resorted to one of those W. C. Fields lines: "Things happen, m'dear." I told her I was not going to do it any more, but that it worked both ways. She realized that I must have had an inkling that she was also cheating.

I saw her with one of her lovers one day and asked her who he was. She said he was a friend from school, but I put two and two together. It became an unwritten understanding that we could cheat as long as it didn't hurt our relationship.

I feel that our liaisons on the side are helping us relate to each other better. But you have to think ahead what might happen in every extramarital relationship.

I don't feel threatened by my wife's affairs. I'm a confident man and I know that if I can recognize a problem early enough, I will counteract it. I've never been in a situation I couldn't get out of. If I feel I am in danger of falling in love, I just stop the relationship. I use the time I fell in love as my bench mark and if I see the same pattern forming again, I stop the relationship. I would never want to end my marriage. A marriage has to be honored. A marriage is a formal thing, regardless if you were married in church or not. That has precedent over any informal relationship.

Jack is a thirty-eight-year-old manager who has been married for fourteen years. He seemed to take great delight in detailing the affairs outside his open marriage and even sent me a graph indicating their progress. His story demonstrates the dangers of open marriage; he is afraid that his wife's sexual experimentation may lead to love.

I used to think marriage meant fidelity but no longer do. Society seems to expect fidelity less. I have had six affairs, ranging from one night to four years. I began cheating with Chris, a thirty-year-old girlfriend of my wife. I saw her two or three times a month in the daytime for sex over the next twenty-five months. Then we broke it off. I then cheated with a close friend of my wife's, Elaine. Elaine came to my house when I was alone babysitting. She almost immediately asked me to take her to bed. After we had sex for an hour, she began to talk. She told me that she had caught my wife Jo in bed with her husband, Will. I don't think Elaine wanted to have sex with me as much as she wanted revenge on Will.

After I had gone to bed with Elaine three times, I told Jo. She had gone to bed with Will three times as well. We each consented to the other carrying on. It was very exciting to both of us, especially me. I blurted out to Jo, "What would you think or do if I told you I was fucking your best friend?" She said nothing for a moment, but my hard-on grew and we were breathing more heavily. Finally she said, "What would you do or say if I told you I was fucking your brother?" I said, "Are you?" and she said "Every time he has visited me." I came by the bucketful. She came beautifully. She had been fucking my brother for over four years. What made me so hot was the thought of his huge cock in her. We then talked about fucking Elaine and Will. We each consented to cheating but not indiscriminately and certainly not to risk VD.

The third person I cheated with was Jacquie, Jo's cousin. Jo knew about the affair. The fourth was with Jacquie's boyfriend, Jim, who caught us together and joined in. Jo would be really shocked if she knew about Jim. My fifth was a stranger I met in a bar. We stayed together for three nights. My sixth was a hooker.

The affairs never bothered me. With all my cheatees sex was

exciting. My sex life hasn't changed because of my cheating, more because of Jo's as she has picked up a bunch of new ideas. I had new experiences because of her cheating. I never knew my nipples were real sensitive until her lover showed her that his were. At times I do feel guilty, right after I have come. But it has always passed. The guilt is characterized by a slightly queazy stomach and a terrific urge to fuck my wife fast.

I wish Jo and I could have a threesome so that everything would really be out in the open. The only thing I dislike about Jo cheating is that her latest lover fell in love with her and wanted to take her away from me. I found out that he wasn't just out to fuck her, but to win her away from me. She had some trouble deciding what she wanted. He has been trying to make her pregnant. I had a vasectomy so he knows that if she is pregnant, I will kick her out. Then he'd like to pick up the pieces. I think affairs can be fun if nobody expects or permits love to develop.

Some open-marriage participants attempt to control the arrangement by either swinging together or by picking each other's sexual partners.

Sheila is a thirty-two-year-old actress who has been married for one and a half years. She and her husband have an open marriage in which he "gives" her to other men.

I believe monogamy is the exception for people and not the rule. We are a promiscuous people who have set up a monogamous society we are unable to adjust to. Before I got married I told my husband I didn't believe in monogamy. I know my husband and I love each other and I realize that both of us will always be attracted to other people. There is nothing wrong with sexual attractions to other people. Or even in following through with the attractions. I do believe we should be up front with those feelings. After the marriage we decided a happy medium to express our sexual needs.

He is free to date, but only does so rarely. He tells me about

> it before and after the date. He can do what he wants when he wants and because he has this freedom, he doesn't do it frequently. Once I stayed at home and read a book while I knew he had a date with someone else. I didn't feel threatened. I am not free to date, but I do tell him about people I am attracted to and he has given me to a friend on occasion, provided that he is allowed to have someone else in return. I would not sleep with someone unless I got my husband's permission. When he has had someone else I find him more sexually attractive to me and relish the new awareness he has for me. Likewise when I have been given to someone else I can't wait to be with my husband again.

Many open marriages which evolve into swinging, ultimately end in the relationship breaking up. Swinging, however, does seem to some of its exponents to provide an alternative to covert infidelity. In 1970, Nena and George O'Neill, now themselves divorced, wrote that some of the married respondents in their survey of swingers "were tired of cheating in secret extramarital affairs but were not yet ready to grant their mate complete sexual autonomy."[1] Swinging to them seems to be a way in which mates can attempt to control their partners' infidelity.

Researcher Betty Fang reports that "the majority of swingers are in their twenties or thirties and can be characterized as white, middle-class, suburban, highly educated, and highly mobile, both geographically and socially." Fang found that there were several motives behind the couple's decision to swing: "Some of the most common ones are boredom and restlessness; a need for new experiences; tired of cheating covertly; need of an ego lift; restriction of marital exclusivity; a means for patching up a failed marriage; and a desire for more sex than the partner gives."[2]

Gilbert D. Bartell, anthropologist, in a report on "Group Sex among the Mid-Americans" also says that swingers often replay a mating game.

They can relive their youth and for many it is advantageous. They can get dressed up, go out together, and attempt a seduction. It is a form of togetherness that they never had before. There is the desire of each partner to reinforce in the other the idea that they are better sexually than any swinger they have encountered. There is a general increase in sexual excitation of both partners due to the possibilities of new types of sexual experience and increase in thought and discussion of sexual experiences.

Bartell goes so far as to indicate that swinging gives both partners a new interest in life, "which can be explored, observed and discussed between themselves and among their new friends."[3]

Although swinging is on the decline, I have interviewed numerous couples who use swinging as a last attempt to salvage their marriages.

The impetus to swing usually comes from the male. My research shows that women often enter group-sex situations to please their mates or to try to control their infidelity by being part of it.

Pam is a twenty-nine-year-old female victim turned swinger.

When Jeff, my husband, suggested we swing together, I was revolted. I didn't know how to react or what to do. I couldn't bear the idea of strange men having sex with me. And I couldn't understand why Jeff would want me to do such a thing. He didn't want straight swinging, you see, he mostly wanted to see me with other men. Also, I said I would only agree to go through with it if he promised me that he wouldn't touch another woman in front of me.

I thought the people at the club were really unattractive. When I looked around I noticed that most of the men were lying back, letting the women give them oral sex while they looked at the other women. I thought it was horrible, I worried about disease, and I didn't want to have anything to do with it.

I couldn't handle the situation. I started crying and Jeff brought me home. The ridiculous part of it all was that I felt guilty. I felt as if there was something wrong with me because I didn't like swinging. But really it's not me that's sick, but the situation.

Controlled cheating, which is how I define swinging, can cause problems in a relationship. Bartell says, "For a couple who are relatively insecure with each other and with themselves, swinging may invoke a great deal of personal jealousy. The man who finds he is occasionally rejected or easily tired physically, may resent his wife's responsiveness to other men. She, in turn, may feel that her partner is enjoying other women more or to a different degree than he enjoys her."

One female swinger I interviewed, Katie, a New York actress, says that she started out swinging because her husband wanted her to. Her story illustrates the pitfalls of swinging.

I did it because I was scared he would cheat on me if I didn't. He said he wanted to see me with another man. I went ahead and had sex with someone in front of him at a club. At first I was cold-blooded about it, and tried to get the whole thing over with. My husband always thought that he was the only man who could really make me react sexually. Until that moment, that is. As I started having sex with the other man, I realized that I was about to react in the identical way that I did with my husband. And I knew that he would hate it. He pretended he didn't care but I knew he did.

We went on swinging for quite a while, but it didn't really work for us. I cheated on my husband outside of swinging. Because we had swung together, because he seemed to like watching me have sex with another man, it didn't seem at all bad if I had sex with another man *without* him watching. He found out and was livid.

I kept trying to explain that it seemed simple for me to have sex with another man and it didn't mean anything to me. I was so used to doing it in front of him; it was only a small step from that to having sex with another man behind his back. But he didn't understand and we divorced.

Dean's story is the male equivalent to Katie's. Dean, a thirty-one-year-old businessman, was married for ten years.

My sex life with my wife was boring and she wasn't coming home on time. It was obvious that she was having an affair. I took a lover in retaliation. My wife caught me in the act. She came home early when she wasn't supposed to be in town. I think I wanted her to catch me because I couldn't stand the pain. She stormed out and didn't come back.

I found out she was having an affair with one of my friends. She told me she felt our sex life wasn't exciting. So we started getting into swinging. It was exciting for a while but it was hard for me. I got jealous. It was hard for me to see her being sexual with a lot of people. I was able to get into it for a while, but then we got divorced.

A classic male approach to swinging is that many men try and persuade their wives to take part in lesbian acts. Fang observes that "many women learn to enjoy it in order to please their husbands or be sociable." Watching two women make love to each other is a common male fantasy, although I have yet to interview women who have the analogous fantasy of watching their husbands with another man. Bartell has observed women in homosexual situations at swing parties and says that men usually initiate this: "In an attempt to 'turn themselves on' the males push their women into having ambisexual relations with another girl. Most of them got the idea from either books or pornographic movies."

Prince Egon Von Furstenberg and his wife Diane had one

of the seventies' most celebrated relationships which ended in divorce.

I talked to Egon about the disintegration of the marriage.

> I don't think open marriages work. Two people that really love each other don't want anyone else. That is what love is. When I was madly in love I didn't look for anyone else. Diane and I were faithful, but after three and a half years of marriage, our sex life became a little dull and we tried to change it by doing other things. A marriage is always a very difficult thing for me because I felt I was in a prison. I like making conquests, it makes me feel secure. I get very insecure with one person. I think cheating is insecurity.
>
> I was supposed to be a playboy. I cheated for four years and Diane was faithful all that time. I don't think women cheat first. When they commit themselves they are much more straightforward. Diane said that after a while it is better to jerk off and I said I cheated on her, in the press. Diane was very upset. She made terrible scenes. She didn't want to know all the details, but she was in tears all the time. If two people marry for love and then they start cheating on each other, then I don't think the love is there anymore. I did try to push Diane into making love to another girl and me. She did that one time to make me happy. I don't think she was.
>
> Diane was very much in love with me and it broke up basically when she found a lover. I suppose I thought she would never leave me. I understood how she felt, though. Open marriages really don't work.

Dr. Neubauer comments, "I've seen people who tried an open marriage and my feeling is that they were already one foot out of the marriage when they tried it." Her experience is paralleled by my findings.

Angie and David Bowie had the archetypal open marriage which ended in divorce. Their story, which Angie has allowed me to quote at length from her autobiography *Free Spirit,* shows the emotional costs of infidelity and the open marriage.[4]

David Bowie, the rock star, started his marriage to wife Angie on the understanding that they would both be free to have sex with other people. Both David and Angie are self-confessed bisexuals. The story of their marriage which began with freedom and rampant sexuality and ended in divorce, is one which crystallizes all the problems and consequences inherent in open marriages.

Angie Bowie and David Bowie began their marriage by pledging that they would never be jealous or possessive. Angie recalls their vows.

> We vowed that infidelity would never threaten our marriage. We vowed that we would never give way to jealousy or possessiveness. We vowed that we would never harbor secrets from one another. We vowed that we would remain together forever and that no one would infringe on our commitment.

David assured Angie that he would always love her, no matter how many other partners he or she had; "David said, 'Whatever happens, you will always be my love. The only person who will still figure in my life when everyone else has gone.' "

The Bowies were almost late for their own wedding ceremony because they were both in bed with the same girl. Angie says that at the beginning she found the idea of David having sex with other people to be "a compliment to my femininity to be married to such a desirable and attractive man."

The marriage began to go wrong for Angie when David fell in love. "But as far as I could see there was nothing I could object to, because I had accepted the role of a dignified and radical thinker on all levels. Now I was lumbered. How could I suddenly become an impassioned wife screaming about infidelity when I myself had not practiced fidelity as part of our marriage vows."

Angie's discomfort with the open-marriage situation deepened when she became pregnant and was worried that the child might not be David's, another consequence of swinging which is easy to disregard in these post-pill days. She told David that the whole affair had made her question where they were going. Finally Angie virtually assumed the classic victim role of wife/mother to a straying son. "I used to feel like David's maiden aunt indulging a favorite nephew as he regaled me with tales of James Bond style escapades. This was all very well except that David disappeared some nights without telling me where he was going or what he was doing. But there was nothing I could do."

Angie was still swinging herself, but again encountered a classic scenario common to many participants of swinging style marriages. She discovered that David was having sex with someone they had both made love to together. "I felt I had to draw the line somewhere. I said to David, 'Somehow that seems more like cheating, because there is an added insult of me having been left out—that now you return to a situation without me.' "

David continued having affairs, but eventually Angie reacted exactly like any other female victim I surveyed. She realized that she couldn't cope with the situation, but was afraid to confront her husband for fear of losing him.

> Fear of losing him stopped me from telling him outright that I could no longer support or deal with this situation. I was no longer able to share him either with black girls, other artists, drag queens or Corrine Schwab; the fantasy had slipped from the frame and was hanging askew. I could not cope with the uncertainties, the loneliness of my plight.

David and Angie Bowie finally divorced, their dream open marriage ending in bitterness and acrimony. In retrospect Angie says that she realizes that the open element destroyed their marriage.

> While I was in love with David and ready to share him with anyone he wanted, I still wanted to hold that privileged and treasured place as his wife. I was prepared to bow to convention that much—I wish now I had submitted to convention more because it would take its natural revenge. My mistake was in not telling David that I would have preferred to live another way, yes, even as a conventional wife, if it would have saved our marriage.

Angie Bowie believes that her open marriage experience taught her something about love and sex.

> I've also learned something about sex. Once I just regarded it as a physical thing and unimportant. Now I know it is something very precious that can only be shared with the one person you love.

Divorce

The new no-fault divorce laws mean that there are no statistics to correlate infidelity with divorce. However, even if the cheater doesn't leave the victim for the cheatee, an affair is often the catalyst for a divorce.

The cheater may leave the victim for the cheatee, but there is no guarantee that he won't cheat again in his new marriage. Dr. Strean implies that a new marriage doesn't necessarily reform an inveterate cheater: "Unless the person faces his or her internal conflicts, changing partners is not going to do much because it is essentially an internal conflict."

Dr. Strean's statement obviously applies to the compulsive

cheater whose infidelity is partially a symptom of his inability to make a commitment. Paul's story supports this perspective. He is a thirty-seven-year-old teacher who has been married three times.

In my first marriage I cheated in a matter of months. They were one-night stands. One woman came round to my house and the other was a friend's sister. I guess I just liked cheating. There was something different about it. A sense of adventure, not like driving a race car or climbing a mountain but of meeting someone new. I guess there is something special about being with a different body. A different body is attractive in the way a body you know is not.

My first wife found out that I was cheating. I told her after she asked me. I didn't like the idea of lying. Everything was idealized in the fifties—songs like "Only You" and "Too Young" and it was very unrealistic. I wanted to be realistic. She didn't say anything, except, Oh. Cheating was a small prelude to the different values we didn't know we had. We grew apart. It was like a tissue on a plant. One part becomes the tissue on a leaf, the other becomes a tissue on a stem and they don't relate anymore.

Our life-styles became very different after I cheated. She became very conservative and voted for Reagan. Totally different from my radical way of life. So we divorced. I don't think monogamous marriage works for most people, there is too much stimulus from too many sources available in too many areas of life. Most people are really diverse and it is difficult to meet people whose range of diversities satisfy each other.

I married my second wife a few months after the divorce from my first wife. I told her I wasn't sure that our marriage would last until death us do part. She said she thought it would. I told her I would tell her if I wanted to have sex with someone else. She was jealous and wasn't too crazy about the idea. After seven years she realized that I was frustrated by not screwing around. I wanted to and it was nerve-racking that I didn't feel free enough to do it. She couldn't deal with the way I felt.

She was unfaithful to me as a kind of punishment. She got involved with someone and I felt really let down. She was very disappointed with herself. She couldn't accept that part of herself. I suggested we become involved with swinging. We knew what fidelity was, so why not try the other extreme—swinging. But that didn't work for us, so we divorced.

In my third marriage we had an open relationship as well. My wife brought home a girlfriend once and I went to bed with her. My wife was going to bed with someone else and I thought it would be a good thing. But it wasn't. We divorced. I don't think I would ever be capable of fidelity.

Helen is a female cheater whose affair led to divorce.

I suppose I got married too young. I loved my husband Don very much but all the same I couldn't help wondering what it would be like to go to bed with another man. I spent most of my marriage fighting those feelings but after seventeen years I gave in and went to bed with another man.

Curiosity made me do it. I'd only ever been to bed with Don and I didn't know what to expect. I found that Al was a much better lover than my husband. I became addicted to him. It got to the point where sex with my husband really revolted me and I couldn't go on. Instinctively I was pushing him away from me. I didn't want to hurt his feelings but Al made me feel that way.

Things got so bad that my husband and I finally divorced and now I am alone. Al didn't want to marry me. He said that an affair is one thing but marriage is quite another. I wish I had never met him. And I think life used to be a lot easier when you married one man and just had sex with him for the rest of your life. That way you had no comparisons and were content with what you had.

Peter is a sixty-two-year-old radar operator. After thirty years of his cheating, his wife also began to have affairs.

> I cheated four years into the marriage. I used the story that I was giving sailing lessons as an excuse. When my wife started cheating, it excited me. I enjoyed my cheating for a time, it got me away from drink and gambling and I even learned to fly a plane from one of my cheatees. But the strain of it all broke up the marriage. I didn't like all the secrecy, all the problems of concealing everything from the neighbors.

Infidelity can corrode a relationship; once one partner discovers that the other has cheated, they often retaliate by having an affair themselves.

Peter, a twenty-five-year-old construction worker divorced his wife after four years of marriage.

> I cheated first, with her sister. The affair went on for a year. I also had five or six other affairs. I'm attracted to a lot of people. My wife was pretty straight. My wife found out. At first she didn't do anything.
>
> Then, one day, I came home and caught her with another man. I got a bit violent with him. I told him to get out and I didn't love her at that moment. She told me she did it to get back at me for the affair I had. We divorced because we didn't trust each other again, but I still love her.

Stan is a thirty-three-year-old executive whose wife's affair ended their marriage.

> I believe in monogamy, in caring and sharing with one person. I noticed that my wife was being different to me. She had unusual moods and rejected me sexually. I wanted to find out what was wrong and I followed her. I found out she was seeing another man. At first I loved her more, but over time I loved her less. I

was very upset and felt terrible. Our sex became less frequent and less satisfying for me. My wife cheating made me feel unhappy and lonely. We divorced. The infidelity was negative and destructive.

Bob, a thirty-seven-year-old insurance investigator, was married for sixteen years and then divorced because of his wife's infidelity.

I started out believing in monogamy. But after ten years of marriage I started picking up women in bars and restaurants. I never fell in love with them and told them all that I was married. I wanted to be honest. I used work as an alibi. I was ambivalent about lying to my wife but thought that my cheating was justified because my needs weren't being satisfied at home. But I felt very depressed and guilty. I never went to bed with the same woman more than twice. They were all terrible in bed and not worth being with. Only about one out of eight was worth being with. None of them ever made me feel like my wife did. She was fantastic. There has never been another woman like her.

After about ten one-night stands I told my wife what I had done because I wanted to hurt her. I felt she didn't take me seriously. I expected her to be hurt but she told me she had done the same thing. I didn't know who it was. I didn't need to know. I did want to kill the other guy, but I was too sensible for that.

My wife claimed that she had cheated because I hadn't fulfilled her needs and she wanted to retaliate. It seemed she didn't cheat for sex. I was shocked. I didn't expect it of her. She claimed I wasn't fulfilling my role emotionally. But I never expected her to cheat. I never thought she would do it. I thought she loved me too much to cheat. So I fell out of love with her because of her cheating. Now I am divorced but I don't want to get married again. I feel marriage is something you only do once. I won't get involved with anyone again. I don't have time for the hassle or the hurt.

Julie is a forty-three-year-old female victim.

My husband and I were married for fourteen years when I found out that he liked to dress up as a woman. He told me all about it. And I was disgusted. I thought he must be homosexual, but he swore that he wasn't. He swore that he had never had sex with another man, but I didn't believe him. He wanted me to talk to a therapist to have him explain to me how dressing up as a woman didn't mean that a man was homosexual. But I didn't want any part of it. I thought it was my husband's problem, not mine.

I tried to forget about the whole thing, then I found out that my husband was having an affair with another woman. He said that when he was with her he used to dress up in female clothes.

The other woman, he said, understood his need to dress up. That made me feel bad. It was the dressing up that turned me off more than the infidelity. Our sex life wasn't great and that compounded the whole thing. We just grew distant. I felt I wasn't sexy enough. We stayed married for another three years, but finally divorced because of the infidelity.

John is a thirty-seven-year-old accountant whose wife divorced him because of his cheating.

I only ever cheated in one-night stands. I didn't like one-night stands, I wasn't into hotels and motels, and I didn't even know why I did it. I had a lot of different partners before I got married. I knew cheating was difficult and complicated but I still did it.

Somehow or other my wife found out about what I was doing. She didn't say anything. But she changed towards me. I began to get suspicious and I followed her. Then I discovered that she was having an affair with my best friend. I knew she was cheating on me, and I knew that I couldn't carry on. I knew that it was the end. I told her that I wanted a divorce. I didn't think I was capable of staying with her. Once her infidelity was out in the open, it was over because I knew about it.

When I think back on it all I realize that I was like a robot. I cheated without thinking. But now I am paying the price. I am getting married again, but this time I have told myself that I won't cheat. The trouble is I don't believe myself.

Patsy, a forty-nine-year-old secretary found her husband cheating and divorced him as a result.

My husband was kind to me, no fights or trouble, but I couldn't spend the rest of my life with him after I found out that he was unfaithful. He broke my heart. I found out that he had been deceiving me for twenty-eight years. I don't trust any man at the moment. I was deeply hurt by my husband and I know there are many men like him. He was fifty-four and trying to be young by chasing girls. Some men are like little boys and have to go out and prove themselves. I know that is what he was doing, but I still couldn't live with him and we had to get a divorce.

Jim found out that his wife was cheating on him after two years of marriage and his story shows some of the psychological consequences of cheating.

I believe in monogamy, in being married to only one woman for life and not having sex with anyone else. But I found rubbers in the bathroom and started watching my wife. I became a detective, which crushed me because I never realized that I would be spying on the person I loved. That was how I found that the person whom she used to bring to our home and claim was a friend of the family was only *her* friend. I was very hurt and stopped having sex with her. I couldn't trust her again because I felt betrayed. I felt very violent, angry, hurt, and resentful. She made me something I thought I would never be—a person who was paranoid and distrustful. I divorced her. I don't think she wanted to hurt me. But that was the result.

The results of infidelity are almost invariably negative. Yet occasionally the cheater does manage to jump off the infidelity carousel and commit to fidelity.

SIX

Why Monogamy Is Better

Reformed Cheaters

I'm a reformed cheater myself and I believe in Dr. Strean's statement, "Often the people who stop are the best at fidelity. There are reformed cheaters, just as there are reformed alcoholics. The pain and the anguish and the hurt and the rejection makes them stop."

Reform may be ideal, but the path from infidelity to fidelity may not be simple and clearly can embrace every possible form of infidelity from the hit-and-run affair, to commercial sex, the secondary relationship, swinging, and open marriages.

Larry, a thirty-two-year-old sales manager, has been married for ten years.

> I cheated in the first year of my marriage. It was a spontaneous automobile experience. Salesmen have a lot of time on the road and what do you do after work is over? I wasn't brought up with monogamy in mind. Everyone cheats. I don't think you can turn around in any group of society without knowing that someone is cheating. I think everybody expects everyone else to be faithful, but the reality is that a lot of people look the other way.
>
> I cheated a lot but never with anyone in my home town. Then

I fell in love. My girlfriend was a business woman and I was attracted to her because she was exciting. We were involved with each other for over a year. She was independent and had a demanding job. We also enjoyed doing different drugs together that I don't do with my wife.

Sex with my wife was better than sex with my girlfriend, probably because of the length of time we have been having sex together. I would have liked to have them both at the same time, I've never been to bed with two women at once. But I tried not to have sex with my wife after I came back from my girlfriend. One problem with cheating is that if you have sex when you come home, the amount of sperm will be less and that is suspicious.

I broke up with my girlfriend because the only person who knew about the affair committed suicide and I felt it was symbolic. Now I've gone through the affair I don't have to fantasize about it and I don't cheat anymore. I have the experience behind me so I know what affairs are: physical and emotional turmoil. Making yourself a little crazy having to care about two women at the same time. I realize that having an affair subtracts from the positive energies.

Bobbie is a thirty-three-year-old female ex-cheater.

When I was a child I found out that my relatives cheated. I was unbelieving at first, yet relieved to know they were human.

I had two cheating affairs in my marriage. One was married and the other helped me through my first divorce. I was afraid of getting hurt and I felt curious about my cheatee's wife. I learned about myself and the art of love through my affairs. I thought my husband would consider me desirable if someone else did, so I told him about the affair and confessed. I didn't like the lying. I couldn't keep my life straight. After a while cheating is no fun.

Danny is a thirty-two-year-old musician. After affairs with other women including his wife's sister, he divorced and now is in a new relationship in which he is monogamous.

I feel that monogamy is the only way. That once you get into anything else, its no good. At one point my ex-wife and I got into threesomes, with other women. It was very exciting sexually but it opened up fears in me. Did it mean that because I was having sex with the other woman, my wife would have sex with other men? Was she going to do it with another man? She did suggest that we make it with another man. I said no. I am not bisexual and I didn't want to share her that way. She suggested that I watch her have sex with the other man. I thought I wouldn't enjoy it because I couldn't control it.

I didn't cheat on my wife just for sexual reasons. As I look back on my marriage, it was emotional stagnation. Now I believe in monogamy because it has the least amount of complications. Going outside of a marriage on a sexual level is more of an emotional commitment. I am now monogamous. I am passionate and romantic but I am trying. It depends on me. I don't think it depends on the woman, it depends on me.

Penny is a thirty-eight-year-old divorcee who remarried six months ago.

I believe that a good male and female relationship demands monogamy and fidelity. Cheaters aren't happy people. I cheated after two months of marriage with someone my husband knew well. My husband initiated it. Our sex life was no good. I knew my husband was cheating. Now I like being faithful in my new marriage. Sex with my husband is fantastic. He is kind, generous, loving, and I will never do anything to hurt him.

Barry, a Hollywood producer, is divorced but no longer cheats on his girlfriends.

I cheated in my first marriage, but I was very young. My wife didn't need sex as much as I did. Possibly if I hadn't cheated the marriage might have ended sooner than it did. My cheating is more European. I had to go elsewhere to find romance. Now I try not to cheat in any way at all and to have respect. Sex is kind of a possessive act. The way I was brought up there is possessiveness and intimacy. If you share intimacy elsewhere, it might turn false. Love is very fragile.

Betty is a nineteen-year-old factory worker with two children who has been married for four years.

I believe in monogamy. You feel it is better for yourself and your relationship. You commit yourself to be faithful. But women have more problems than men do in being satisfied. I had one lover on and off for two years. It started out as sex, then developed into love. He was best man at our wedding, my husband's best friend, and I met him again at a party. I never wanted to break up the marriage. But the other man was more romantic and more gentle than my husband. But I felt uncomfortable and guilty about cheating. Really, because of tradition.

Then my husband told me that he had been unfaithful. I felt hurt and I loved him less. I constantly watched him after that and had others watch him. We had more sex and if we didn't have sex I felt he didn't love me anymore. I trust him now. I went back to my cheatee after my husband confessed the affair. I confessed because of guilt and confusion. My husband acted hurt and our relationship changed. We had a lot of doubt.

Cheating has given me more experience and made me grow up a lot. It was sometimes exciting, but I didn't like the lying or the hurt. I don't recommend cheating to anyone. What starts out as a casual relationship often turns to love and causes too much pain, confusion, aggravation, and hurt on both sides. Now I want just to be a wife to my husband. I resolved never to cheat again. But though I regret having cheated there was still the thrill of knowing that you can still excite more men than your husband.

David is a thirty-four-year-old attorney who has been married for nine years.

I cheated after the third year of marriage. I got involved with a client. I was handling her divorce. I felt guilty about it because it was difficult to relate to my mate for a couple of weeks. Every time I was with her, I was thinking about the person I was cheating with. I confessed to my wife. She was devastated.

I asked her if she wanted to end the relationship and she said, "I will forgive but I won't forget." About a year later, she told me that she had had a casual relationship with a professor. My reaction was "it took you a year and you got even." I felt it was a wild west situation. I had fired the first shot and she fired the second.

We opened up the marriage and dated other people. After I dated I didn't like it. Lying didn't please me. There were hurt feelings. My wife told me "I had so much faith in you." I never fell in love. But now I don't cheat and I believe in monogamy. I think that if you truly love somebody then there is really no need to cheat. And if you do cheat, you don't really love the person.

Richard's story runs the entire gamut of infidelity through to monogamy. He is a fifty-year-old lawyer who was married for twenty-one years.

When I got married I intended to have lady friends and fool around, to see prostitutes and have a variety of sexual partners. I thought one woman couldn't satisfy me. Maybe it was an ego thing, I don't know. It was the idea of forbidden fruit. The excitement of a new woman, the adventure of it. I cheated with about three hundred women. I never had to give an excuse, I always did it in daytime. I always told the women that I was married. I always play it safe. I'd rather turn down a potential liaison with a woman than risk trouble. I always had two rules about cheating. One, never get involved. If I found a woman getting involved with me or vice versa, I cut. Two, wake up every morning alongside of my wife.

I never felt guilty and I never worried that she might be cheating on me. She had her hands full with the children. I think my wife suspected that I was cheating, but she didn't say anything until we had been married for fourteen years. We lived the suburban life in New Jersey. I was a Little League coach and in the PTA. I was a prosecutor in the town where I lived and I led a double life.

When we had been married for nine years, a friend said, in front of my wife, "There's not a married man I know that doesn't cheat." I kicked him under the table because he was blowing my racket. My wife said that from that moment on she suspected me. She was very upset. Then, after we had been married for fourteen years, we got drunk one night and she suddenly asked me if I had ever cheated. I said yes. She was very upset and she questioned whether or not she wanted to end the marriage.

My wife loved me, but over a period of time she felt if you can't beat them, join them. We got into swinging. We started with clubs, went four times before we made a contact. She had a couple of drinks. I don't think she really enjoyed the swinging scene. I was secure when she was having sex with a man, I always felt very confident with her. Maybe it's an ego thing, but I thought I was a very good husband. She was very much in love with me. I don't know that swinging was constructive. It may have brought us closer together, bringing things to each other that we learned from other people. That went on for seven months. It wasn't really my thing because all the forbidden fruit was gone. I was still cheating on the side because swinging wasn't nearly as much fun as cheating.

My wife found out that I was cheating and she was exasperated. We went to a marriage encounter weekend, when you write to each other constantly. We became very close, very communicative. She finally decided, "Go ahead, cheat, but don't get involved." We developed an open marriage in which we would swing but not necessarily together. She would go out occasionally and she would come home afterwards and tell me what had happened.

I remember being on a date, once, and the young lady asked if I had ever been in love. I said, "Are you out of your mind? No way. I've got this nice little racket; happily married, three kids, a thriving law practice, politically active." But then one day I met this fantastic woman, Alice, the most sexually exciting woman that I had ever met in my life. She wanted a casual relationship. She was divorced with two children, she had a history of abandonment in her life because her mother died when she was seven, she was deserted through death by her foster mother, and her husband left her when she was pregnant. She felt that if she loved someone, he would leave her. So I was ideal, because I was "happily married." We were going to see each other every six weeks, have dinner and screw our brains out. We were dynamic together. Every six weeks got to be every three weeks, then once a week, then staying over. Then we realized we were in love.

After three months, my wife Mary said, "It's *one* of us, who is it going to be?" My wife knew Alice. She and my wife gave me a birthday present of a ménage à trois. I went to bed with both of them at once. They knew I would love it. My wife wasn't too into it. Alice is bisexual, but my wife isn't. That night my wife was passively bisexual.

If you had asked me at the time if I loved my wife, I would have said yes. But looking back, I never loved her. I loved Alice. I told my wife that I loved her *and* Alice and that I wasn't prepared to give up either. We were away for the weekend in West Hampton and she said, "Let's take a walk on the beach." I said no, I didn't feel like it. She went on the beach and I phoned Alice. My wife came back, blew up, and said which one is it, me or Alice. I said Alice.

Alice and I got into a relationship that got more and more exclusive and then for a year was monogamous. It was a tumultuous, tremendous hurricanelike relationship. Fights and passion like you wouldn't believe. Then I discovered that I had heart disease and I had open heart surgery. It blew Alice's mind. I was going to live with her after the operation. Hospitals were terrifying to her after her mother's death. I went to stay with her and after five days, it was over.

I was shattered. I was thinking about suicide. I was truly shattered. My law practice went to hell. I started owing money and screwing everything that walked. Now I have met a woman who I am very attracted to. She's great and I am faithful to her. It's a combination of what she brings out in me, and my situation. I want to be monogamous now. I'm tired you see. And what else am I going to prove about my sexuality.

Rose is a forty-five-year-old reformed cheater.

I didn't want to hurt my husband or my children when I fell in love with Mark, but I just couldn't help myself. He made me feel like a woman and not just a dull wife and mother. Up till then I felt as if I had lost myself, that I wasn't a person in my own right, just a wife or a mother. Mark made me come alive again. And I loved him for it.

I had an affair with Mark for five years; then Wanda, my oldest daughter, saw us together, having lunch. I tried to cover everything up but I know she guessed the truth. She was only twelve at the time and I could see the hurt in her eyes. She began acting bitchy and nasty towards me and I knew that she didn't feel the same way about me. I couldn't take the look in her eyes, the contempt that I believed she felt for me.

Wanda and I never discussed my affair but I think she knows that it's over. I wouldn't hurt my kids for all the world, so that's why I stopped cheating. And I am never going to do it again.

Mike is a forty-seven-year-old reformed cheater.

In my first marriage I cheated all the time. My marriage ended because I had an affair with a co-worker that lasted for six months. I didn't just want to have sex with her, I wanted to get to know her, talk to her, and get close to her. So I divorced.

Another reason for the divorce was the inability of my wife and I to communicate and accept sexual needs.

The tables were completely turned when I married for the second time. My wife is afraid to love someone, she is afraid of becoming attached for fear of losing them, so her sexual liaisons and her marriage are very shallow and cold and unsatisfying. She spent years having quite obvious affairs and taunting me with the details. She tried to turn on my best friend and seduce him. Then she called up *his* best friend and went after him.

I was so angry and miserable about my wife's ongoing affairs and I finally came to grips with my feelings. I confronted her, and told her that I wouldn't put up with her affairs any longer. She broke down and told me everything, far too much, and at first refused to agree to stop. She quickly retracted that and went on to tell me that she wasn't sure of the paternity of my daughter. I still love my daughter, she is precious and delightful and didn't bring this on herself. She needs all the love she can get from me.

Now my wife and I are divorced and I want to be in a monogamous relationship. The depth of a relationship with trust and sincerity and love is where it's at for me. That means being very vulnerable and subject to loss, pain, and hurt should the partner die or leave. But without mutual vulnerability people only pass time together. I need a deep and richly rewarding relationship. Affairs are fun, but briefly so, and often, even at their best, they are negative. So now I am going to be faithful. A single rose is still, to me, far prettier and more expressive than a dozen roses.

Jim is a thirty-three-year-old writer. He was married, ten years ago, for two and a half years.

I grew up in the late sixties. I was into the whole flower-child thing, it was all free love. If you wanted to make love with someone, you did it because you liked them and you didn't have any moral obligation. I embraced that for a while. I cheated eleven months after our marriage. I was in love with the cheatee.

I felt terrible about lying. I felt that I was doing something wrong but I knew we were on the rocks. It was a way of hanging on in a crisis. I didn't cheat for sexual reasons but for comfort and because I was afraid of being alone.

I was quite certain my wife was having a major flirtation. Then she became pregnant and a couple of friends suggested that she might be pregnant by another man. I knew for a fact that she had spent a night at this man's house. I wanted her to say that the baby was mine, and she did. But when I confronted my wife the divorce was pending, and she said she knew that my asking was the last straw; we would never trust each other. I felt badly but I knew I had to ask her directly because of the baby.

After the marriage broke up, I went into relationship after relationship. Each one was meant to be *the* one. Then I learned from one, so I thought the next one would always be better. I wasn't faithful. I feel that my tendency was always to look for another woman in a period of crisis. The cheating made me very skeptical about such a thing as eternal love and happily ever after.

Then, over a period of years, I found myself getting more and more reactionary. Now I feel like a fairly old man. I feel such a capacity for jealousy. I have been in a relationship now for ten months and I haven't been unfaithful. I don't think she has been unfaithful, but I am afraid of it. I find myself jealous of her nameless, faceless friends. I ask a lot of questions. I am nosier than I was; whereas before I wouldn't ask. I felt before I didn't want my freedom impinged upon, but right now I feel I don't mind. I feel I need constant reassurance. I feel like a little boy. I am ashamed of those feelings. I ask insulting questions like "Where were you, who were you with?"

Ten years ago I was the opposite. It was almost as if I didn't care. I set up my relationships by saying, "This is who I am. This is where I am going. Come along if you like. If you don't, get lost." Now it is, "I'll do anything. Please don't leave me." I feel as if I am doing a good thing, being faithful.

Of course, monogamy has its problems. There are a lot of

> people in the world. A lot of people are attractive. There is a lot to like about people. There are a lot of possibilities. It seems that one person won't fulfill everything. You have to have friends. There is a lot of temptation. It seems that all the odds are against monogamy. It is a primal attitude to say, "Give in to the instincts." You have to realize the instincts are there, but the real deeper meaning of what a relationship is about has to do with commitment. You choose a framework to work in. You choose some kind of social or moral ethic and you set it up yourself. You just have to work at it. I think it gives life structure and order. I think it makes you feel that man is not the measure of all things. It also makes you strive for something bigger than yourself. It is almost impossible to be faithful so it is reaching for the impossible. Monogamy is stretching the possibilities of what it is to be human.

Jim and I are exactly the same age, representatives of a generation that was nourished on freedom, and guiltlessness, and discovered that none of it leads to happiness. We both started out reckless and determined to sample every sensation available. In my wild uncommitted years, I strongly identified with D. H. Lawrence's Ursula from *The Rainbow,* who fell in love with Skrebensky but didn't want to marry him and cried, "As an end in itself, I could love a thousand men, one after the other. Why should I end with a Skrebensky? Why should I not go on, and love all the types I fancy, one after the other, if love is an end in itself."

But in my thirties, I found the answer to Ursula's impassioned cry and realized that love isn't an end in itself, that sensation isn't everything, that wildness isn't happiness, and that love certainly is not all you need. There is commitment and security, comfort and tenderness, loyalty and trust. And, as we have seen, infidelity is the enemy of all these things.

In today's chaotic world, relationships are more important

than ever. The family and religion have dramatically disintegrated and relationships are often the only anchor providing men and women with security, so that anything that undermines our relationships creates unhappiness. Throughout all my interviewing I didn't encounter anyone who found that infidelity led to everlasting happiness. The fruits of infidelity range from confusion to pain, from passion to divorce, from sexual experimentation to hurt and betrayal. A thousand other elements were mentioned in interviews but no one ever claimed infidelity was the key to ultimate happiness.

Everyone, as I said in the introduction, wants to know how to keep the one they love faithful. And there aren't any foolproof answers or formulas. I do believe, however, that it may help to categorically state both your feelings about infidelity and your potential reactions, right at the beginning of any relationship. Perhaps in the form of "If you cheat, you'll be hurting me. So you will have to decide what is more important to you: your desire to cheat or not to hurt me. And if you do cheat, I will react in one of two ways, either by cheating myself or by leaving you."

Dr. Neubauer advises that at the beginning of your relationship both partners discuss fidelity and explain exactly how they feel; "Talk it over and say something like 'If you were unfaithful I would feel so hurt, I don't know if I would trust you again and it wouldn't help the relationship.' " By ignoring the issue of fidelity altogether both partners are lulling each other into a false sense of security that enables them to believe that cheating will have no consequences.

Another possible route to fidelity might be that men and women start learning from one another. If women learn from men how to confront and deal with problems more effectively, perhaps many women who play ostrich politics in the face of their partners' infidelity might be able to cope better. Just as women need to learn from men how to confront their partner, perhaps men too, should learn from women how to confront themselves.

Men are no longer compelled to act out the masculine stereotype, so perhaps they can now learn to cultivate some of the "feminine" attributes of introspection and analysis and examine their own emotions and behavior. Today, men need women as much as women need men; it may be time for men to examine their concepts of love and to think about the consequences of their infidelity. Men no longer commit to women just because of financial or social pressures. The majority of men commit to women out of free will. Perhaps they will now begin to take responsibility for the relationships they choose instead of drifting into infidelity and helping to destroy them.

Is there any hope for monogamy in the future? Dr. Neubauer believes there may be. "I think everything is going to equalize out. We are in a societal change. We are just in the beginning. It won't happen yet. The power is still on the male side. The world is changing, but it is going to take some time. I find the younger generation of men is different. It may be the wave of the future but it will take many generations till it gets there."

And while we wait for all those centuries to pass, we still have to cope with today. We may persist in reading our children fairy tales that end with the words "And they lived happily ever after," but nevertheless 50 percent of us don't. Infidelity creates distance and corrodes intimacy. And it is only by commitment and closeness that we may perhaps begin to crack what Kafka terms "the frozen sea inside us."

AFTERWORD

Herpes, AIDS, and Infidelity

The AIDS and herpes epidemics of the eighties were raging round about the time that I began to research this book. Not a month passed without newspapers or magazines carrying sensationalist headlines on AIDS deaths and how millions of Americans were suffering from herpes. The reports were full of terms like leper, scourge, scarlet letter, and the Moral Majority's revenge. Yet throughout all my interviews with the cheaters of America, only about two people even mentioned the dreaded herpes and AIDS epidemics at all.

Although the Moral Majority had proclaimed that AIDS and herpes were the judgment of God on the promiscuous that would drive cheaters back onto the path of fidelity, it appeared that none of my interviewees believed this applied to them. They continued to cheat, oblivious to any dangers from disease. However, during my original research I hadn't directly broached the subject with the interviewees waiting instead to see if they themselves alluded to it. And at the time, talking to the cheaters of 1982, it seemed as if herpes and AIDS were nonexistent.

In an attempt to specifically explore whether or not herpes and AIDS had altered the behavior patterns of cheaters all over America, I talked to John Graves of the Herpes Resource Center in California (an organization that exists to provide information on herpes) and to Don Meriwether of the AIDS Resource Center in New York (an organization that exists to get financial help and shelter for people with AIDS). Both Graves and Meriwether confirmed that no statistics on the relationship between AIDS, herpes, and infidelity exist. In an attempt to collect some data on the subject, I placed an advertisement in *The Village Voice* (in September and October of 1983) which read: "Attention Cheaters: Has the current herpes and AIDS epidemic stopped your cheating or not?"

At the time that I placed the advertisement, I was also studying the current facts and statistics available on AIDS and herpes, in the belief that it would only be possible to evaluate cheater's responses to the diseases if I had a thorough understanding of them myself. The degree to which cheaters are, or are not, influenced by the epidemics needs to be compared to the reality regarding AIDS and herpes. I wanted to discover as best I could what caused the diseases, what their symptoms and consequences were, and how dangerous AIDS and herpes really were to the majority of the population.

I am grateful to Don Meriwether and John Graves for the following facts and statistics on AIDS and herpes.

The first cases of AIDS, which stands for Acquired Immune Deficiency Syndrome, were first discovered in New York at the end of 1978. From that time, until September 26, 1983, according to the Center of Disease Control in Atlanta, 2,374 cases of AIDS had been reported. Meriwether notes, however, that AIDS cases don't have to be reported to the CDC by law, so that there could be many more AIDS victims in America. Out of the reported 2,374 AIDS victims, a total of 989 people had died.

The majority of AIDS victims are male. In New York, which comprises 50 percent of AIDS victims, 898 males and 81 females have suffered from AIDS since 1978. That 10 percent-plus ratio of women holds up nationwide. The major risk groups remain homosexual or bisexual men and intravenous drug users. A much smaller percentage are Haitians and hemophiliacs. The majority of women who have contracted AIDS have been intravenous drug users.

The rate of AIDS victims doubles every six months, so that it is projected that in October 1984 there will be 9,496 people suffering from AIDS. The average incubation period of the disease is fourteen months. However, there was the case of the Massachusetts prison in which one of the inmates came down with AIDS. None of the prisoners had been incarcerated for *fewer than* three years, therefore that postulates that AIDS can have an incubation period that lasts as long as three years.

The definition of an AIDS victim, according to the Center for Disease Control, is someone with a drastically impaired cellular immunity level and who has also developed one out of a list of specific diseases. Since researchers have not, as of October 1983, discovered what exactly AIDS is, it is postulated on models of how other diseases work. Hepatitis B, which has been rather epidemic, especially among gay people, is spread through shared needles. It is also spread through those body fluids that have been contaminated or derived from blood, sperm, feces and urine. Although you will get a trace of the cytomegliovirus CMV viruses in saliva and blood, that is not at the highest level. The virus remains at its highest levels (for as long as a year) in urine and sperm. So there is some reason to believe that sperm may be the most hospitable host for the infection.

Researchers seem to think that the easiest root of transmission of AIDS is through anal sex, because the sperm can enter the bloodstream, and it is common in anal sex for minor lesions to develop in intestinal linings. If, in contrast, a woman has sex with an AIDS victim vaginally, there is a chance that the sperm is not going to be a major problem. There are no blood vessels or capilleries in the walls of the vagina which would absorb the sperm. In oral sex, if the sperm is ejaculated and swallowed, it goes through the strong acids in the mouth which might lessen the risk, but there still is a chance of transmission.

Wearing condoms during sex and not swallowing semen is thought to stop the transfusion of AIDS. But the disease can also be caught through dirty needles and blood transfusions, as in the case of the Long Island grandmother who had no other relation at all with any other possible root of transmission save for a blood transfusion she had received two or three years prior to her diagnosis.

It appears that AIDS is caused by multiple contacts with an infected person or persons. There is, of course, says Meriwether, a possibility that there is an unlucky individual somewhere who had sex once with an infected person and then came down with AIDS, but no one researching the disease really thinks that is possible. If AIDS were spread by casual contact (one time) many more people would have AIDS by now. Victims would also be more spread across the general population rather than in the risk groups which are currently documented.

While research on the causes and transmission of AIDS is in its infancy, much work has been done on investigating herpes. The word *herpes* derives from the ancient Greek, meaning *to creep.* In 1982, American health authorities estimated that between five million and twenty million people contracted the disease in one of its two forms: Herpes One (oral herpes) or Herpes Two (genital herpes). Herpes One is a virus related to chicken pox and is the most common kind of herpes. Herpes One causes cold sores to appear on the face. Approximately 90 percent of people have Herpes One, but far fewer than this get the accompanying lip sores that go with it. Herpes Two is basically cold sores on the genitals. The first attack lasts two to four weeks. First there is pain and itching, then there are flulike symptoms: fever, swollen lymph glands, pain on urination. Blisters develop. The virus then moves away from the genitals along the nerve pathways into the dorsal root ganglion at the base of the spinal cord. It stays there ready to reappear on a future occasion.

At the time of writing, herpes is incurable.

Women who have had genital herpes face an increased risk of developing cervical cancer years later. Pieces of genetic material from the genital herpes virus have been found in the cancer cells of 40 to 50 percent of women with cervical cancer. Several hundred babies die each year in the United States because they have been infected with genital herpes during birth. About 70 percent of their mothers had no idea that they were carrying the disease.

The average incubation period for herpes is six to seven days. There is a tingling, forty-eight hours before the sore is visible, at which time the person is contagious. The blisters then stay from two to seven days. However, not all herpes carriers are easily identifiable by blisters. Dr. Michael Truppin (*Cleo,* June 1983) says that 4 to 5 percent of women are herpes carriers and that they shed from the cervix with no sores being visible. Dr. Harry Keyserling (*Cleo,* June 1983), an assistant professor of Pediatrics, says that men too can be herpes carriers. The virus can come from the urethra without the person having any visible symptoms.

Herpes is contagious just before the sores develop as well as when they are visible. If someone has recurrent herpes and goes to bed with someone who has active genital herpes, they may actually get a fresh infection. If two people have herpes and one has a recurrence, they should still avoid contact. If both have genital herpes and have oral sex, they run the risk of passing the virus to their mouths. Ninety-nine percent of cases are caused by contact with an infected person. There are plenty of theories prevalent, such as the belief that herpes lives in toilet seats, mascara, swimming pools, and towels. However, reports from the Centers for Disease Control and the National Institute of Health show that the transmission of genital herpes through a nonsexual medium has never been proved. While the possibility of transmission through contact with toilet seats may exist, the possibility is remote.

There are two ways of avoiding herpes: condoms and celibacy. Condoms help avoid transmission, but Graves says that if you have an outbreak of herpes, you shouldn't have contact with an uninfected person. Dr. Keyserling advises that condoms as a way of avoiding transmission are suspect. He points out that there are no good studies in terms of condoms. If a woman is shedding herpes in her vaginal secretions, it won't stop her from shedding on a man's scrotum or buttocks.

These, then, are the basic facts about AIDS and herpes, currently available (as of October 1983). Both diseases can kill. AIDS can kill the victim; herpes an infant, after delivery through a vaginal canal infected with herpes. While most of my interviewees were aware that herpes endangered a newborn baby's life, and that AIDS could kill homosexual men, very few of them knew much else about the diseases. I had countless calls from cheaters (and even from a female prostitute) asking what exactly herpes and AIDS were.

It is difficult to gauge how the epidemic has affected the population en masse. The best analysis of a group's reaction and behavior in the light of the epidemic, came from Don Meriwether, of the AIDS Resource Center, who has observed the patterns of the more extreme sections of the gay community in New York City during the AIDS epidemic.

> During the winter of 1982, there was quite a noticeable drop in attendance at the baths and gay clubs. They were losing hundreds and thousands of dollars. But in the late spring and summer of 1983, people started going back and doing more. It is the same phenomenon that happens in individuals. You deny for a while that a problem exists. Then you go excessively in the direction of preventing it. Then you decide that nothing is moving fast enough and you dabble in it again and see if you can get away with it.

If you can judge people's fear of something by what they refrain from doing that they used to do (because of it), very little has changed. Male hookers hustling men haven't stopped. It is going on as much as ever. Most of the male hustlers are young kids who have run away from home. They hustle to get food and shelter for the night. They don't have the luxury of saying, "This is no longer healthy." The customers haven't changed, though they may give a closer eye to someone's health.

Gay men may have been forced to become more monogamous but not completely monogamous. There is also a new phenomenon as a result of AIDS—"Jerk-Off Clubs," where gay or bisexual men wear leather, watch porno movies for visual stimulation, masturbate but don't have oral or anal sex. But a lot of people have made the decision that they are willing to take whatever comes.

The only parallel in the heterosexual world in regard to the effect of herpes and AIDS on the sexual behavior of a large social group is the swing clubs where people gather en masse. Statistics on business aren't available, but it is rumored that attendance at the clubs decreased as a result of the epidemics and that more voyeurism than participation now takes place. A female swinger told me that she and her boyfriend rarely have ménage à trois sex with men anymore, in case the man is bisexual and a possible AIDS carrier. At the same time, she admitted that her fear of the epidemic had caused her to become more bisexual and have sex with women at the clubs because she wasn't afraid of herpes.

The general effect of herpes and AIDS on people's sex lives is one of being "a little bit pregnant," there is no sign yet of celibacy, yet people are being more careful. Rosie, a hooker who answered *The Voice* advertisement, told me that *before* the epidemic, her customers (most of them married) were often unwilling to wear a condom during intercourse with her, nowadays they all were more than willing to wear one. Rosie hadn't noticed any marked drop in business; but a frightening footnote on herpes, AIDS, and prostitution came from Don Meriwether who told me that the majority of female AIDS victims were IV drug users and that since many prostitutes take drugs intravenously, there is currently concern that the disease will be spread through prostitution.

As well as talking to respondents to my *Voice* ad, I also re-interviewed some of the original cheaters from my research. Not one cheater claimed to have stopped cheating as a result of the epidemic. However, all of them admitted that they were afraid and had changed their method of infidelity. Typical responses were "I'm afraid, I don't cruise the bars anymore. I pick people to cheat with through social gatherings." "I look for married people, I get very put-off if someone is single and may be sleeping around. . . ." "I have to know a lot about someone before I go to bed with them, about their life-style and sexual habits."

The irony of the AIDS and herpes epidemics is that although they may have caused the death of the one-night stand, they have also provided fertile ground for secondary-relationship cheating. Cheaters now feel that in order to reassure themselves about AIDS or herpes, they have to really know the cheatee well before being unfaithful. Previously infidelity could easily be compartmentalized into the quick hit-and-run sexual experience; whereas fear of AIDS and herpes obliges many cheaters to spend more time with the cheatee. And spending more time, as we have seen, can lead to involvement.

A thirty-five-year-old married male cheater says,

> I have stopped having one-night stands or pickups. I need to get involved. Because of herpes and AIDS I no longer have an emergency feeling about my sexuality. I don't want any more one-night stands. I am looking for a caring lover. I want to get close to the person I have sex with, before I have sex with her.

It may be farewell to the one-night stand, but the era of the virgin hasn't returned completely. The days of the zipless fuck (to use Erica Jong's phrase) and the anonymous instant sex of *Last Tango in Paris* may be gone, but none of that has been replaced by chastity or fidelity. Just more caution and a longer time span leading up to sex.

A thirty-seven-year-old married woman told me,

> I have to know someone's life-style before I cheat with them now. If they are sleeping around a lot they may have had sex with a woman who had a bisexual boyfriend, then I would risk getting AIDS. I only cheat now with someone I know well. Preferably with someone who is married. I don't cheat with single people at all.

A few formerly rampant cheaters are turning down sexual opportunities for fear of contracting disease.

> The opportunity is there, but I often hold back. I can take it or leave it. If I think someone goes to swingers' clubs or parties I stay away from them. And if someone goes to bed with me too quickly, I am not interested. They probably have been to bed with too many other people and might have something. I watch their economic background and dress and usually pick more refined women. I figure that they will be a little more careful to protect themselves.

Pete, a male cheater, talked about his fear of herpes (very few straight men were afraid of AIDS, believing it to be solely a homosexual disease).

> I am sexually active, but now I am not looking. Women pick me up and if the opportunity is there, fine. But sometimes I see the most beautiful women and if they have a little sore on their lips, I just get turned off. I didn't know anything about herpes and

AIDS till I read about them in *Time* magazine, I am careful now. I have to get to know a person before I cheat with her, to know she is trustworthy and hasn't got it. Now I get involved with a woman I cheat with. I don't want a quick fuck. All this herpes and AIDS stuff has slowed me down a lot. I know I am taking a chance when I am unfaithful these days. It is really shaky out there. You have to watch what you are doing. Then you have to sweat it out. When it comes down to it I know I am gambling every time I am unfaithful.

Bruce, a male cheater whose first interview appears in Chapter Five was still cheating a year later, although with some reservations.

I don't fool around much. Hardly at all. I only go out with people that are clean. You can just tell. This has stopped me having one-night stands. I wait till I get to know the person before I cheat with them—spend a lot of time with them. My wife and I hardly swing as much as we used to. Only with people we know. It is scary, herpes and AIDS. You don't want to get it. I fool around hardly any. But I still fool around.

The hit-and-run cheater has to worry about herpes; the bisexual cheater, about both herpes *and* AIDS. Darren, a broadcaster, grapples with both problems as he is bisexual.

I have been living with Peggy for five years, but I have never been faithful to her. I have a very high sex drive and there is no way in the world she can satisfy that need in me all the time. I don't think anybody could. She doesn't know I am unfaithful to her. She would be very upset. I don't know if she would leave me, but I think she would if she viewed my cheating as an emotional involvement. If she were unfaithful to me I would be pissed.

I am bisexual so I have sex with both men and women. I am always concerned with women if they have something on their lips because I do like to get head. I don't wear rubbers (I hate rubbers) but I am very selective now. I try to make some kind of appraisal about what kind of a woman I am with. I look at her complexion and if she has any sores. I am worried about getting herpes from a woman because I find that women tend to be more affectionate in their lovemaking. I find that when I am with a male I have no contact with him. I just stick it in.

I am not so concerned about getting AIDS because I am the active partner. I am entering the man's body and he is not entering mine. So I don't think I am in any danger because I am the one doing the penetrating. I think people who get AIDS are really very unhealthy. I am not a drug user, I am a super healthy person. My thing is sex. I don't consider myself to be a homosexual. But what I like about men is that they are anxious to fulfill an animal drive. I find a woman is not nearly as turned on by the fact that I have a male member as homosexuals are. They get very hot. While most women are not enthralled by sucking your cock, most men are crazy about it. It is easy and it is hot. I like sex with a man. It is so "right to it."

I think sex for men is very cock-oriented. You would be surprised how many straight men are willing to do a man who is sexually aggressive. I make it clear to some of my male straight friends that I don't mind if they suck my cock. And it is surprising how many of them do. They love it. They are so into it. I don't have the desire to be faithful to anyone. But I am emotionally faithful to Peggy though.

Darren's remarks on male and female attitudes toward sexuality, his very male approach that he can be unfaithful but if his girlfriend is, he will be upset, are paralleled by his belief that he can control herpes and somehow avoid it. Just as most male cheaters believe that their wives won't find out about their infidelity, the majority also believe that they won't get herpes or AIDS. When Pete said he was gambling when he was unfaithful in the current era of herpes and AIDS, I felt that he was partially seduced by the romance and challenge of gambling, that he believed he was so powerful that he would avoid all obstacles to his pleasure, such as herpes. I continually encountered male cheaters who made excuses like "I am not worried about AIDS. I don't get into anal, so it doesn't really affect me." "It has crossed my mind once in a while, herpes and AIDS, but you can be crossing the road and be hit by a car too and you are not going to stop crossing roads."

Female cheaters, on the other hand, seemed more deterred by the idea of herpes (most were unaware that a woman could get AIDS). The majority were uncomfortable about discussing the subject, but the feedback I did get included a single's bar cheater who had given up going to single's bars; a woman who stopped cheating after she saw her friend's marriage destroyed when her husband discovered she had been cheating when she got herpes; and Rosie, the hooker, who was on the verge of giving up hooking because she was afraid she would get herpes and her boyfriend would discover her hitherto secret profession.

Fear seems to be the key to people's behavior patterns when faced by the possibility of AIDS or herpes. However, when it comes to fear of infidelity being discovered because of herpes or AIDS, men react in the same way as they do to the idea of their infidelity being revealed; it won't happen to them, but if it does, they will be able to cope. They treat the possibility as a game, something which can be successfully negotiated. I asked one cheater what he would tell his wife if he got herpes. "I don't know," he replied, flippantly adding, "Do you have any ideas?" Another male cheater told me, "I just hope herpes will never happen to me. You just take a chance and hope it won't happen to you. But if I did get herpes, I would make a deal with the doctor so he would tell my wife it wasn't really herpes but another kind of infection."

The herpes/AIDS issue again highlights the different attitudes men and women have toward their spouses. Most of the women I talked to felt that their husbands couldn't be fobbed off by excuses if they got herpes, were afraid of the consequences, and often stopped cheating altogether. Yet men were confident that they would be able to cope with any herpes-related consequences of their infidelity. The hesitance of many female victims to confront men has made the majority of men justifiably unafraid of their wives' reaction to their cheating.

Of course, men who are aware of the dangers of herpes during childbirth, or who have bisexual encounters, may worry about the consequences of their infidelity in terms of disease, but their fears don't seem to change their behavior. Marilyn, the call girl previously interviewed, says that many of her clients worry about the disease, but still patronize her.

> When most men call me for an appointment, they say, "If you have AIDS or herpes, I don't want to meet you." That is ridiculous. I don't have it, but I wouldn't tell them anyway. Business is down, but the guys still come to me. They are going to a prostitute because their wives won't put out anymore.
>
> I think I am more afraid of getting herpes than my clients are. If I think someone is promiscuous, I don't have sex with them. If a man tells me he hangs around bars and picks up young girls, I say, "Listen, Mister, I don't need your money." I meet men in my private life by advertising in *The Village Voice* for married men. That way, I meet people like presidents of corporations. They are married, they take me out and we have fun. I don't want to go out with someone who is paying alimony and is crying into their beer. A woman I talked to in Westbury told me she also put an ad in for married men. Three hundred replied. But I am careful now. Herpes and AIDS are around.

There is no scientific way of proving whether or not herpes and AIDS have caused people to return to monogamy. Judging by my small sample, I don't think so. It seems that men are more selective and avoid one-night stands; women, according to my research, have always been cautious about one-night stands when cheating. Women appear to be more worried about consequences; in the same way as they are aware and worried about the general consequences of their infidelity.

Although many cheaters do feel that they are playing russian roulette with their sexuality, the lure of the game still seems to override the danger. And there is always human nature's proclivity toward playing ostrich politics. "What will I do if ever I get herpes and my wife finds out?" mused Jack, a married cheater. "That is a bridge I don't want to cross until it happens. But I don't think it ever will."

As Don Meriwether pointed out, "Everyone thinks herpes and AIDS won't happen to them. It is the same as with auto accidents, they can happen to everyone else, but not to me." Herpes and AIDS may be here to stay, but even the dangers of those diseases cannot eclipse human nature and every individual's faith in his own invincibility. Herpes and AIDS, they fervently believe, will never "infringe on" the pursuit of their own personal pleasure. And neither will infidelity, its consequences, and the possibility of divorce. Despite all the scare surrounding the herpes and AIDS epidemics, nothing ultimately changes or affects human optimism.

Notes and Sources

INTRODUCTION

1. *Playboy* survey, November 1982.
2. Lynne Atwater, *The Extramarital Connection* (N.Y.: Irvington, 1982).
3. William Shakespeare, *Antony and Cleopatra.*

CHAPTER ONE

1. Alfred C. Kinsey, Wardell Pomeroy, and Clyde Martin, *Sexual Behavior in the Human Male* (Philadelphia: Saunders, 1948).
2. Lewis Yablonsky, *The Extra-Sex Factor* (N.Y.: Times Books, 1979).
3. Shere Hite, *The Hite Report on Male Sexuality* (N.Y.: Knopf, 1982).
4. Alfred C. Kinsey, Wardell Pomeroy, and Paul Gebhard, *Sexual Behavior in the Human Female* (Philadelphia: Saunders, 1953).
5. *Redbook* survey, September 1975.
6. Linda Wolf, *The Cosmo Report* (N.Y.: a Bantam Book published by arrangement with Arbor House, 1981).
7. Lynne Atwater, *The Extramarital Connection* (N.Y.: Irvington, 1982).
8. David C. Weiss (Rutgers) and Michael Slosnerick (Pan Handle Medical Center), "Attitudes Toward Sexual and Nonsexual Extramarital Involvement among a Sample of College Students," *Journal of Marriage and Family* (May 1981).
9. Ira L. Reiss, Ronald E. Anderson, and G. C. Sponaugle (Uni-

versity of Minnesota, Dept. of Sociology), "A Multivariate Model of the Determinants of Extramarital Sexual Permissiveness," *Journal of Marriage and Family* (May 1980).

10. Minako K. Maykovich (California State University at Sacramento), "Attitudes versus Behavior in Extramarital Sexual Relations," *Journal of Marriage and Family* (November 1976).
11. Lionel Tiger, "Omnigamy—the New Kinship System," *Psychology Today* (July 1976).
12. Richard A. Kulka and Helen Weingarten, "The Long-Term Effects of Parental Divorce in Childhood on Adult Adjustment," *Journal of Social Issues,* Vol. 35, No. 4 (1979).
13. James Hassett, "Report on Cheating," *Psychology Today* (November 1981).
14. Ira L. Reiss, Ronald E. Anderson, and G. C. Sponaugle, "A Multivariate Model of the Determinants of Extramarital Sexual Permissiveness," *Journal of Marriage and Family* (May 1980).
15. Lee H. Bukstel, et al., "Projected Extramarital Involvement in Unmarried College Students," *Journal of Marriage and Family* (May 1978).
16. Norval D. Glenn and Charles N. Weaver, "Attitudes Toward Pre-Marital, Extramarital and Homosexual Relations in the U.S. in the 1970's," *Journal of Sex Research* (May 1979).
17. Reiss, Anderson, and Sponaugle, op cit.
18. Robert N. Whitehurst, "The Violence Potential in Extramarital Sexual Responses," *Journal of Marriage and Family* (November 1971).
19. Ibid.
20. Hartnett, Mahoney, and Bernstein, "The Errant Spouse," *Perceptual and Motor Skills,* Vol. 45 (1977).
21. Kitty Kelley, *Elizabeth Taylor, The Last Star* (N.Y.: Simon & Schuster, 1981).
22. Ingrid Bergman and Alan Burgess, *My Story* (N.Y.: Dell, 1980).
23. Kitty Kelley, *Jackie Oh!* (N.J.: Lyle Stuart, 1978).
24. Alan E. Gross, "The Male Role and Heterosexual Behavior," *The Journal of Social Issues,* Vol. 34, No. 1 (1978).
25. D. Byrne, "Social Psychology and the Study of Sexual Behav-

ior," *The Personality and Social Psychology Bulletin,* No. 3 (1977).

26. Gross, op. cit.
27. Gilbert D. Bartell, "Group Sex Among Mid-Americans," *The Journal of Sex Research* Vol. 6 (May 1970).
28. Whitehurst, op. cit.

CHAPTER TWO

1. *Playboy* sex survey (January 1983).
2. Shana Alexander, *Very Much a Lady—The Untold Story of Jean Harris and Dr. Tarnower* (Boston: Little, Brown and Company, 1983).
3. Diana Trilling, *Mrs. Harris, The Death of the Scarsdale Diet Doctor* (N.Y.: Harcourt, Brace, Jovanovich, 1981).
4. Alexander, op cit.
5. *Playboy,* op cit.
6. Dr. Herbert Strean, *The Extramarital Affair* (N.Y.: The Free Press, a division of Macmillan, 1980).
7. Robert N. Whitehurst, "The Violence Potential in Extramarital Sexual Responses," *Journal of Marriage and Family* (November 1971).
8. Strean, op. cit.
9. D. W. Gurgul and F. Furstenberg, "Marital Infidelity," Northeastern University, 1969.
10. Dr. Robert Athanasiou, et al., "Survey on Sex," *Psychology Today* (1970).
11. Shirley P. Glass and Thomas L. Wright (Catholic University of America), "The Relationship of Extramarital Sex, Length of Marriage and Sex Differences on Marital Satisfaction and Romanticism; Athanasiou's Data Re-Analyzed," *Journal of Marriage and Family* (November 1977).
12. Ibid.
13. Minako K. Maykovich, "Attitudes Versus Behavior in Extramarital Sexual Relations," *Journal of Marriage and Family* (November 1976).
14. Robert R. Bell, Stanley Turner, and Ronald Rosen (Dept. of Sociology, Temple University), "A Multivariate Analysis of

Female Extramarital Coitus," *Journal of Marriage and Family* (May 1975).
15. Kingsley Davis, "Sexual Behaviour," *Contemporary Social Problems*, eds., R.K. Merton and R.A. Nisbet (N.Y.: Harcourt, Brace and World, 1966).
16. Duane Denfield and Michael Gordon, "The Sociology of Mate Swapping; or the Family Swings Together Clings Together," *The Journal of Sex Research* (May 1970).
17. Joseph Harry (Assistant Prof., Dept. of Sociology, Northern Illinois University), "The Marital Liaisons of Gay Men," *Family Coordinator,* October 1979. Also refers to Gagnon and Simon's *Sexual Conduct* (Chicago: Aldine, 1973).
18. Athanasiou, op. cit.
19. Alfred L. Kinsey, Wardell Pomeroy, and Paul Gebhard, *Sexual Behavior and the Human Female* (Philadelphia: Saunders, 1953).
20. Athanasiou, op. cit.
21. *Quick* interview with Flora Carabella, 1982.
22. Glass and Wright, op. cit.

CHAPTER THREE

1. Marion Zola, *All the Good Ones Are Married* (N.Y.: Times Books, 1981).
2. Wendy Leigh, *What Makes a Woman G.I.B. (Good in Bed)* (N.Y.: New American Library, 1978).

CHAPTER FOUR

1. Gordon Clanton and Lynn G. Smith, "The Self-Inflicted Pains of Jealousy," *Psychology Today* (March 1977).
2. Janice L. Francis, "Toward the Management of Heterosexual Jealousy," *The Journal of Marriage and Family Counselling* (October 1977).
3. Marilyn Laron Funt, *The Other Half* (N.Y.: Dial, 1980), serialized in *Ladies Home Journal* as "Are you Anybody?"

4. Abigail Van Buren, *The Best of Dear Abby* (N.Y.: Pocket Books, 1981).
5. Dr. Robert Seidenberg, "Fidelity and Jealousy," *The Psychoanalytical Review,* No. 54 (Winter 1967).
6. Kitty Kelley, *Jackie Oh!* (N.J.: Lyle Stuart, 1978).
7. Kitty Kelley, *Elizabeth Taylor, The Last Star,* (N.Y.: Simon & Schuster, 1981).
8. Joseph Pleck, "The Male Role: Definitions, Problems and Sources of Changes," *Journal of Social Issues,* No. 3 (1976).
9. Albert Goldman, *Elvis* (N.Y.: McGraw Hill, 1981).

CHAPTER FIVE

1. Nena and George O'Neill, "Patterns in Group Sexual Activity," *The Journal of Sex Research,* Vol. 6 (May 1970).
2. Betty Fang, "Swinging in Retrospect," *The Journal of Sex Research,* Vol. 12, No. 3 (August 1976).
3. Gilbert D. Bartell, "Group Sex Among the Mid-Americans," *The Journal of Sex Research,* Vol. 6 (May 1970).
4. Angie Bowie, *Free Spirit* (London: Mushroom Books, 1981).

Bibliography

Magazine Features

Adams, Virginia, "Getting at the Heart of Jealous Love." *Psychology Today,* May 1980.

Athanasiou, Dr. Robert, et al., "Survey on Sex." *Psychology Today,* 1970.

Clanton, Gordon, and Smith, Lynn, "The Self-Inflicted Pains of Jealousy." *Psychology Today,* March 1977.

Funt, Marilyn Laron, *The Other Half.* (N.Y.: Dial, 1980) (as serialized in *Ladies Home Journal*).

Hassett, James, "Report on Cheating," *Psychology Today,* November 1981.

People interview with Bobby Bouton and Nancy Marshall, June 1983.

People interview with Moya Lear, by Nancy Farber, November 1980.

"The Playboy Survey," *Playboy,* November 1982.

"The Playboy Survey," *Playboy,* January 1983.

Quick interview with Flora Carabella, 1982.

"Redbook Survey," *Redbook,* September 1975.

Tiger, Lionel, "Omnigamy—The New Kinship System." *Psychology Today,* July 1976.

Books

Alexander, Shana, *Very Much a Lady—The Untold Story of Jean Harris and Dr. Tarnower.* Boston: Little, Brown and Company, 1983.

Atwater, Lynne, *The Extramarital Connection.* N.Y.: Irvington, 1982.

Bergman, Ingrid, and Burgess, Alan, *My Story.* N.Y.: Dell, 1980.

Bernard, Jesse, *Jealousy and Marriage.* Essay in Gordon Clanton and Lynn Smith's *Jealousy.* N.J.: Prentice Hall, 1972.

Bowie, Angie, *Free Spirit.* London: Mushroom Books, 1981.

Davis, Kingsley, "Sexual Behaviour," in *Contemporary Social Problems,* R.K. Merton and R.A. Nisbet, eds. N.Y.: Harcourt, Brace and World, 1966.

Gagnon, John, and Simon, William, *Sexual Conduct.* Chicago: Aldine, 1973.

Goldman, Albert, *Elvis.* N.Y.: McGraw Hill, 1981.

Hite, Shere, *The Hite Report on Male Sexuality.* N.Y.: Knopf, 1982.

Kelley, Kitty, *Elizabeth Taylor, The Last Star.* N.Y.: Simon & Schuster, 1981.

Kelley, Kitty, *Jackie Oh!* N.J.: Lyle Stuart, 1978.

Kinsey, Alfred C., Pomeroy, Wardell, and Gebhard, Paul, *Sexual Behavior in the Human Female.* Philadelphia: Saunders, 1953.

Kinsey, Alfred C., Pomeroy, Wardell, and Martin, Clyde, *Sexual Behavior in the Human Male.* Philadelphia: Saunders, 1948.

Leigh, Wendy, *What Makes a Woman G.I.B.* N.Y.: New American Library, 1978.

Strean, Herbert, *The Extramarital Affair.* N.Y.: The Free Press, a division of Macmillan, 1980.

Trilling, Diana, *Mrs. Harris, The Death of the Scarsdale Diet Doctor.* N.Y.: Harcourt, Brace, Jovanovich, 1981.

Van Buren, Abigail, *The Best of Dear Abby.* N.Y.: Pocket Books, 1981.

Wolfe, Linda, *The Cosmo Report.* N.Y.: A Bantam book published by arrangement with Arbor House, 1981.

Yablonsky, Lewis, *The Extra-Sex Factor.* N.Y.: Times Books, 1979.

Zola, Marion, *All the Good Ones Are Married.* N.Y.: Times Books, 1981.

Periodicals

Bartell, Gilbert D., "Group Sex Among the Mid-Americans." *The Journal of Sex Research,* Vol. 6., May 1970.

Bell, Robert R., Turner, Stanley, and Rosen, Robert, "A Multivariate Analysis of Female Extramarital Coitus." *Journal of Marriage and Family,* May 1975.

Bukstel, Leo H., et al., "Projected Extramarital Involvement in Unmarried College Students." *The Journal of Marriage and Family,* May 1978.

Byrne, D., "Social Psychology and the Study of Sexual Behavior." *The Personality and Social Psychology Bulletin,* No. 3, 1977.

Denfield, Duane, and Gordon, Michael, "The Sociology of Mate Swapping; or the Family That Swings Together Clings Together." *The Journal of Sex Research,* May 1970.

Fang, Betty, "Swinging in Retrospect." *The Journal of Sex Research,* Vol. 12, No. 3, August 1976.

Francis, Janis L., "Toward the Management of Heterosexual Jealousy." *The Journal of Marriage and Family Counselling,* October 1977.

Glass, Shirley P., and Wright, Thomas L., "The Relationship of Extramarital Sex, the Length of Marriage and Sex Differences on Marital Satisfaction and Romanticism; Athanasiou's Data Re-Analyzed." *Journal of Marriage and Family*, November 1977.

Glenn, Norval D., and Weaver, Charles N., "Attitudes Toward Pre-Marital, Extramarital and Homosexual Relations in the U.S. in the 1970s." *Journal of Sex Research,* May 1979.

Gross, Alan E., "The Male Role and Heterosexual Behavior." *The Journal of Social Issues,* Vol. 34, No. 1, 1978.

Gurgul, D.W., and Furstenberg, F., "Marital Infidelity." Northeastern University, 1969.

Hartnett, Mahoney, and Bernstein, "The Errant Spouse: A Study in Person Perception." *Perceptual and Motor Skills,* Vol. 45, 1977.

Kulka, Richard A., and Weingarten, Helen, "The Long-Term Effects of Parental Divorce in Childhood on Adult Adjustment." *Journal of Social Issues,* Vol. 35, No. 4, 1979.

Maykovich, Minako K., "Attitudes Versus Behavior in Extramarital Sexual Relations." *Journal of Marriage and Family,* November 1976.

O'Neill, Nena and George, "Patterns in Group Sexual Activity." *The Journal of Sex Research,* Vol. 6, May 1970.

Pleck, Joseph, "The Male Role: Definitions, Problems and Sources of Change." *Journal of Social Issues,* No. 3, 1976.

Reiss, Ira L., Anderson, Ronald E., and Sponaugle, G. L., "A Multivariate Model of the Determinants of Extramarital Sexual Permissiveness." *Journal of Marriage and Family,* May 1980.

Seidenberg, Robert, "Fidelity and Jealousy." *The Psychoanalytical Review,* No. 54, Winter 1967.

Weiss, David C., and Slosnerick, Michael, "Attitudes Toward Sexual and Non-Sexual Extramarital Involvement Among a Sample of College Students." *Journal of Marriage and Family,* May 1981.

Whitehurst, Robert N., "The Violence Potential in Extramarital Sexual Responses." *Journal of Marriage and Family,* November 1971.